A GUIDE
TO MANAGING
INTEREST-RATE RISK

A GUIDE
TO MANAGING
INTEREST-RATE RISK

Donna M. Howe, CFA

New York Institute of Finance

New York   London   Toronto   Sydney   Tokyo   Singapore

Library of Congress Cataloging-in-Publication Data

Howe, Donna M.
    A guide to managing interest-rate risk / Donna M. Howe.
        p.   cm.
    Includes index.
    ISBN 0-13-470733-8
    1. Interest rate futures—Case studies. 2. Risk management—
Case studies.   I. Title.
HG6024.5.H69   1991
332.63'23—dc20   91-17819
                                                              CIP

© 1992 by NYIF Corp.
Simon & Schuster
A Paramount Communications Company

Printed in the United States of America
10 9 8 7 6 5 4 3 2 1

To Howie and Gracie, for being good sports

Contents

Preface

Interest-rate risk management is becoming more and more common in today's corporate America. This is primarily in response to increased competition and the availability of tools to manage the risk. This text is designed as an aid to decision making. Risk management has few hard and fast rules. It is mostly a process of calculating risk, determining the degree of undesirability attached to the risk, and the most cost-effective manner of reducing it.

The book is designed to follow a decision-making tree so that those unfamiliar with the topic can be introduced to the concepts underlying the numbers and specific areas of concern. Accordingly, in Chapter 1, we will begin with the definition of risk, its sources and its measurement. As an adjunct the topics of volatility, variability, delta, and gamma will be examined.

To help those who find the mathematics rough-going, there is a short appendix to the first chapter that deals with elementary probability and statistics from a pragmatic viewpoint.

After successfully defining risk, in Chapter 2 we will look at the process of transferring it to another party or reducing it through internal policy changes. This chapter will look at the choice of hedge instruments, the calculation of the hedge ratio, the measurement of duration, and the various basic financial instruments designed to manage risk. We will look at forward rate agreements, futures contracts, options, and swaps. As well, in Chapter 3 some of the newer instruments will be evaluated such as caps and floors, collars, swaptions, compound options, and dual-currency instruments. There is a discussion of how altering cash flows can change the risk profile for a corporation or division.

The bulk of the text lies in Chapter 4 where several commonly occurring risky situations are discussed and evaluated. Several basic strategies are advanced as alternatives to reducing the risk for each situation.

In a brief fashion taxation, commission, and manpower costs are reviewed in Chapter 5. Sometimes these additional costs change a risk-management program from attractive to too costly. These hidden costs should be evaluated seriously.

The text takes a minor side-path at Chapter 6. Since expectations play a major part in strategic thinking, and since expectations can quickly turn acceptable risks into unacceptable risks, I wanted to overview the forecasting process. The chapter will look at two different but accepted methodologies for forming a price or economic forecast as well as review the pricing mechanics for derivative securities. By knowing the variables affecting the price of derivatives, sometimes below-average cost hedge programs can be implemented.

The book concludes with a summary of key points and issues in managing risk from a pragmatic point of view. Again, the purpose of this text is to help anyone whose responsibility is management of risk to make better decisions. In becoming more knowledgeable about the major factors leading to a reduction of risk, better trade-offs can be made between precise risk-reduction and cost. Today, the successful corporate officer is one who can manage costs. Reducing downside volatility, having disaster protection, and paying lower outside brokerage fees all add to the bottom-line.

CHAPTER 1

A Discussion of Risk

This book is intended to be a decision-making tool. The building blocks of risk management currently exist in several forms: futures, options, synthetics, swaps, and the like. The challenge is how to use these devices most effectively. Few people are expert in this field, as it is relatively new and the base of users is still expanding. That means that an uninformed user is at the mercy of others acting in an advisory capacity such as a broker or a consultant hired specifically to help organize the risk-management process. This text will help to explain the important issues in the process and to clarify the variables that are most likely to add to uncertainty. The knowledge the text provides will lead to better, more cost-efficient risk management.

RISK: EVENT, PROBABILITY, AND TIME HORIZON

Risk is a sufficiently common but ambiguous term that it often leads to confusion. The key to risk is uncertainty and undesirability. It can be best understood as the probability that a situation will have an undesirable outcome. So to evaluate risk one needs to evaluate the degree of acceptability associated with an undesired outcome as well as measure the probability that it will occur. Depending on the specific circumstance and the specific investor, an undesirable outcome can be defined as the occurrence of a loss. To others it might be an unacceptable level of volatility in the market price. This can lead to additional tax costs and additional man-hours spent monitoring the position. To yet other investors, an occasional loss is acceptable but *sustained* losses are undesirable. Second, since we can assume that any event is possible, one generally tries to evaluate the *probability* of it happening. The use of statistics has been a helpful addition to finance in measuring and monitoring the likelihood of the occurrence of certain events. Therefore the first steps in evaluating the initial risk position involve defining what events are unacceptable and therefore to be avoided. Then one measures the probability that such an event will occur within a specific time period. Since the future cannot be accurately forecasted, the probability of an event occurring should be periodically re-measured. Lastly, the time period for management must be specified since it is tied to measuring the probability of an event occurring.

When speaking of risk management we mean the act of reducing the probability of an undesired result. By transferring rights and obligations to specific future cash flows if interest rates change, one can alter the probability of these possible but unattractive outcomes. In some cases risk can be virtually eliminated from a position by transferring the risk to others. The process of shifting risk from investors to speculators is a primary force in the markets. However, risk should be managed only when the risktaker is not being paid for the exposure to the risk. Generally speaking, additional risk is acceptable as long as it is offset by additional return. Therefore, depending on the field of business, or the department in a company, or even the individual preferences of a manager, the choice of a risk management strategy will vary. After all, risk management tools can often be interchanged, and the solution may be more a question of cost and how general or specific is the risk that is to be managed.

Measuring the probability of an event's occurrence can be complex, so the science of probability and statistics is used to make the wealth of data understandable. Fortunately, it is not necessary to be an expert statistician to use the concepts or techniques of statistical analysis. A discussion of methods follows and the basic concepts and definitions are explained in the Appendix to Chapter 1.

MEASURING RISK

A quick intuitive picture of risk is obtained by graphing the potential or possible outcomes against the probability that each possible outcome will occur. See Figure 1.1. The various outcomes tend to converge around a consensus outcome. This consensus is the weighted average of the range of probable outcomes and is defined as the expected outcome. The expected outcome of an event is therefore the outcome most likely to occur. On the graph this will result in the average outcome being indicated by the highest point, and other outcomes spreading out to either side. The lower the point on the graph, the less likely the event is to occur. More favorable events are graphed to the right side of the expected point and less favorable outcomes are graphed to the left side of the expected outcome. As a standard, we assume that the range of probable outcomes will lie along the normal curve. A normal curve has an average of zero, with the bulk of probable outcomes lying between negative one and positive one. Using the normal curve makes it possible to evaluate the risk of individual investments by offering a standard of comparison. As the possible outcomes diverge from the expected outcome, their occurrence becomes less likely. However, less probable does not eliminate the *possibility* of their occurrence. This is where the degree of undesirability of the possible outcome must be considered as well as the probability of its happening. There are three ways to look at any particular initial situation: (1) the event is somewhat undesirable but the probability of occurrence is slight so it is not worthwhile to incur the costs of managing the risk; (2) the event is undesirable and the probability of its occurring is sufficiently high—say greater than 25%—to make hedging it important; (3) the event is extremely undesirable so that even though the probability of occurrence is small, it is worthwhile to hedge.

Sometimes the distribution of probabilities ceases to follow the normal curve. One type of variation is called a *skew* distribution. Skew occurs when the most probable outcome no longer lies half-way be-

Figure 1.1.   Comparing Probable Price to Possible Price

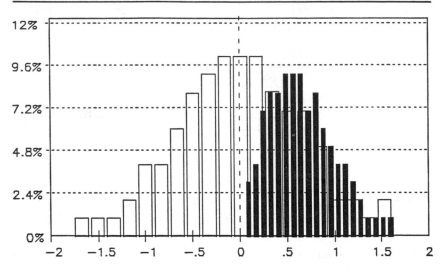

In this picture, the probability of occurrence for a value is charted on the vertical, or y-axis and the actual value is charted on the horizontal, or x-axis. The white bars show a *normal distribution*, which is the range of possible prices for a random event. The black bars show the probable, or likely price distribution for a specific event. In this case, the event is the percentage return for a security over a period of time. The ratio of probable prices to possible prices is a measure of the risk incurred by owning the security.

Generally, the smaller the value of probable-to-possible price, the more risky is ownership of the security since a change in an influencing variable can alter the expected return. This is analogous to inferring a greater risk measure on a security with a lower standard deviation of return. This measure is used instead because there may be a non-normal or skewed price distribution.

tween the most favorable and least favorable outcomes; which is a property of the normal curve. Note that a skewed distribution can be desirable from an investment point of view. For example a positively skewed probability distribution implies that the most likely outcome is closer to the best outcome rather than the worst outcome. This translates as a greater chance of earning a positive return. The difficulty with a skewed distribution is that it cannot be meaningfully compared to a normal curve without a great deal of additional complexity.

The Ratio of Probable Price Range to Possible Price Range

In looking at probability distributions it becomes clear that the range of possible outcomes is distinct from the range of probable outcomes. Theoretically anything is possible so the range of possible outcomes can reach from minus infinity to positive infinity. However to limit this range the usual practice is to assume a riskless-arbitrage condition. That is, the possible high and low range of price or interest rates is determined by the level at which it becomes profitable to buy or sell without incurring any risk. It is the ratio of probable outcomes to possible outcomes that offers one way to measure the degree of risk. For example, if the price of a corporate bond can range from 98–10 to 102–15 (the range limited by riskless arbitrage opportunities at both ends) but the range of probable prices is 100–00 to 101–04, then the risk ratio is 1 and 4/32 divided by 4 and 5/32, or .27. The smaller the ratio, the larger the risk involved. If the distribution of prices is a perfectly normal curve with symmetric price expectations, then the ratio is .67. This is sort of the "base line" for this ratio. See Figure 1.2 for an example. The **expected** price is the average of the range of probable prices, as described above. This is also the **mode,** or most probable value of the price distribution in a normal curve. The areas where price moves are possible but unlikely are the areas where risk is most acute for any specific outcome. This is mostly because the unlikely prices will occur in times of greater than usual uncertainty. That is, for exactly those circumstances when security is desired due to an uncertain view of the future, the less probable prices occur due to changing notions of acceptable prices.

For purposes of using the laws of probability and statistics, we assume that prices follow a normal distribution curve. However, we know that this is not always the case. Consider labor costs, for example. Wages tend to move upward in times of shortage much faster than they decrease when the shortage eases. This sort of "sticky" price movement translates into a **skewed** price distribution curve. Sometimes this skew can help—if you are the specialist at a high salary.

Figure 1.2.   An Example of a Normal Curve

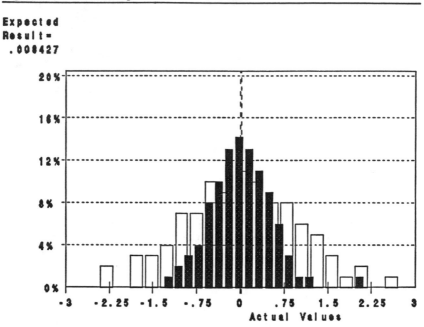

This graph again has the probability of each occurrence plotted on the y-axis (vertical) and the actual value of the return plotted on the x-axis (horizontal). The black bars show the probable prices for a normal distribution, while the white bars show a random price distribution for possible prices. The ratio is calculated by taking the range of values along the x-axis. For a normal curve, this value is ⅔, or .6667.

Sometimes this skew can hurt—if you are the manager who pays the salary.

The holder of a position must determine whether or not to limit, or **hedge** the risk. Hedging is the procedure for managing risk by altering the distribution range of possible outcomes, thereby reducing the uncertainty. See Figure 1.3. In business, and specifically in finance, the outcome of an event is generally the price of an investment. Whether this investment is the purchase of raw materials or an investment portfolio, a change in the price of the investment subjects the purchaser to risk. We will examine risk in a variety of ways, but for interest-rate risk it all boils down to price changes—acceptable or otherwise.

Figure 1.3. Changing the Price Distribution Curve

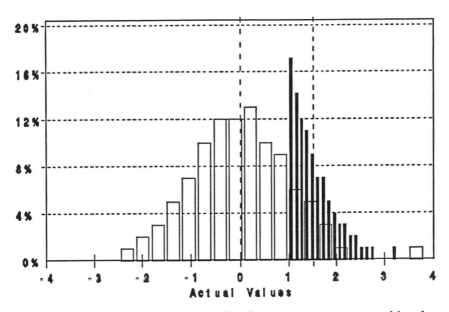

This graph overlays a new price distribution curve, represented by the black bars, over the original price distribution curve, represented by the white bars. Again, the probability of occurrence is graphed on the y-axis with the actual price graphed on the x-axis. By using this hedge strategy, all negative returns have been avoided. However, the cost of implementing such a hedge strategy is high.

THE ROLE OF FINANCIAL
RISK MANAGEMENT

Regardless of the specific source of risk, there are two undesirable outcomes on a corporate level. One does not want the net worth of the corporation to be subject to sharp declines, and one also wishes to minimize the volatility of the corporations's net worth. If either of these events occurs, there is an impact of higher borrowing costs. All corporations borrow to some extent, either to cover short-term needs or in the longer term to finance improvements to capital. Equally, both of these two events can cause dilution of the corporation. If the stock of the corporation is perceived as being less valuable due to higher volatility of market price or chance of a loss, then more shares need to be issued to garner a given amount of additional capital. To avoid these two undesirable events, we introduce interest-rate risk management. The business process impacts on either the asset side of the balance sheet, the liability side of the balance sheet, or the income statement. The assets are composed of items where you have a right to certain cash flows. Liabilities are securities where you have an obligation to provide other cash flows. The difference between the assets and the liabilities for a specific time frame is referred to as a **gap.** It is indeed a gap between the cash amounts you are entitled to versus the amount you are obligated to supply. The corporation generally wishes to reduce the volatility of the income sheet as well. A more stable income flow is generally regarded as being more desirable by analysts evaluating the worth of the corporation.

The risk management for these undesired outcomes is directed towards interest rates. All future cash flows, whether obligations you must meet or rights due to you, need to be adjusted for the time value of money. Essentially, a dollar to be paid in the future is worth less than a dollar paid today because there is no absolute certainty that it will be paid in the future. There is a discussion on present value in Chapter 2.

SOURCES OF RISK

There are various ways to classify risk. We can define it according to the source of uncertainty, such as political risk, or we might choose to define it according to where it occurs in the business process, such as inventory risk. We might also define it in terms of a variable that causes the uncertainty, such as basis risk. Figure 1.4 categorizes a number of these sources of risk.

PROCESS RISK

In the entire cycle of the business process, there are specific places where changes in price create risk. Figure 1.5 diagrams five major risk points: (1) the initial purchase of raw materials, (2) the change in the value of stocks held, (3) any change in costs for processing raw mater-

Figure 1.4.   Sources of Risk

Risk Incurred Initially	*Additional Hedging Risk*
Process Risk	Price Correlation Risk
Operating Leverage	Basis Risk
Sales Variability	Event Risk
Financial Risk	Spread Risk
Level of Interest Rates	Inexact Hedge Risk
Non-parallel Shifts	
Expectations of the Future	
Distribution Risk	
Changes in Probability	
Changes in Price Ratios	
Non-normal Price Distribution	
Highly Undesirable Outcomes	
Volatility	
Variability	

Figure 1.5.   Areas of Risk in the Business Process

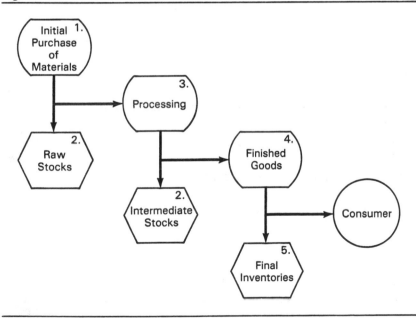

ials into finished goods, (4) any change in the final sale price, and (5) the effect of a change in final price on inventories held. This is a simplistic view, but it aids in analyzing real hazards to profit margins and pinpointing where risk-management techniques are most needed. When dealing with interest-rate risk management, we are really dealing with the whole business spectrum. Changes in interest rates and in expectations of changes in interest rates affect the behavior of market participants throughout the entire cycle.

Initial Costs

Of course there are ways to manage these risks without using financial instruments. After all, protecting a company from these price changes has long been the concern of its managers. Except for commodities that deteriorate with time, like fresh vegetables, the amount of stocks held has depended on whether there is an anticipation that prices will rise or fall. Like the consumer who buys on sale, managers will load up on non-perishables when there is a perceived short-term dip in prices. However, by using risk-management techniques, the manager can avoid or minimize a loss if this "down-tick" is instead the harbinger of a new downward trend in prices. Much of this stock management was the impetus for the creation of our current futures markets. Its beginning was in agriculturals and physical commodities, although financials get the press these days.

Changes in Inventory Value

When stocks held change in their market value, there are accounting implications. When the final good is sold, its cost must be determined to calculate the company's profit or loss on the good. Part of this cost results from the value of the inventory. It can be evaluated at either the historical cost or the current market price. The use of one or the other can determine whether or not the good is profitable or not from an accounting viewpoint. As well as raw materials, quite often a corporation will have an investment account or accounts holding various fixed-income or equity securities. These too must be evaluated in an ongoing fashion. Just as the inventory cost of a good helps to determine the profitability of a product, the costs of financial securities contribute to the investment return for a corporation. The company that uses financial risk-management tools to keep the average cost of the product below that of its competitor will earn above-average returns in times of above-average costs.

Changes in Processing Costs

Changes in input prices for the processing of raw materials can be broken down into fixed versus variable inputs. Managers generally attempt to convert as many variable inputs into fixed inputs as they can—assuming that the fixed price is favorable. This, for example, is the essential reason for labor contracts. When the fixed price is no longer attractive, management prefers to work from week to week. Management wins so many labor disputes because they are paid to take the risk of dealing with workers on the short term when the long-term price is not favorable. There is a decent chance that negotiations will provide an opportunity to lock in a good price for the longer term. Generally speaking, the longer the contract, the more underpriced managements feels the labor costs are. This attempt to establish fixed prices also applies to capital inputs. Accounting practices are designed to even out cash flows. In this way, although machinery requires a large one-time output, the cost is recognized only gradually. This is also a reason that the leasing of equipment has come into fashion. By leasing, the costs are fixed over the term of the contract and the cash flows are minimized.

Changes in Price of Final Goods

Changes in the price of the final product are not really in the control of the company. Whether or not the public likes the price, or indeed whether they buy quantities of the product at any price, depends on the market. Whether or not the item is a necessity or a luxury, the availability of substitutes, and the price of any potential complements are some of the factors that will affect the volume of the product that will be sold. The volume sold of a necessity with few acceptable substitutes will be greater than that of a luxury item with many alternatives. For example, many more paperclips than teak desks are sold. Similarly, even in an economic downturn, telephone and electric companies will see continued demand for their services, while a small company that builds yachts might wish to manage more of its risk.

Final Price/Inventory Effect

There is also **process risk** in the amount of inventory held of the finished or end-product. In times of quickly changing technology, one might prefer to keep low inventories of the final product but build up the inventories of intermediate products. For example, Chrysler may hold fewer cars but stock more spare parts. Spare parts with multiple uses may come in for special scrutiny and be kept at even higher levels. On the other hand, if the product has few or no substitutes, the company may opt to hold high levels of inventory for its finished product.

Keep in mind that the rising cost of a segment of the process chain is less important then the ability to pass along the rising costs to the consumer. If a manufacturer can feed all of its price increases to the consumer, then an increase in cost is good for business. Much of the ability to pass on the price moves is dependent on the nature of the product. After all, if fresh tomatoes go up in price, we can substitute another vegetable or use fewer tomatoes in the salad. On the other hand, heating oil users can only make use of a substitute by making changes in capital equipment, which will be very expensive.

In the case of process risk, not all businesses will have the same demand for reduced risk at all points of the chain. Some businesses will have done some backward integration and so will have purchased the suppliers of their raw materials. In this case, while the price of raw materials will not be fixed, the variation in price will be reduced, as the captive supplier will not be able to pass along 100% of its price increase. In such an instance, an increase in the price of raw materials may actually be a benefit, because it might hurt competitors more than the business itself.

Measuring Process Risk: Sales Variability & Operating Leverage

Regardless of the specific area of process risk, the net effect can be measured. It can be broken into two components, the sales variability and the degree of operating leverage. **Sales variability** is measured as the adjusted standard deviation of sales over time; that is, the standard deviation of sales devided by average sales.

$$\text{Sales Variability} \ = \ \frac{\text{Standard Deviation of Sales}}{\text{Average Sales}}$$

The equation is as follows:

$$\text{Sales Variability} = \frac{\sqrt{\dfrac{\Sigma (S_i - \overline{S})^2}{N}}}{\Sigma \dfrac{S_i}{N}}$$

where Σ = addition function
S_i = dollar amount of sales in period i
$\overline{S}$ = average or mean of sales
N = number of periods

As mentioned above, the sales level for the product is mostly outside the control of the company since it is dependent on consumer demand. The effect of consumer demand can be maximized through niche marketing of course, but long-term demand cannot be created where none exists. Consumer demand is a difficult variable to evaluate since it depends on such diverse factors as consumer debt levels, disposable income, and expectations of future economic growth.

The degree of operating leverage is heavily dependent on the production function, which in turn is related to the inventory processing costs. Both are determined by the mix of fixed-cost and variable-cost inputs. In fact, operating costs volatility is dependent on the proportion of fixed-costs to total costs. A higher proportion adds to volatility of costs by not decreasing when production volume decreases but not increasing as quickly when production volume increases. Variable costs do not add to volatility of sales because they are always some fixed proportion of total sales. Since changing the production function is extremely difficult and can be costly, the uses of financial risk-management tools such as swaps can alter the proportion by turning fixed-costs into variable costs and vice versa.

Operating leverage is defined as the percentage change in operating earnings divided by the percentage change in sales over a period of time. The equation for operating leverage is as follows:

$$\text{Operating Leverage} = \frac{\Sigma \left| \dfrac{\%\Delta OE}{\%\Delta S} \right|}{N}$$

where ΔOE = change in level of operating earnings
       ΔS = change in level of sales per period
       N = number of time periods over
           which measure is taken
      $|x|$ = absolute value of x

By adding together the sales variability measure and the degree of operating leverage we obtain a measure of the business process risk that can be used for comparison purposes and also to calculate the effects of risk-management programs after they have been implemented.

FINANCIAL RISK

Another broad-based risk is financial risk. This involves managing assets and liabilities including payables and receivables and lost opportunity cost that is incurred by letting funds lie idle or by locking up too high a percentage of cash in long-term investments. One form of risk arises when the return on funds is incorrectly calculated. For example, if the yield of an investment has been calculated on a yield-to-maturity basis, then a major portion of the return is tied up in the interest-on-interest portion. However, if the investment was chosen for its income stream which will be diverted into some other need, then the return on the investment is really much smaller. This is demonstrated by the income calculations in Figure 1.6. This is a sufficiently involved topic that we will be discussing it in detail in later chapters: Chapter 4 gives a number of examples of asset/liability hedging and the minimizing of borrowing costs is discussed in Chapter 2.

While the underlying causes are examined later, here we will look at the way to measure the corporation's exposure to financial risk. It consists of three different variables: (1) the level of nominal interest rates, (2) any non-parallel shifts along the yield curve, and (3) an expectations component that anticipates future events.

Level of Interest Rates

The absolute level of nominal interest rates is measured by the average risk-free yield available. This is calculated by taking the rates on government securities and dividing by time. The calculation is as follows:

$$\text{Average Interest Rate} = \overline{I} = \frac{\Sigma\, tI_t}{T}$$

where t = maturity of the security
        I = nominal interest rate for the security
        T = total time periods

This interest rate affects the borrowing costs for the corporation as well as having an impact on the availability of funds to borrow and investment in the secondary market.

Delta i

The second component, the non-parallel shift in the yield curve, is referred to as the sector risk or Delta i. Often when interest rates move,

Figure 1.6.   Breakdown of Yield-to-Maturity as Income: U.S. Treasury Note 8.5% due September 1994—Purchased at 100.00% (Par)

Principal	$1,000,000.00 at maturity No capital gains earned
Interest	$85,000 annually for five years $425,000 total interest income
Compounded Interest-on-interest	$16,256.25 ($42,500 @ 8.5% for 4.5 years) $14,450.00 ($42,500 @ 8.5% for 4.0 years) $12,643.75 ($42,500 @ 8.5% for 3.5 years) $10,837.50 ($42,500 @ 8.5% for 3.0 years) $ 9,031.25 ($42,500 @ 8.5% for 2.5 years) $ 7,225.00 ($42,500 @ 8.5% for 2.0 years) $ 5,418.75 ($42,500 @ 8.5% for 1.5 years) $ 3,612.50 ($42,500 @ 8.5% for 1.0 years) $ 1,806.25 ($42,500 @ 8.5% for .5 years) $81,281.25 interest-on-interest earned

When calculating return based on yield to maturity, there is an assumption that all the subsequent interest payments will be instantly re-invested at the initial rate of the yield to maturity. So if there are any coupon payments used as cash income rather than being reinvested, the total return on the security is reduced. Note that even under conservative assumptions, the interest-on-interest component of return is almost 20%. This loss would reduce the actual return on the security from 8.5% to 8.3%.

some sectors see a yield appreciation while other see a yield depreciation. Owning the appreciating sector in a depreciating environment can lead to capital losses as well as offering poor investment performance when compared to a broad-based index. It is calculated as the difference between the maturity sector you are concerned with and the absolute level of interest rates. So the equation looks like this:

$$\text{Sector risk} = \Delta i = \overline{I} - i_t$$

where $\overline{I}$ = average level of interest rates
       i_t = interest rate for the maturity sector

The Expectations Premium

The last component is a non-stable part of the measure because it depends on the investor's optimism or pessimism as well as the state of the economy. The expectations premium is the additional amount of yield required to make investment attractive at any particular time. It can have either a positive or negative effect. For example, if you think interest rates are going to drop in future, you may take a lower rate on an investment than you would otherwise find acceptable. Equally, you may pay a slightly higher rate to borrow short-term if you think you will be compensated by doing that and borrowing longer-term later in the year. The expectations premium is a major reason why you may choose to transact a deal at other then theoretically attractive levels.

Process risk and financial risk when taken together account for the major portion of risk under most circumstances. As a result, the most work has been done on the measurement of these two areas.

DISTRIBUTION RISK

This category of risk refers back to the basic definition of risk early in the chapter. Risk was broken into the probability of an event occurring and the degree of acceptability associated with that outcome. In general there are four situations in which we talk about distribution risk: (1) when the probability of an event occurring changes over time, (2) when the ratio of probable price to possible price changes, (3) when the price distribution varies significantly from the normal curve, and (4) when a low probability event has a high degree of undesirability attached.

The risk that the probability of an event occurring will change over time is less of a risk than a certainty. After all, at the outset any single event will have a cumulative probability of no more than 50%. That is the nature of the normal curve. However, as the time period draws to a close, the event will occur with a 100% probability. This risk is managed by simply re-evaluating the situation periodically. While there are Act-of-God events such as cyclones or political assassinations that cause large jumps in probability, usually this probability changes gradually over time.

In looking at the distribution of possible prices, if the range of possible outcomes is more narrow, we say that the outcome is less risky since the absolute change in price will be minor for any probable event. Equally, a wider range of possibilities is associated with a higher degree of risk as even a minor error in forecasting can lead to a large price change. However, the range of possible prices is determined by arbitrage possibilities. If the price where a riskless opportunity occurs changes due to contingent events, then the range of possible prices will change. As a result the ratio of probable-to-possible prices can change dramatically as well. This type of risk is known as spread risk.

One other type of distribution risk that occurs is when the price distribution is skewed but the investor or analyst treats it as being a normal curve. When this arises, the likelihood of events occurring is inaccurately measured. So the initial risk of the situation is being mismeasured as well. There are a number of computer programs available today that allow the past history of prices to be recorded and compared to a normal curve. In this fashion a potential skew condition can be spotted early on. While non-normal curves cannot be meaningfully compared to normal ones, simply being aware that a non-normal distribution is present is often sufficient. As a general rule, positively skewed price distributions are attractive and negatively skewed distributions are not.

It seems fairly obvious that the wider the range of possible outcomes, the more risk is associated with choosing the "wrong" outcome. However in many cases, there is no large penalty if the actual outcome is different from the forecasted or best-preferred outcome. Quite often there is range of more or less acceptable outcomes. In many cases, there is only a small range of completely unacceptable outcomes, and they often have a small likelihood of occurring. Since the level of risk remains relatively constant over the range of outcomes, with variation only in the extreme ends of the distribution range, this is exactly the type of circumstance that is easiest and cheapest to manage. Specifically, this type of distribution risk is known as event risk. The name was derived from the way in which only certain and specific events are hedged.

VOLATILITY AS RISK

Volatility can also be a risk. In finance, volatility is defined as the historic degree of price change and it is measured by averaging the net changes in the price of an investment over time. Because the elements of volatility are variables, it is not a stable measurement. For example, volatility for the June 1991 bond futures contract can vary as the length of time for the measurement changes. Using the values in Figure 1.7 we can see that the result changes when using weekly data or daily data. In addition to actual volatility we look at implied volatility. The difference between the two is an exceptional factor. Implied volatility adds in a component to forecast the future. For example, if monetary figures are due out tomorrow and the market expects these figures to change the consensus outlook for the economy, then the **implied volatility** can be greater than the actual volatility. This is a difficult item to measure and is also difficult to protect against.

Measures of Volatility

Another way to measure volatility is to use standard deviation. *Standard deviation* is the average absolute difference from the average value that can be experienced at any time. To calculate it, we square the difference between any point and the average, then sum them and take the average of those differences. The equation is as follows:

$$\text{Standard deviation} = \sigma = \sqrt{\frac{\Sigma \, (X_i - \overline{X})^2}{N}}$$

where X = price or interest rate
        i = the particular time period
        $\overline{X}$ = the average level of X
        N = total time period for the measurement

Figure 1.7. Price Volatility Measures: June Bond Futures, Daily & Weekly

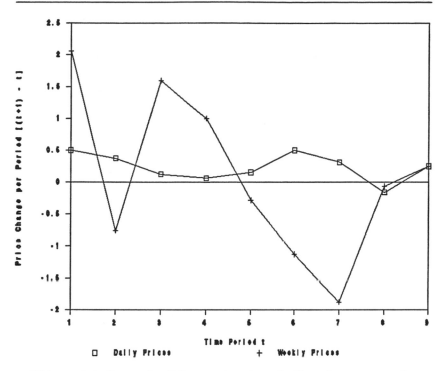

This graph indicates the difference in price volatility when measured over different time periods. When measured daily, the June 1991 Bond Futures contract shows much less volatility for this period than when measured on a weekly basis. Volatility on a daily basis is calculated as 9.7% whereas volatility measured on a weekly basis is calculated as 21.0%.

Standard deviation assumes that due to random events, the actual price or interest rate will not equal the average. However, it assumes that the fluctuations will occur in an unpredictable manner and follow the normal curve for distribution. So the average is the best forcast for the future. This is not unreasonable when the average is calculated using a long historical period. However if the past history is short, inaccuracies can rise from using these assumptions. The advantage of using standard deviation is that it allows comparisons between different investments or costs. We can assume a high probability that returns in any given year will fall between the average minus the standard deviation, and the average plus the standard deviation. This is known as the *confidence interval*. For more detail, see the Appendix to Chapter 1.

The size of the standard deviation is dependent on the size of the mean return. So as a way of adjusting standard deviation when the average levels are vastly different, we use variability. *Variability* differs from volatility by being adjusted by the average level of returns. That is:

$$\text{Variability} = V - \frac{\sigma_x}{\overline{X}}$$

Where x = variable being measured
$\overline{X}$ = average level of returns for x
σ = standard deviation of returns for x
V = volatility

Low volatility or a small standard deviation is often associated with tight probability ranges for an investment, but not always. This depends a good deal on the absolute levels of interest rates. Price changes are more violent for a given yield change if the cash flow or coupon is higher. Quite often, the implied volatility is greater at the extreme ends of the range than it is around the average value. This is because at the extremes expectation of fundamental changes in capital controls and supply/demand factors come into play. In addition, some markets have a higher base level of volatility than others. Although there is no proof (indeed, there is little proven absolutely when it comes to volatility), there is a general assumption that volatility increases with speculative participation. Since speculators can enter and leave markets according to their anticipation of abnormal profits, it becomes clear that volatility increases when an individual investment or a market enters a new price range. Given the expectational component, the implied volatility can increase whenever the market of investors feels a repricing of the item is possible, perhaps due to changing demand/supply for the item.

It is particularly important to note that the individual market players will not have the same opinion of market volatility at any given time. The range of volatilities can vary by 2% or 3% around a market consensus. This has quite an effect on opinions of what is an attractive price for both the **underlying** cash markets and the **derivative** hedge markets.

Delta. One measurement closely associated with the concept of volatility is delta. Delta is the rate of change in the price of the hedge instrument as the price of the underlying security changes. We will look at delta as a hedge ratio in Chapter 2. For volatility, delta can also be interpreted as acceleration. Delta for different put options is graphed in Figure 1.8. Figure 1.8 is derived from Figures 1.9 and 1.10 where we look at the price of the hedge for different prices of the underlying. Since the relationship does not follow either a straight line or a gentle curve, it is an additional proof that volatility is seldom constant except within small defined ranges. A graph of acceleration must increase at a decreasing rate to keep the volatility constant. This will be discussed in more detail in both Chapter 2 and Chapter 5. However, keep in

Figure 1.8.　Delta as a Rate of Change Measure for Puts with Different Strike Prices

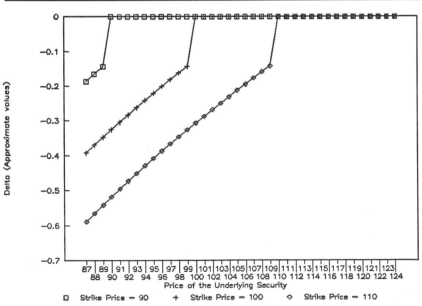

Figure 1.9. Call Option Prices at Different Strike Prices

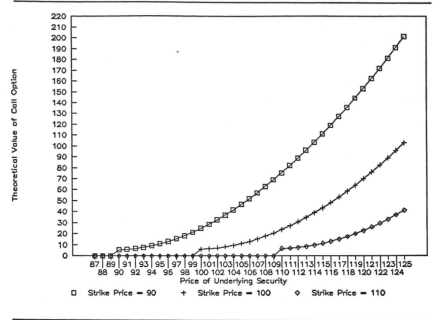

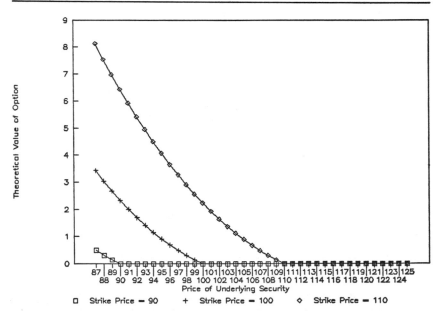

Figure 1.10. Put Option Prices at Different Strike Prices

mind that measuring the acceleration of volatility may help make sense of implied volatility measures. It may also change the distribution of possible outcomes for the event. Unfortunately, this is not a static field. If it were, managing risk would be much less expensive.

Gamma. A second measurement associated with volatility is gamma, a way of measuring the skew of the distribution curve. It is most used with the options market and has been described as the curvature or second derivative of the option. In other words, just as delta is the rate of change of volatility, gamma is the rate of change of delta. It is an important risk measure in that it tells you if your option is behaving like the underlying future. If your future is acting as a close proxy for the underlying market—where the risk actually exists—then the protection is good. Otherwise, spread risk comes into play. Unfortunately, gamma is a non-directional measure, so it can indicate *when* the market price is undergoing skew, but it does not indicate the direction. As a result, gamma is not a forecasting tool.

CORRELATION RISK

The gamma and delta measurements are associated with an additional risk known as as correlation risk. This risk only exists after one starts to manage risk. It is the degree of price correlation that exists between the original position, the underlying, and the hedge. It is a fact that the financial instruments on the market are not exact substitutes for the underlying investment. As a result, an exact amount of protection often cannot be obtained and over-hedging or under-hedging is the name of the game. In addition, in unusual market conditions the future or option often does not act like the underlying security. As a result, although the returns are highly correlated and monotonic in the long run, as is shown in Figure 1.11, they may vary significantly in the short run. For example, all those managers with equity portfolio insurance at the time of the 1987 stock market crash experienced a case where the short-run price changes varied distinctly from the long-run expectations. See Figure 1.12.

Measures of Correlation Risk

We can measure correlation risk by measuring the correlation between price movements of the underlying security and the hedge vehicle.

Figure 1.11.   Long-Term Price Correlation: Bonds vs. Bond Futures

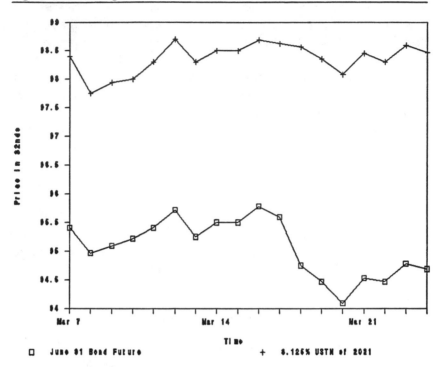

Note that despite small variations in the difference in price, over the longer term, the price of the futures contracts is highly correlated with the cash bond. The difference between the two prices is known as the *basis*. This is another source of risk when instituting hedges.

However, the measure becomes more standardized by dividing this correlation by the variance of the hedge instrument: this measure was initially used in the stock markets and is known as *beta*. The calculations for correlation and beta are similar.

$$\beta_{x,y} = \frac{\text{Covariance}_{x,y}}{\text{Variance}_y}$$

$$\beta_{x,y} = \frac{\dfrac{\Sigma(X_i - \overline{X}) * (Y_i - \overline{Y})}{N}}{\dfrac{\Sigma(Y_i - \overline{Y})^2}{N}}$$

Figure 1.12.   An Example of Short-Term Price Correlation: IBM and the
S&P 500

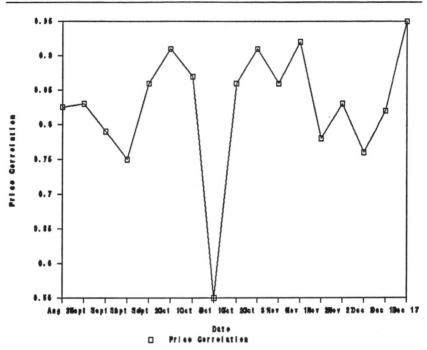

The correlation of the price of IBM common stock to the Standard &
Poor's 500 equity index was measured over a period of time in 1987. Although the price correlation was excellent for most of that period, during the
stock market crash the correlation worsened dramatically. This is an example
of an added risk when implementing a hedge program.

They differ, however, in that beta uses the price action of the hedge
instrument as the determining factor while correlation uses the underlying security. Correlation has the advantage of lying in a range from
positive one to negative one. So it is easily used in comparing price
action between a number of combined securities. Beta is more useful
when looking to measure the price action of an individual security versus a portfolio or index of other securities. So beta sees use in performance measurement or when derivatives are being used to hedge a portfolio of securities. Correlation is used on a security by security basis.

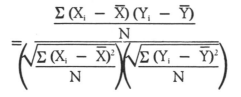

$$\text{Correlation} = \frac{\dfrac{\Sigma (X_i - \overline{X})(Y_i - \overline{Y})}{N}}{(\sigma_x)(\sigma_y)}$$

$$= \frac{\dfrac{\Sigma (X_i - \overline{X})(Y_i - \overline{Y})}{N}}{\left(\sqrt{\dfrac{\Sigma (X_i - \overline{X})^2}{N}} \right) \left(\sqrt{\dfrac{\Sigma (Y_i - \overline{Y})^2}{N}} \right)}$$

THE PROCESS OF RISK MANAGEMENT

All types of risk need to be examined before any major plan to manage risk can be implemented. After all, many risks may effectively cancel each other out, and it is unlikely that all risks will be in the same direction. After the management plan is selected, you must consider how to implement it in the most cost-effective way; that is, the cheapest way that gets done what you want to get done. After that, you must evaluate the correlation risk in order to see how likely it is that the protection will actually work when needed.

However, risk is additive in that it causes the range of possible prices to be wider. Spread risk might add plus *or* minus 10 basis points to possible prices, even though the *expected* change would be only plus or minus 5 basis points. Risk usually increases the possible price potential more than the range of probable prices.

When the management plan is actually implemented, we call the resulting chart a **risk profile.*** A risk profile consists of two parts: (1) a comparison of the initial distribution of returns and the hedged distribution of returns, and (2) a comparison of hedged returns in theory and including costs and additional risks. See Figures 1.13A and 1.13B. Many of the numbers in the risk profile are "soft" numbers, that are subject to change. As a result, the risk profile should be re-evaluated

---

*I would like to caution that the phrase might be misinterpreted. This differs significantly from what other authors have defined as risk profiles. Smith, Smithson, and Wilford in *Managing Financial Risk* refer to a risk profile as a graph of change in value of assets versus change in real interest rates or price (pp. 22–26).

Figure 1.13.A.   Risk Profile: Initial vs. Hedged Returns

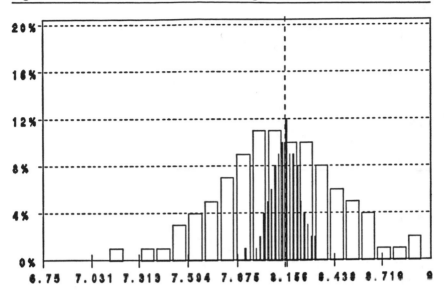

This graph shows the probability of an event's occurrence on the vertical axis, and the specific return expected on the horizontal axis. The white bars indicate the return distribution anticipated initially, before a hedge program is implemented. The black bars show the distribution after a hedge is initiated. Note the tighter distribution of returns, indicating lesser volatility. Also, the returns are now positively skewed, for a greater likelihood of a positive return on the investment.

on a regular basis. There will also be a number of areas of risk that will be effectively zero when risk management is done on a departmental level, so the categories should be customized somewhat to reflect the business involved.

The idea behind the risk profile is to point out the areas of highest risk, that is, the largest spread between probable price and possible price. Therefore, if you are not receiving adequate reward for taking on these risks—also called **assuming an exposure**—then management will be worthwhile.

In this period of increased market volatility, there are opportunities for abnormally high profits. However, this volatility also increases the

Figure 1.13.B.   Risk Profile: Theoretical vs. Actual Hedge Return

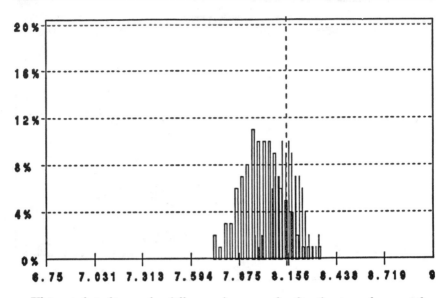

This graph indicates the difference between the distribution of returns for the theoretical hedge, and the distribution of returns after including the costs of the hedge, and any additional risks incurred through hedging. The probability of an event occurring is plotted on the vertical axis, and the result itself is plotted on the horizontal axis. The black bars are the theoretical hedge and the white ones show the hedge including costs. Note that the cost-inclusive hedge is less positively skewed and has a wider range of returns.

---

chance of a disaster. I tend to feel that the dangers are due less to increased volatility and more to the way that volatility levels fluctuate. However, this fluctuation and the increased number of players in the various markets mean that we can almost always achieve an acceptable level of risk management with acceptable prices.

APPENDIX 1.A

Probability and Statistics

In finance, when we look at the price of an asset, we generally like to look at how the price behaved in the past over time so that we can identify what affected the price in the past. Creating this price history produces many individual values for each asset. Since the price behavior exists over a period of time, this set is called a **time series**. This historical analysis applies the laws of statistics to the price action of assets. The purpose of descriptive statistics is to compare and contrast different series of numbers in a meaningful manner. To make the comprehension of the mass of detail as easy as possible, there are ways to represent the series with one particular number. Some of these numbers describe how similar the elements of the series are to one another: they are **measures of central tendency.** Other representative numbers stress the differences within the series: these are **measures of dispersion.**

MEASUREMENT TECHNIQUES

Many of the measures of central tendency will be familiar. The primary measures are **mean, median,** and **mode.** The mean is the average value of the series. To calculate the mean, all the members of the series are added together and then are divided by the number of members in the series. The equation appears as follows:

$$\text{Mean} = \overline{X} = \frac{\Sigma x_i}{N}$$

where Σ = the addition function
x = element of the series
i = the time period of the element
N = the number of elements

The mean is also known as the average in everyday speech and the same measure is used to determine the expected value in finance.

The mean is the number halfway between the high and low of the series. The median, on the other hand, is in the middle of the data points themselves. That is, the median is the number such that half the members of the number series lie above it and half the members lie below. The mode is the most common value, or most common range of values, regardless of where along the range it lies. The mode can be at the low end, near the high end, or anywhere in between. See Figure 1.A.1 for an overview of the measures of central tendency.

The measures of central tendency seek to identify a representative member of the series. When an attempt is made to forecast the next member in the series, one of these measures should not be too far off. In the absence of any other information, using either the mean, median, or mode will give an estimate that should be close to the actual level. To improve the degree of accuracy, however, other methods of analysis such as regression analysis, are employed. There is a difficulty in using a measure of central tendency as a forecast. To achieve any degree of accuracy, the series needs to have already traded near or at both the long term high and low. When the series is seeing a directional move over time we refer to a **trend condition,** where the use of a measure of central tendency is subject to potentially large errors.

This concept of using one of these measures for forecasting purposes, usually the average, is called **regression to the mean.** This implies that there is a normal or "correct" value and that the members of the time series will fluctuate around this value. See Figure 1.A.2. As an example, we can take the price of a man's cotton shirt. Sometimes the

Figure 1.A.1.   Measures of Central Tendency

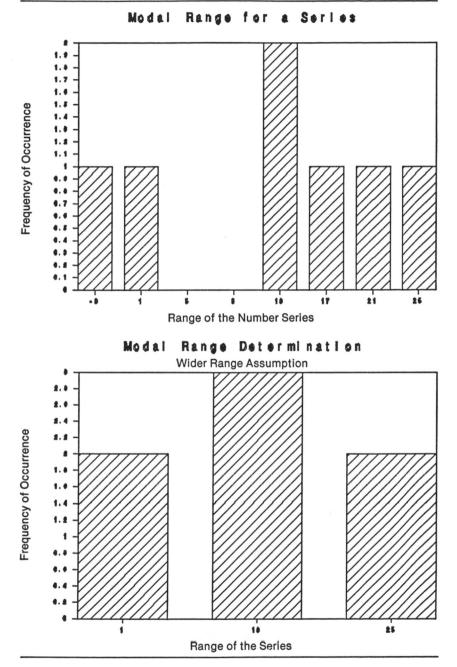

Figure 1.A.1.   Measures of Central Tendency *(continued)*

The *Mean*

$$\text{Mean} = \overline{X} = \frac{\Sigma\,(x_1)}{N}$$

As an example, take the number
series A = {12, 15, 22, −3, 17, 2, 27}

There are 7 elements in the series, so N = 7. When we add the individual elements in the series together, the sum is 92 so the mean is 13.142.

The *Median* is calculated by placing the elements in numerical order as follows:

$$[-3,2,12,15,17,22,27]$$
$$\uparrow$$

The median is 15.
Half the data lies above it, half the data lies below.

The *Mode* is the most common value, or most common range of values. In this series, there is no repeated value, but we can designate ranges. See the Figure 1.A.1 graphs for examples of modal frequency. You can see that the mode is heavily dependent on the width chosen for the range. In both of these cases though, the mode is 13.

So when choosing a single number to represent this series, we arrive at similar answers; 13.14, 15, and 13.

---

price is higher than usual due to cotton shortages or mill strikes. Sometimes the price is lower than usual due to oversupply of cotton or increases in inventories. However, there will always be a usual price. While this concept is helpful in times of stable markets, the current volatility or change in interest rates makes it more doubtfully useful for forecasting financial prices. Therefore, when attempting to forecast in the financial markets, you must be very cautious of using the average price to guess the next number in the series, for it will be no more accurate than a guess under most circumstances.

The measures of dispersion indicate how different the members of a series are from one another. For instance, two series might have the same average, but be very different. Their respective measures of dis-

Figure 1.A.2. Regression to the Mean: June 1991 Bond Futures

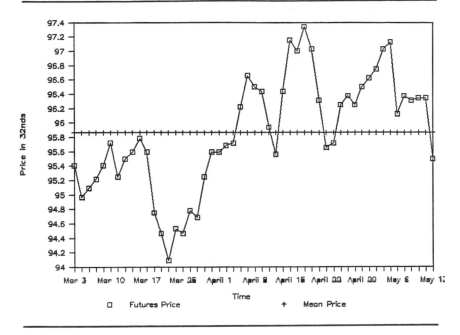

persion are probably quite different as well. The three common measures of dispersion are **range, variance,** and **standard deviation.** The standard deviation is the most commonly used measure of dispersion.

The range is the size of the breadth of the series. It is measured by taking the difference between the high value of the series and the low value. The equation can be stated as follows:

$$\text{Range} = R = x_H - x_L$$

where x = element of the series
       H = high value
       L = low value

A small or tight range indicates that there is less chance that a forecast will be significantly wrong.

The variance is the sum of the squared deviations from the mean divided by the number of items in the series. That is, the difference between each member and the mean is calculated and squared, then these calculations are added together and divided by the number of members of the series. This results in a sort of average squared deviation from the mean. The squaring process is important because it makes small deviations even smaller and minimizes their difference from the mean. However, it magnifies a large difference from the mean, in effect making a large deviation easier to spot. The equation is as follows:

$$\text{Variance} = \sigma^2 = \Sigma \; \frac{(X_i - \overline{X})^2}{N}$$

where Σ = the addition function
       X = element of the series
       i = time period of the element
       $\overline{X}$ = mean
       N = number of elements

The standard deviation is the easiest calculation to make. It is the square root of the variance, which eliminates one awkward use of variance. Variance is measured in units-squared, which has no real meaning. By putting the dispersion measure back into standard units, the measure becomes more conceptually useful. It essentially indicates the amount of variability in the members of the series. The full equation is as follows, using the same symbolism as previously:

$$\text{Standard Deviation} = \sigma = \sqrt{\frac{\Sigma \, (X_i - \overline{X})^2}{N}}$$

As an example, see Figure 1.A.3.

EXPRESSING PROBABILITY

An event with different possible outcomes is a random variable. To examine the likelihood of occurrence for each possible outcome, we construct a **probability distribution curve.** This plots the various possible outcomes against the probability of their occurrence. For instance, the outcome of tossing a coin is a random variable. In this case,

Figure 1.A.3.   Measures of Dispersion

The *Range* is simply the difference between the high value of the series and the low value. Taking the series from Figure 1.A.1,

$$A = \{12, 15, 22, -3, 17, 2, 27\}$$

The range is the difference between 27 and −3, or 30.

The *Variance* is a method of calculating the amount any individual element of the series will differ from the mean. In our example, with $N = 7$,

$$\sigma^2 = [\,(12 - 13.142)^2 + (15 - 13.142)^2 + (22 - 13.142)^2 + (-3 - 13.143)^2 + (17 - 13.142)^2 + (2 - 13.142)^2 + (27 - 13.142)^2\,]$$
$$\overline{\hspace{6cm}}$$
$$7$$

Variance = $674.856/7 = 96.408$ units-squared

The *standard deviation* is simply the square-root of the variance, so that the answer is quoted in regular units. In this case, the standard deviation = 9.819 units.

The standard deviation is used in constructing a *confidence interval*. This provides a range of values for a forecast of the next element in the series. The confidence interval is determined by both adding and subtracting the value of the standard deviation to the mean. For instance,

$$\text{Confidence Interval} = \overline{X} \pm \sigma$$
$$13.142 \pm 9.819$$
$$3.323 > x_i > 22.96$$

which means that the next element can fall between 3 and 23, and still comfortably fit within the series.

---

the range of outcomes is small. The heads/tail outcome can be transformed into a 0/1 outcome for the graph when we assign the value of zero to a heads outcome and a value of one to a tails outcome. When we draw a probability distribution curve for this event, it consists of two points, zero and one, each with a .50 probability. See Figure 1.A.4 for an example.

As the number of outcomes increases, a **bell curve** takes shape. Fig-

Figure 1.A.4.   Probability Distribution for Tossing a Coin

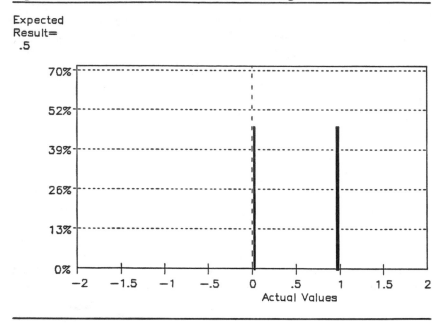

ure 1.A.5 shows a variety of bell curves. The highest probability of occurrence is at the mean or expected value of the possibilities. As the deviation of the specific outcome deviates from the mean, the probability decreases. The actual probability associated with the mean will vary from event to event, but is usually somewhere around .25 or 25%.

The **normal curve** is a standardized version of the bell curve probability distribution. The mean is set at 0, and the standard deviation is one. The range for the normal curve runs from negative infinity to positive infinity and is symmetric around the mean. A key figure to remember is that there is a 67% probability that an event's outcome will fall between plus and minus one. That is, the outcome for an event will fall within one standard deviation of the mean. See Figure 1.A.6 for a picture of the normal curve.

The beauty of a standardized curve is that the event's outcome is expressed in terms of standard deviation. Specific distribution curves can be transformed to the normal curve so that one series of numbers can easily be compared to another. A series of outcomes for an event

Figure 1.A.5.   Types of Bell Curves

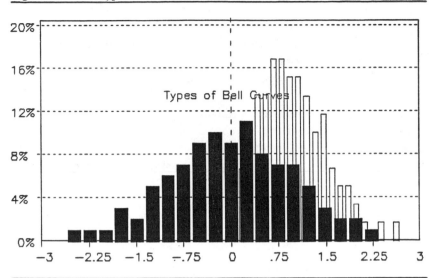

Figure 1.A.6.   An Example of a Normal Curve

Expected
Result=
 4.070015

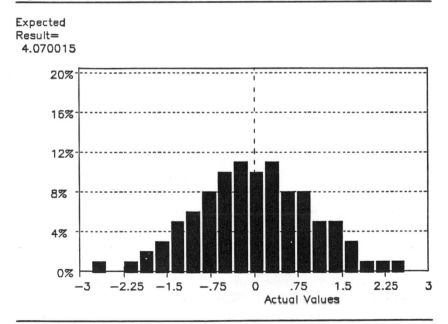

that results in a rather flat distribution curve with a wide range can be compared with a series of outcomes that results in a tight range and a more "humped" profile. We can do this because the mathematics transforms the curves to permit a comparison based on the respective standard deviations. For each point on the distribution curve that is to be tested, the mean of the series is subtracted and this resulting figure is divided by the standard deviation. The calculation is called a **Z-transformation.** The Z-number tells how many standard deviations away from the mean that corresponding point falls on the normal curve. If the Z-number is negative, it falls to the left of the mean and if the Z-number is positive it lies on the right side of the mean. The formula is:

$$Z = \frac{(X_i - \overline{X})}{\sigma_x}$$

where   Z = Corresponding point on the normal curve
           σ_x = Standard Deviation of series x

The laws of probability can tell us the likelihood that a particular outcome will occur. This will depend on where along the normal curve the transformed outcome will fall. The transformation can also be used as a test to check the probability of occurrence for a range of outcomes. It measures the proportion of the area under the normal curve between the mean (which is zero) and the potential outcome. The maximum possible value for this test is .50, which would be a measure from zero to plus infinity. Generally, the transformed Z-value should be between zero and one to be most likely, as this means the outcome falls within one standard deviation of the mean. An outcome is statistically possible if the transformed value is between 0 and 2. This translates as a specific point falling within two standard deviations of either side of the mean. However, if the outcome produces a Z-value greater than two, we are talking about a very small chance of occurrence unless conditions change. For a Z-value of 2 or more, there is only about a 3% chance for the outcome to happen. See Figure 1.A.7 for an example of the use of the test.

The notion of the symmetry of the normal curve is important, as it introduces the concept of *skew*. Skew occurs when the distribution of returns is asymmetric, or not symmetric to the mean. The normal curve implies that a return better than the average is as likely as a return worse than the average. When positive skew is introduced, the likelihood of doing better than average is greater than the chance of doing worse. Also, by examining the returns and recognizing negative skew conditions, they can be avoided. We can use a number of derivative products to change the distribution of a security's returns from symmetric to skewed. Particularly, a positive skew is desired because it gives a higher probability of a neutral to positive return at the expense of negative returns. This is a very desirable distribution because it has the effect of "weighting the dice" by moving the mode away from the mean. Any investment looks more attractive if there is a smaller chance of losing money, so if the most common return becomes greater than the average return, there is a lesser chance of seeing below-average returns. This protection is generally paid for by a sacrifice of some of the potential positive returns.

CONDITIONAL EVENTS

Previously, we looked at distribution curves as if outcomes were independent, or not influenced by any outside forces—as if they were a law unto themselves. Obviously, this is not the case. When we choose to examine the outcome of any event in terms of another event, the events are dependent. This is where **Bayes' Rule** comes into play. Bayes' Rule is a formula for calculating the probability of an outcome associated with a different, separate event. See Figure 1.A.8. We can look at "if . . . , then . . . statements" to put the event series in English and use Bayes' Rule to find the **conditional probability** for the combined events. For example, "if the price of oil increases, then bond prices will fall" may be your model. By multiplying the conditional probability (which is the likelihood of bond prices moving up or down) by the probability of the conditioning variable (which is the likelihood of oil moving up or down), we get the probability for this particular combined event. By doing this calculation for every combination of the two events (both up, both down, the first one up and the other one down, and the first one down and the other one up) we can develop a probability distribution of returns for this conditional case. See Figure 1.A.9. Therefore, even when two variables are dependent, derivatives can be used.

Figure 1.A.7. Using the Z-Test

Using the series in Figures 1.A.1 and 1.A.3, we can use the Z-test to examine how likely it is that the next number in the series will be 5.

$$A = \{12, 15, 22, -3, 17, 2, 27\}$$

$$\bar{X} = 13.142 \qquad \sigma = 9.819$$

To determine the probability that the next number in the series is 5 or greater, we calculate Z as

$$Z = (5 - 13.142)/9.819 = -.829$$

Using the normal distribution table, we find that the probability of the next element in the series being *less* than 5 is .2033 or 20.33%. So the chance that the element will be greater than 5 is $100 - 20.33 = 79.67\%$. In using this test, we measure how many standard deviations away from the series' mean the element falls. In this example, 5 falls .83 standard deviations below the mean.

A partial Normal Distribution Table follows. Use it by moving down the vertical axis until you reach the first digit of the Z-calculation, then move horizontally across until you reach the second digit. The value at the intersection of horizontal and vertical is the probability that the next element in the series will be the forecast or smaller.

Z	−.00	−.01	−.02	−.03	−.04	−.05	−.06	−.07	−.08	−.09
						Normal Distribution Table				
0.0	0.5000	0.5040	0.5080	0.5120	0.5160	0.5199	0.5239	0.5279	0.5319	0.5359
0.1	0.5398	0.5438	0.5478	0.5517	0.5557	0.5596	0.5636	0.5675	0.5714	0.5753
0.2	0.5793	0.5832	0.5871	0.5910	0.5948	0.5897	0.6026	0.6064	0.6103	0.6141
0.3	0.6179	0.6217	0.6255	0.6293	0.6331	0.6368	0.6406	0.6443	0.6480	0.6517
0.4	0.6554	0.6592	0.6628	0.6664	0.6700	0.6736	0.6772	0.6808	0.6844	0.6880

z										
0.5	0.6915	0.6950	0.6985	0.7019	0.7054	0.7088	0.7123	0.7157	0.7190	0.7224
0.6	0.7257	0.7291	0.7324	0.7357	0.7389	0.7422	0.7454	0.7486	0.7517	0.7549
0.7	0.7580	0.7611	0.7642	0.7673	0.7704	0.7734	0.7764	0.7794	0.7823	0.7852
0.8	0.7881	0.7910	0.7939	0.7967	0.7995	0.8023	0.8051	0.8078	0.8106	0.8133
0.9	0.8159	0.8186	0.8212	0.8238	0.8264	0.8289	0.8315	0.8340	0.8365	0.8389
1.0	0.8413	0.8438	0.8461	0.8485	0.8508	0.8531	0.8554	0.8577	0.8599	0.8621
1.1	0.8643	0.8665	0.8686	0.8708	0.8729	0.8749	0.8770	0.8790	0.8810	0.8830
1.2	0.8849	0.8870	0.8888	0.8907	0.8925	0.8944	0.8962	0.8980	0.8997	0.9015
1.3	0.9032	0.9049	0.9066	0.9082	0.9099	0.9115	0.9131	0.9147	0.9162	0.9177
1.4	0.9192	0.9207	0.9222	0.9236	0.9251	0.9265	0.9279	0.9292	0.9306	0.9319
1.5	0.9332	0.9345	0.9357	0.9370	0.9382	0.9394	0.9406	0.9418	0.9429	0.9441
1.6	0.9452	0.9463	0.9474	0.9484	0.9495	0.9505	0.9515	0.9525	0.9535	0.9545
1.7	0.9554	0.9564	0.9573	0.9582	0.9591	0.9599	0.9608	0.9616	0.9625	0.9633
1.8	0.9641	0.9649	0.9656	0.9664	0.9671	0.9678	0.9686	0.9693	0.9700	0.9706
1.9	0.9713	0.9719	0.9726	0.9732	0.9738	0.9744	0.9750	0.9756	0.9761	0.9767
2.0	0.9772	0.9778	0.9783	0.9788	0.9793	0.9798	0.9803	0.9808	0.9812	0.9817
2.1	0.9821	0.9826	0.9830	0.9834	0.9838	0.9842	0.9846	0.9850	0.9854	0.9857
2.2	0.9861	0.9864	0.9868	0.9871	0.9875	0.9878	0.9881	0.9884	0.9887	0.9890
2.3	0.9893	0.9896	0.9898	0.9901	0.9904	0.9906	0.9909	0.9911	0.9913	0.9916
2.4	0.9918	0.9920	0.9922	0.9925	0.9927	0.9929	0.9931	0.9932	0.9934	0.9936
2.5	0.9938	0.9940	0.9941	0.9943	0.9945	0.9946	0.9948	0.9949	0.9951	0.9952

Figure 1.A.8.   Bayes' Rule
_____

This rule is used to determine the likelihood of an event, once another event has occurred. It is used in finance to calculate the probability that a price will occur once a particular price in another, dependent market has been observed. The equation is as follows:

$$P(E_i/A) = \frac{P(E_i)\,P(A\,/\,E_i)}{\Sigma\,P(E_i)\,P(A/E_i)}$$

In plain language, the probability that E will occur once A has occurred is the probability that both events will occur divided by the probability that A (the conditional event) alone will occur.
_____

This sort of conditional event is useful in the process of options pricing, since there seem to be two types of price movement. One type is essentially random, since it depends on day-to-day minor supply/demand fluctuations and is not a sustained price move. The other type is a change in the value of the security. It tends to be sustained, and it will depend on major shifts in supply/demand for both the security itself and on close substitutes. Therefore, while short-term moves can be treated as independent events, usually longer term moves are conditional on some other event.

Determining the mean or expected value for a conditional event is actually a simple process. The expected return is denoted as E(R) and is the sum of the separate scenarios. The probability for one combination of events is multiplied by the associated expected return. This calculation is done for all the combinations or scenarios, and the results are added together. The resulting figure will be the expected value. See Figure 1.A.10.

The mean deviation is calculated similarly. The difference between the scenario return and the expected return is squared, then multiplied by the probability that that scenario will occur. This is done for all the scenarios, and the results are added together. The result is the **variance** for the series. The square root of the variance equals the standard deviation of return for the conditional series. See Figure 1.A.11.

Figure 1.A.9. Conditional Probability

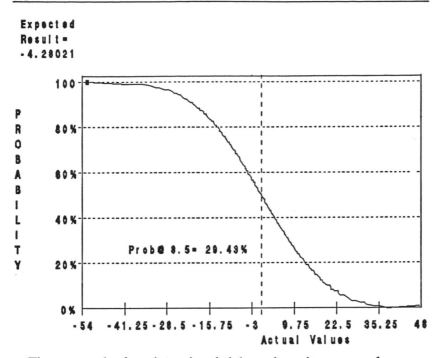

This is a graph of conditional probability, where the returns of an event are dependent on a secondary event. In this case, the mean return is almost zero (−.00428). However, if the secondary event occurs, then the chance of this security achieving a return of 8.5% or greater is 29.43%. While this does not appear to be too unfavorable, it implies that the likelihood of achieving a result of less than 8.5% is 70.57%. Therefore, if the 8.5% is a target level, the chance of the secondary event occurring should be carefully monitored.

MEASURES OF ASSOCIATION

When we speak of conditional events, it brings up the notions of correlation and covariance. These are measures of association between two different variables. They measure the similarity of the price directions of two separate events. The **covariance** is the sum of the multi-

Figure 1.A.10.   Calculating the Expected Value of a Conditional Event

Suppose that under three different economic conditions, there are three separate forecasts for a security's return. Each separate economic scenario has a different probability of occurrence under current conditions. By multiplying the expected result for each scenario by the probability of its happening, we arrive at a cumulative expected return for the security. For example:

Scenario #1	Mean Return = 12.5%	Probability = 35%
Scenario #2	Mean Return = 7.75%	Probability = 40%
Scenario #3	Mean Return = −.50%	Probability = 25%

$$(.125 * .35) + (.0775 * .40) + (-.050 * .25) = .06225$$
or 6.225% cumulative expected return

plication of the differences between one variable and its mean, and the other variable and its mean. The formula is:

$$\text{Covariance} = \text{Cov} = \Sigma \frac{(X_i - \bar{X})(Y_i - \bar{Y})}{N}$$

where   X = element of series A
            Y = element of series B
             i = time period of the element
            $\bar{X}$ = mean of series A
            $\bar{Y}$ = mean of series B
            N = number of elements each series contains

The **correlation** is a standardized version of the covariance that ranges from negative one to positive one. It is calculated by taking the covariance and dividing it by the standard deviations of the two series. See Figure 1.A.12. This idea of a standardized covariance measure has important implications in connection with conditional probability measure. It affects the conditional probabilities, because if the returns are highly correlated, the probability distribution will be wider and flatter since there will be higher probabilities associated with the extreme values. On the other hand, if there is no correlation and the measure is near zero. then the higher probabilities will be clustered around the mean, reflecting random events.

Figure 1.A.11. Conditional Variance and Standard Deviation

As calculated in Figure A.10, the conditional mean return is 6.225%. To calculate the *variance*, or *mean deviation*, for the series, the single expected results are subtracted from the conditional expectation. This number is then squared, and multiplied by the likelihood that the scenario will occur. The separate variances are then summed to arrive at the conditional variance. For example,

$$
\begin{array}{l}
(.1250 - .06225)^2 * .35 \\
+ \ (.0775 - .06225)^2 * .40 \\
\underline{+ \ (-.050 - .06225)^2 * .25} \\
.004618
\end{array}
$$

Thus *Variance* = .004618

The square root of this variance is the *conditional standard deviation*. For this example, it equals .06800.

When examining variables to see if two or more of them are associated in any way, we also need to look at the series itself to see if it is representative. That is, we want to know if the part of the total series that has already occurred is a fair sample for the rest of the series that we are trying to forecast. If a series of returns is not representative, then we might draw incorrect forecasts for how the security's price will respond to different circumstances. For example, if the first five years of returns are lower than average, we might underestimate returns for the next five years. Equally, if the returns are higher than average, we might overestimate returns. Overestimation might lead us to think that a security is a more attractive investment than it really is, while underestimation might provide better-than-expected returns. Thus, being conservative on estimates of future prices offers the best upside potential. The series of historical returns drawn from the past may well not be representative. When the historical series is moving toward an unknown long term average, it is called a **price trend.** In that circumstance, any assumptions of regression to the mean are likely to be inaccurate.

We handle the question of potential misrepresentation mostly by using common sense. We need to look at the series and see if the price

Figure 1.A.12.   Examples of Covariance and Correlation

Using series A from Figure 1.A.1, and creating series B, we have:

$$\text{series A} = \{12, 15, 22, -3, 17, 2, 27\}$$
$$\text{series B} = \{6, 9, 15, 17, 20, 21, 23\}$$

The mean of A = 13.142, and the mean of B = 15.857, N = 7

$$
\begin{aligned}
\text{Cov} = \ &(12-13.142)\,(6-15.857) \\
+\ &(15-13.142)\,(9-15.857) \\
+\ &(22-13.142)\,(15-15.857) \\
+\ &(-3-13.142)\,(17-15.857) \\
+\ &(17-13.142)\,(20-15.857) \\
+\ &(2-13.142)\,(21-15.857) \\
+\ &\underline{(27-13.142)\,(23-15.857)} \\
&33.11
\end{aligned}
$$

$$33.\frac{11}{7} = 4.73$$

Thus, the covariance of the two series is 4.73 units squared.

To calculate the *correlation*, simply take the covariance and divide it by the standard deviation for each series. This standardizes the number to fall between negative one and positive one.

$$\text{Correlation coefficient} = \frac{\text{Cov}}{\sigma_A * \sigma_B} = \frac{(4.73)}{(9.819*5.866)} = +.082$$

moves are what we would expect. If they are not, we must know why. At times, there may be a third factor that only occasionally influences returns. At other times, we may find that the relationship between to variables is accidental, not **causal,** and that an apparent relationship can be explained by coincidence. This is where logic and common sense are key. Thus, while probability and statistics offer new tools to manage risk by altering the probable distribution of returns, there is still very much a place for the fundamental investor. These methods are additions to the tools of the investment analyst, not replacements for other methods.

CHAPTER 2

Hedging

Hedging is the act of managing a particular type of risk, where managing is generally understood to be an attempt to reduce the risk for which there is not enough additional return. Often one is able to separate out the sources of risk and transfer the undesirable portion to another market participant with more appetite for risk. The usual process is using a similar type of financial instrument to take the same position in an opposite direction, so that a level of return can be assured for the combined outcome. A simple example would be selling Treasury bond futures contracts to hedge an underlying position in government securities. The hedge instrument is usually not an exactly offsetting match. Therefore, hedging is not like arbitrage, where a profit is locked in. Instead, hedging narrows the probability distribution of outcomes. See Figure 2.1.

The ultimate offset between the risky position and the hedge will depend on the relative **price path** of the securities. A price path is the behavior of the price of a security over time. See Figure 2.2. For example, we assume that certain futures and options prices will tend toward a known price at a certain date, like at-the-money options tending towards zero at expiration or futures contracts prices converging toward

Figure 2.1.   How Hedging Alters the Probability Distribution Curve

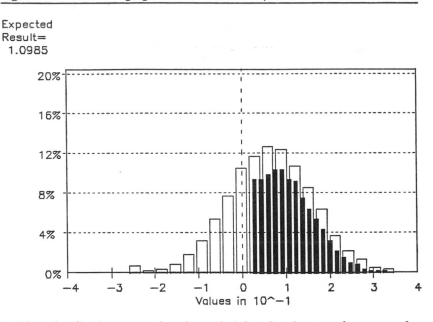

The role of hedging is to alter the probability distribution of outcomes for a risky situation. In this example, the white bars show the original probability distribution, and the black bars show the probability distribution after a hedge program was initiated. Notice that the chance of a positive outcome has greatly increased, and the negative returns are truncated at zero.

the cash price at expiration. However, the exact path the price will take at any particular time is unknown. This is dependent on day-to-day supply/demand shifts, liquidity, and, most importantly, an expectational factor we can only begin to measure. One security might show a steady decline in price until an abrupt upward move occurs near expiration, while another might show a more regular move toward zero, edging there a bit more every day. With another security there may be violent gyrations or no movement at all. All of these price behaviors are possible, and all of them would imply an inexact match between the asset and the hedge instrument. How narrow the distribution of outcomes can become will depend on the specific hedge instrument and strategy chosen.

Figure 2.2.   Price Path of a Security: June 1991 Bond Futures

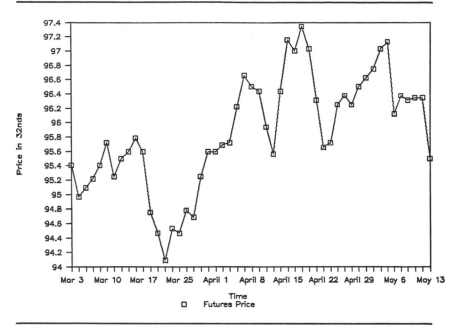

There seems to be an assumption that hedging a risk eliminates risk completely, but that is far from the truth. How much risk is transferred to another party and how much is retained depends on (1) what instrument is used as the hedge vehicle, (2) how closely the price movement of the hedge instrument correlates with the underlying security, and (3) how closely the amount hedged matches the amount of the risk. After all, risk does not normally occur in round, even lots. A risky asset may have a very specific present value in dollars and cents while the risk can be hedged cheaply only in large, round-number lots.

Indeed, sometimes the amount of risk exposure is neither exact nor certain. For instance, suppose you are an importer. You have a view that domestic interest rates will increase in the next six months, but you are uncertain what effect that will have on demand for your products. However, you do know that an increase in rates will increase your borrowing or funding costs. In such a case, you may choose to fine-tune the management of your assets and liabilities. You may opt to transfer more of the risk in any mismatch to others by duration

Figure 2.3.   Decision Path for Placing a Hedge

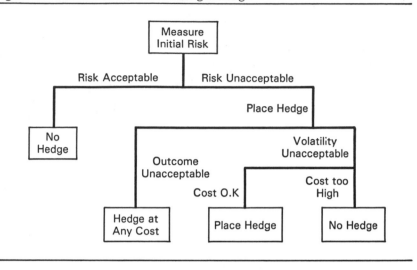

hedging or using swaps. This would mean that any increase in your borrowing costs would be exactly offset by increases to your investment account. As an alternative, you might choose to institute a new policy of making purchases by cash but allowing more leniency in your receivables. In this way, your interest costs would be lessened but you would be paid more interest by others. As a third alternative, you might choose to take a small "short" position in some interest-rate futures contract or purchase a put. Sometimes, though, the consequences of a change are ambiguous. Some risk protection is sought to avert the downside, but total protection might well lose you an attractive upside opportunity. That is why the decisions about risk management really are most effective when made in conjunction with an overall view of the business or department concerned. Figure 2.3 illustrates a decision path for placing a hedge.

CHOOSING A HEDGE VEHICLE

One factor in the choice of a hedge vehicle will be how closely the price movements of the vehicle match with the underlying security. Sometimes the hedge will match closely for small moves, but less well for large ones. This can actually increase the risk, as a large move in price may cause losses in both the primary position and in the hedge. An example of this might be hedging a Eurodollar denominated bond you own by selling Eurodollar futures. For large price moves, the price of one or the other is likely to "overshoot" theoretical value. If you are short the futures contract, you may experience a larger loss than the gain from owning the underlying cash security. You also should break out the components of price moves, if you can. For example, if you want to compare price movements of longer-term corporates with U.S. bond futures contracts, it is a good idea to separate out the credit spread. Corporate bonds are generally priced by looking at the comparable maturity government bond and adding some number of basis points to compensate for the additional credit risk. This additional yield is usually measured in basis points (bps) and is known as the **spread.** For instance, a 10-year corporate bond may be priced at +110 bps over Treasuries. That means if 10-year government notes are yielding 8.06%, a typical corporate security would yield 9.16%. This pricing spread above Treasuries is a variable separate from movements of absolute interest rates. Depending on the degree of credit risk, it might move from +30 bps to +225 bps. Figure 2.4 shows a graph of the spread over time. The credit spread moves from +30 bps to +160 bps in a six-month period.

It is also a good idea to look at the **duration** of your corporate security or portfolio of securities versus the duration of the bond futures. The duration is the weighted average of the cash flows for the security. If there are few or small cash flows in the near future and most repayments are near the maturity date, then the duration will be longer than that of a security with more and larger payments in the near-term. A mismatch here may well throw off any planned asset-liability management. If your obligations (liabilities) are owed soon (short duration-weighted) and the obligations owed to you (assets) are long duration-weighted, then we have what is known as a **gap.** Figure 2.5 shows a time-line with incoming and outgoing payments represented by arrows. The diagram depicts a positive gap where the incoming monies are received before outgoing monies are due. However, even a positive gap is less than desirable because either the payments received sit idle earning no interest, or they must be re-invested at a less than optimal interest rate. A common personal example is when a family's bills are due on the 15th of the month but the wage-earner is not paid until the

Figure 2.4. Credit Spreads Over Time: GM 8.125% due 4/16 vs. Generic 30y Tsy

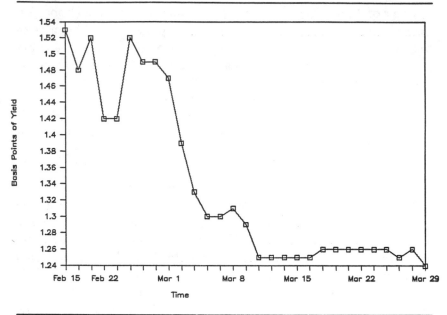

30th. Either the bills are paid early, losing the time-value of the funds, or they are paid late, incurring interest charges.

Another factor in the decision of which vehicle to use will be **commission costs.** Some of the more custom hedges have a higher commission simply because the party who assumes the risk for you will have higher costs in passing on the part of the risk he chooses not to keep. Think of risk as something concrete. It cannot be eliminated, but it can be divided up and passed along to others. If one party must accept a larger piece than desired to obtain any at all, they may charge a higher price to transact. Also, since risk may consist of either positive or negative **price sensitivity,** which is the direction you do not want price to move, some risks can be "matched up" so that they are neutral. Passing a risk of a decline in price on to someone who already has a risk of an increase in price causes the combined risk to become neutral. The party that can neutralize risk and receive fee income from the commission may well lower his price. This type of transaction is thus the cheapest way to hedge. However, since it is not usually clear who

Figure 2.5.   Asset/Liability Gap: Cash Inflows vs. Cash Outflows

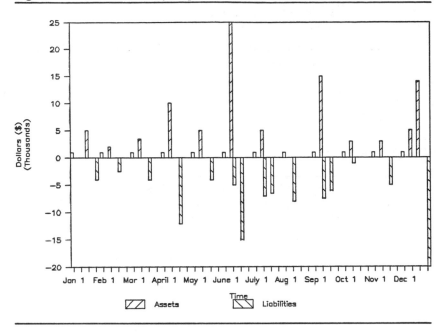

needs what type of price risk to move to a neutral position, this is difficult to do. Comparison of prices and bid/ask levels is the only way to get a feel for this. When a broker/dealer does not want a particular position, he becomes less aggressive by raising his selling price and lowering the buying price. This means that few or no deals will be done, since the other party wants to buy from the seller at a lower price and sell at a higher price and will go elsewhere to transact the deal. However, for a position this broker/dealer would like to have, he will set the selling price lower so that more buyers will be attracted. If the broker/dealer wants to buy, he raises the acceptable bid so that more sellers are attracted.

An additional strategy may be to exchange one type of risk for another. Instead of eliminating risk, choosing strategy A over strategy B would give you an exposure to a different type of risk that might be more acceptable to your purposes. You might consider hedging your corporate bond by selling futures contracts against it or by entering an interest-rate swap to fix the level of the cash flows. The swap is a more exact hedge, but it limits participation if rates move favorably. The futures strategy is a less exact hedge, but it covers the general interest-rate risk. If you are comfortable with the credit-spread risk, or if the commission is less, and this alternative exposure to credit-spread risk is acceptable, this might be the best choice. See Figure 2.6 for a diagram of how commissions affect the probability distributions.

A factor similar to commissions costs is processing costs. **Processing costs** are composed of security settlement costs, margin calculations and their settlement, and financing costs. The more complicated the deal, the higher the processing costs. Generally the term **back-office costs** is also used, but this does not take into account the number of man-hours required by the front-office in checking limits and executing the deal. A customized hedge with a fixed term, perhaps a forward agreement or a swap, needs much less ongoing care than an exchange-traded future or option, which needs constant marking-to-market and rolling over. Also, a standardized product may not provide an exact

Figure 2.6.　The Effect of Commissions on Probable Price Distribution

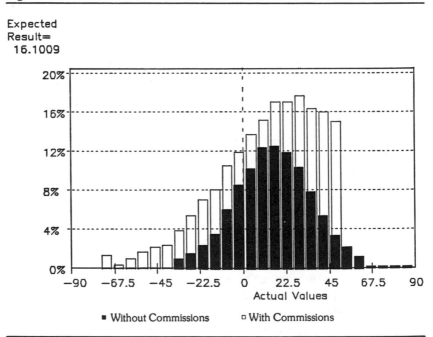

match in dates. For example, you may want protection over the weekend, while the exchange product may mature the Friday before.

The last concern in deciding on a hedge vehicle is the amount of protection offered. Generally, a range of possibilities is available. An exact match can be provided by a customized forward. The match will be much less exact if an exchange-traded product is used. When the protection purchased is for a value greater than the risky position, we refer to it as an **overhedged case.** If the protection is provided for only a percentage of the risky position, we speak of an **underhedged case.** When a position is overhedged, it is as though the excess hedge is a new, unhedged position. If the hedge provides only partial protection, then the investor is assuming more risk than is optimal.

CALCULATING HEDGE UNITS

The equation for determining the necessary number of units of the hedge vehicle is fairly simple. Units refers to the smallest standard size of the underlying security. For fixed-income securities, this is usually $1,000,000. However many derivative securities have a minimum size of $10,000. So there is a need to compare the underlying security to the hedge vehicle to calculate how many units of the underlying security can be hedged with one unit of the hedge vehicle. This calculation is done by taking the face value of one unit of the underlying security and dividing it by the face value of one unit of the hedge vehicle. For Treasury bonds, the value is 10, because the face value of the cash is $1,000,000 and the face value of the futures is $10,000. This figure is the number of futures contracts needed to hedge one cash bond. This figure is then calculated by the hedge ratio to derive the exact number of futures contracts needed to offset the underlying security.

$$\# \text{ of units} = \frac{\$ \text{ face value of position be hedged} \times \text{Hedge Ratio}}{\$ \text{ face value per unit of hedge vehicle}}$$

However, the number of units so determined may not be an even number. When you need 4.6 units to place a hedge, but can purchase only full units, then of necessity you must be either overhedged or underhedged.

Hedge Ratios

The hedge ratio is a factor that attempts to account for the relative price volatilities between the underlying and the hedge instrument. The magnitude of a price move is usually not the same for the underlying security and the hedge, even when the direction is the same. There are a number of different ways to determine the hedge ratio. Most of these methods were designed for futures contracts, but they can be expanded to encompass other hedge instruments. These methods can be classified by whether or not their use requires a directional view on prices.

Naive Model. The naive hedge model is aptly named. It contains very naive ideas of price behavior and assumes an exact correlation in price movements between the underlying security and the hedge vehicle. For this model, the hedge ratio is always one. That is, it assumes that an exact match in face value between the underlying and the hedge will offer perfect protection. See Figure 2.7 for a diagram of how the naive model pictures price adjustments.

Conversion Factor Model. The futures market often uses a conversion factor model to calculate the hedge ratio. The hedge ratio is set equal to the futures conversion factor. The conversion factor is the price of a security that provides an effective 8% yield. This allows all government bonds to be easily compared despite differences in coupon and maturity. The 8% coupon bond is used as a standard because the long bond contract specifies an 8% coupon security. However, to keep supply liquid other coupon securities can be used in the futures delivery process. The conversion factors were devised to allow securities with coupons other than 8% to be delivered to settle a short futures position at expiration.

The underlying position you want to hedge may also not have this 8% coupon, or indeed, any constant cash flow that replicates any fixed bond coupon. For example, the risky position might be a floating-rate loan. The conversion factor model is a bit more sophisticated than the naive model in that it acknowledges that price moves are of differing magnitudes when the coupon is different. For a given change in yield, two otherwise identical securities will see a different magnitude of price change depending on their coupon. A higher coupon security will see

Figure 2.7. Price Behavior Assumptions: Naive Hedge Model

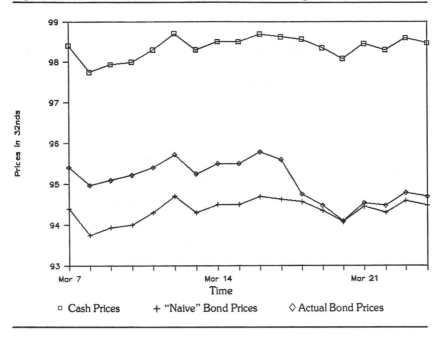

larger moves than will a smaller coupon security. While the conversion factor accounts for the greater volatility associated with a higher coupon, it assumes that coupon is the only variation. Usually, however, this is not the case. The time remaining to maturity, the credit quality of the security and how much the coupon level differs from current interest rates all affect price moves. After all, if the two securities were identical in all other ways, then the coupon would not have to vary significantly. The coupon is the price the issuer needs to pay to borrow the funds. If two bonds are identical, their issuing price should be very similar. The hedge ratio for this model is the conversion factor calculated by the Chicago Board of Trade. A higher conversion factor implies a greater volatility as measured against the standard 8% coupon of the contract. For example, a factor of 1.30 indicates that the security to be hedged is 1.3 times as volatile as the 8% government bond. This means that you will need more futures contracts to offset owning the underlying position. It also means that the commission is increasing, since futures commissions are based on the number of futures contracts bought or sold. Figure 2.8 diagrams how the conversion factor model assumes prices move.

Basis Point Model. The basis point model is used in the futures market to address the mismatch between the security to be hedged and the cheapest-to-deliver security for the appropriate futures contract. Its name comes from the fact that the model measures relative changes in price for a given change in yield, that is, per basis point. In general terms, the change in dollar value of the security or portfolio to be hedged is adjusted by a factor that is intended to make prices between the hedged security and the futures contract correlate more closely. In futures terms, this adjustment is the dollar-value change for a unit of yield change divided by a volatility term. In the futures market, this volatility term is the conversion factor for the cheapest-to-deliver. If the hedge vehicle is not futures, this model could still be used. In that case, the volatility effect would be measured from a zero-coupon, instead of using the 8% bond as a base.

Figure 2.8.   Price Behavior Assumptions: Conversion Factor Model

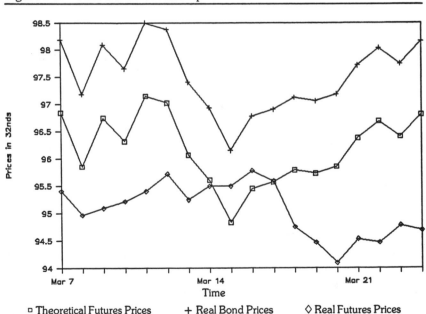

The basis point model works by comparing the relative volatilities between the risky security and the hedge security and adjusting them for a closer match. For example, if the hedge instrument is more volatile, then you need less of it to match the lower volatility underlying security. As a result, this model gives the best results for small changes in yield, but is really not suitable for a change larger than half a percentage point or so.

This model has a close correlation to the acceleration of volatility expressed as **delta,** which was discussed in Chapter 1. As delta continuously changes, so does the relative volatility. Therefore, this model generates high processing costs. The basis point model must be monitored continually and the hedge vehicle rebalanced often. As a result, futures and options are the hedges most often applied with this model. Moreover, because of the rebalancing, the total commission costs can be fairly high. This is particularly true in environments where volatility changes quite often. Since this type of market is difficult to forecast in advance, you should allow for higher-than-estimated commissions when initially evaluating whether to use this model. See Figure 2.9 for the equation, examples, and a diagram of the estimation process and price path expectations.

Duration-based Model. A model that has gained some recent popularity due to its universal applications is the duration-based model. Again, the most common use is when the hedge vehicle is futures or options, but this model is readily applied to other hedge instruments. The duration-based model is popular largely because duration matching has become common in asset-liability management. In this model, the hedge ratio is determined by the change in price of the position to be hedged divided by the change in price of the hedge vehicle:

$$\text{Hedge Ratio} = \frac{\Delta \text{ Price Position of Risk}}{\Delta \text{ Price of Hedging Instrument}}$$

Since this can be re-written in terms of duration, this becomes a simple equation with known inputs. The change in price for a given change in yield can be looked at as the price times the duration of the instrument. Since we can calculate the duration for any type or combination of cash flows, this model is applicable for portfolios with irregular cash

Figure 2.9.   An Example of the Basis Point Model

(A) Calculation of Yield Beta: GM 8-1/8 due 4/16 vs. Tsy 9-¼ due 2/16

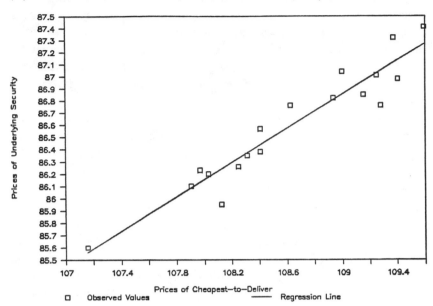

Prices of Cheapest—to—Deliver

□ Observed Values   —— Regression Line

(B) Basis Point Model: GM 8.125% of 4/16 vs. Futures

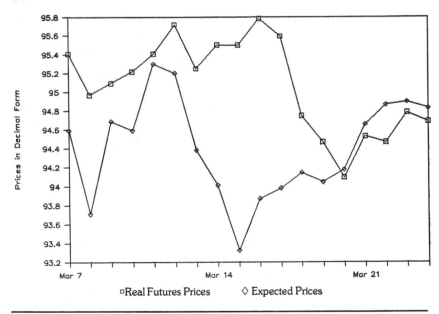

□ Real Futures Prices   ◇ Expected Prices

Figure 2.9.   An Example of the Basis Point Model: *(continued)*

The Hedge Ratio is calculated by comparing the relative price volatility of the underlying security to the price volatility of the hedge instrument. This ratio is then discounted by the conversion factor of the cheapest-to-deliver bond and multiplied by the *yield beta*, or relative volatility of the change in yield. This whole formula becomes:

$$HR = (\frac{BVC_{us}}{BVC_{ctd}}) * CF_{ctd} * \beta$$

Where BVC = Dollar value change per basis point yield change
  us = Underlying security
  ctd = Cheapest deliverable security for the bond
    futures contract
  CF = Conversion factor
  β = Relative yield change volatility

The BVC can be calculated by taking the dollar change in price of a $100,000 face value security when a one basis point change in yield occurs. The yield beta is calculated by plotting the cheapest-to-deliver bond against the underlying security. The slope of the line formed this way is the yield beta. It calculates the speed of the yield change of the underlying security to the cheapest-to-deliver security.

Let's look at an example. Suppose you own $1,000,000 face value of the General Motors 8.125% due 4/15/16. This is the underlying security. You wish to use the bond futures contract to hedge. This means that you will be selling some amount of the bond contract. You have further decided to use the Basis Point Hedging Model to calculate the hedge ratio to determine how many futures contracts to sell.

To use this model, first we need to determine the relative yield change volatility. Using a recent month and taking daily prices, the regression line in Figure 2.9A is formed. It gives a slope of about .7000. We will use this value for the Yield Beta.

Next, we need to calculate the basis point value for both the underlying security and the cheapest deliverable security for the futures contract. For a $100,000 face value, the General Motors security moves .10 in price. The cheapest-to-deliver security is currently the U.S. Treasury 9.25% due 2/15/16. For the same time period, it moves .0872 in price for a one basis point change in yield. So the ratio of basis point values is .1/.0872 or 1.1468.

Lastly, we take this ratio and multiply it by the conversion factor of the cheapest-to-deliver (1.1334) and multiply it then by the yield beta of .700. This gives a total of .9098, per equation 2.

Figure 2.9.   An Example of the Basis Point Model: *(continued)*

$$HR = (1.1468)*(1.1334)*(.7) = .9098$$

Once the hedge ratio is calculated, we derive the number of futures contracts to sell by multiplying the hedge ratio by the face value of the underlying
security ($1,000,000) and dividing by the face value of the futures contract
($100,000) to arrive at 9.098. In other words, to offset the risk of owning the
underlying position, we need to sell 9 futures contracts. This will leave us
underhedged by .098 contracts, or slightly less than 1%. A mismatch of 1% is
acceptable since there may be an error at least that large in estimating any of
the variables used to calculate the hedge ratio itself.

The calculation of the hedge ratio assumes a certain price action by the
futures contract. See Figure 2.9B for a diagram of how this model will expect
futures prices to behave, versus the historical reality.

---

flows such as real-estate, as well as equity or fixed-income portfolios.
Therefore, the equation for the hedge ratio becomes:

$$\text{Hedge Ratio} = \frac{\text{Portfolio Price} \times \text{Portfolio Duration}}{\text{Hedge Vehicle Price} \times \text{Hedge Vehicle Duration}}$$

Since all of these numbers can be measured, this version of the hedge
ratio is more precise. The hedge must still be rebalanced with some
frequency, since the price will change in response to market conditions
and the duration will change as cash flows are received. However, rebalancing will be required less often than under the conversion factor
model. Also, the basic hedge for the duration model, can be a customized vehicle, if you prefer, and the rebalancing can be done through
the futures or options market. Figure 2.10 shows the equation for
Macaulay's duration which is currently the industry standard. However, it is being overtaken by **Modified Duration** which adjusts for
the current level of interest rates.

Regression Model. The regression model for determining the hedge
ratio has gained some popularity due to the capability of numerous
analytical systems to do regression analysis. By plotting the historical

Figure 2.10.   Duration: Macaulay's and Modified

Macaulay duration is the weighted average time-to-maturity for the cash flows of a security or portfolio. It is calculated as follows:

$$D = \Sigma \frac{(t \times PVCF_t)}{(k \times PVTCF)}$$

$$= \Sigma \frac{(t \times \dfrac{CF_t}{(1 + r)^t})}{(k \times (\Sigma \dfrac{(CF_t)}{(1 + r)^t})}$$

Where D = Duration
        t = time period
   PVCF = Present Value of the Cash Flows
        k = Number of Periods Annually
 PVTCF = Present Value of the Total Cash Flows
     CF = Cash Flow
      Σ = The Addition Function

In plain English, the current price is the present value of the security's cash flows. Duration then weights each of the flows by the proportion of total price that the cash flow represents. For example, a cash flow that is worth half the current value of the security has a weight of .50. In this fashion, the larger cash flows that occur sooner are weighted more heavily than smaller cash flows owed farther in the future. Duration is a method of calculating the time you will have recovered half the value of the security, using the current price as a measure of value. So as time moves forward and payments are received, the duration of a security will change.

Modified duration adjusts the Macaulay measure to take into account the different interest-rate sensitivity for securities selling at a discount or premium. Modified duration is calculated as follows:

$$D* = \frac{D}{(1 + \dfrac{YTM}{k})}$$

Where D* = Modified Duration
      D = Macaulay's Duration
  YTM = Internal Rate of Return
      k = Number of Annual Time Periods

Both of these measures are related to other bond price volatility measures as well. For example, the Price Value of a Basis Point, used in the Basis Point Hedging Model, can be approximated using Modified Duration.

Figure 2.10.   Duration: Macaulay's and Modified (continued)

$$PVBP \approx \frac{D* \times P}{10,000}$$

Where P = Price of the Bond

And if trading near par,

$$PVBP \approx \frac{D*}{100}$$

These measures help to set the price moves for securities with different types of cash flows and different magnitudes of coupon payments more nearly equivalent.

---

prices of the position to be hedged against the historical prices of the hedge vehicle, a constant relationship may be found. The slope of the line of this relationship should approximate the hedge ratio.

Since most systems are able run a regression and since good data bases of historical prices for a number of securities are available, this process has become more simple than it was five or ten years ago. However, there are some problems. First, the regression assumes that whatever relationship held in the past will continue to hold in the future. However, due to changing regulations or supply/demand factors, this may not be true. Second, the regression also assumes that the relationship is a straight line. Therefore, if this assumption is not true, it is best to rebalance often so that the calculation will not differ greatly from the true relationship. Third, the regression is most accurate for small changes in yield. A number of seemingly solid relationships have changed when large jumps in price caused demand curves or credit considerations to shift.

Theoretically, the regression model has some merit. It is based on an examination of the correlation of price moves between the risk position and the hedge instrument. It also contains a factor that includes relative volatility between the two. Its major drawback is its description of a past relationship without evaluating systematically whether that relationship will continue to hold. In addition, the mathematics are rather simplistic, in that the relationship is always assumed to be a straight line, even though there are very few straight line relationships in finance.

Yield Forecast Model. The yield forecast or **multi-scenario model** attempts to account for expectational considerations, but it is most often used to add a "fudge factor" to the hedging process. The "soft" number in this process is the estimation of carrying costs. An additional drawback is the need to set a definite time horizon. While the other models let the time of the hedge vary, the yield forecast model requires an assumption for the length of time the hedge will be in place. If the length of time changes, then the calculation for the hedge ratio must be re-run. Fortunately, though, this model is well suited to a range of assumptions. You can use a fixed time horizon and consider different carrying costs, or you can keep the cost of carry fixed and vary the time periods. If you do both before actually placing the hedge, then you can determine if time or carry rate is the more sensitive variable. A variable is more sensitive if it changes greatly in value for a small change in the associated factor. For example, a bond is interest-rate sensitive if the price changes greatly for a small change in interest-rate levels. By calculating both variables, you can determine which will have the greater effect on your hedge.

The hedge ratio itself is calculated as the change in cash price divided by the change in the hedge instrument price for a given change in yield. This process is the same as for the regression model, duration model, and conversion factor model. The difference is in how the prices are calculated. In the conversion factor model, the hedge instrument is assumed to trade at a constant volatility difference in price versus the risky position. In the regression analysis model, the assumption is that prior historical relationships will continue to hold. In the duration model, the volatility differences are offset by relative durations. In the yield forecast model, on the other hand, the hedge vehicle price under different circumstances can be open to miscalculation. If using futures, the futures price is calculated using a model of cash-to-futures arbitrage. There is an assumption that the two prices will converge as the delivery date of the futures expires. Calculating a "base case" futures price in this way involves taking the cash price, adding in carrying costs, and deducting income flow. If the position to be hedged has varying cash flows or if assumptions on carrying costs vary too widely, this model can become very complicated. The source of error can easily be twice the magnitude of the answer obtained using the model. However, despite its problems, the yield forecast model does offer a chance to look at how the hedge ratio will change as the conditions of the hedge change. See Figure 2.11 for an example of using this model and a matrix of hedge ratios.

Since all the models try to incorporate slightly different world views, I recommend calculating the hedge ratio using each model. Wide variations of value would show where the greatest sensitivities lie. Particularly,using the yield forecast model shows the range of the size of the hedge before it is actually placed. This can help make an estimate of commission costs and give a clue as to the amount of management this position will need. A wide range of hedge ratios implies that more management will be required. A closer range of hedge ratios would mean that you can probably get by with fewer re-evaluations.

Practical Considerations

Now, suppose that for a specific hedge vehicle we need 4.06 units to offset the specified risk. This is equivalent to saying that we need to buy 4.06 futures contracts, or 4.06 options, or 4.06 of whatever hedge vehicle is to be used. This result is an example of a common occurrence in using quantitative methods in finance. The answer is more precise than we can use. Unfortunately, this also means that we are left either underhedging or overhedging our risk. If we buy 4.0 contracts rather than the 4.06 specified by the model, we are hedging only 98.5% of the risk. This means that we are changing the distribution of outcomes on 98.5% of the position, but not changing the distribution of outcomes at all on 1.5% of the position. If we overhedge, then we are adding another source of risk exposure. In effect, it is like going short or long a new position.

Being able to hedge 98.5% is a very close fit. Quite often the mismatch between the risk position and the hedge vehicle permits only 75% to 85% of the position to be hedged without going over. The decision as to what portion of the risk position to hedge is very important. If you feel that too much upside opportunity is being lost, then a smaller hedge may be in order. If you want to gain as much protection as possible because the downside is considered so unattractive, then a variety of hedge vehicles might be used in combination to achieve a full 100%. For example, in the above case with a hedge offset of 4.06

Figure 2.11.   Yield Forecast Model

The Yield Forecast Model is used primarily to examine the sensitivity of the hedge ratio itself to various price and yield changes. The accompanying table shows an example of its use. Again, we own $1,000,000 face value of the General Motors 8.125% due 4.16 and want to hedge it with bond futures contracts. A hedge ratio is calculated using the change in price of the underlying security divided by the change in the futures price.

The table examines price moves of the futures contract and the General Motors security under various economic scenarios. The scenarios are *Growth, Stability,* and *Recession.* Within each economic scenario, the table further examines the factors that influence the ultimate price change. For the futures price, the major factors are the price of the cheapest-to-deliver security, and the financing rate. For the underlying security, the major factors are the reinvestment rate which affects the present value of the cash flows, and the spread above treasuries.

There are two cases of price reaction for each economic scenario. In one the market anticipates the move, and in the other, the market is caught unawares. So there are differences in the magnitude of credit spread change, and in the expectations premium.

Essentially, the hedge ratio falls within a range of .50 to 1.50 except for two specific circumstances. When the price correlation of the underlying security and the futures contracts becomes negative, the hedge ratio becomes negative. In these cases, using futures as a hedge vehicle can cause losses in both the hedge and the underlying security. Under those circumstances, another hedge instrument must be chosen. In the table, both cases occur in a recessionary environment when a bullish market bids up the price of the futures contract with increasing expectations, but the credit spread for the underlying security also increases due to the anticipation of poor corporate earnings.

By being aware of the economic conditions that will cause large changes in the hedge ratio, hedges can be re-constructed using different instruments. Also, by knowing the expected range of values for the hedge ratio, an estimate of commission costs can be made. If there are a number of possible alternative hedge instruments, a table can be constructed for each possibility. The instrument with the least sensitive hedge ratio will require the least amount of adjustment and so may be cheaper for a long-term hedge.

Figure 2.11. Yield Forecast Model (*continued*)

Example of Use of Yield Forecast Model

	Factors Affecting the Price of the Hedge Vehicle (Futures)			Factors Affecting the Price of the Underlying Security			Hedge Ratio
	Price of CTD	Financing Rate	Change in Futures Price	Reinvestment Rate	Credit Spread	Change in Price	
Growth	108.750	5.00%	−0.625	6.00%	+65 bp	−0.563	0.900
	108.250	5.50%	−1.125	6.50%	+80 bp	−1.125	1.000
	108.000	6.00%	−1.500	7.00%	+95 bp	−1.563	1.042
	107.625	6.50%	−1.750	7.50%	+115 bp	−1.938	1.107
	108.750	5.00%	−0.250	6.00%	+115 bp	−0.313	1.250
	108.250	5.50%	−0.625	6.50%	+95 bp	−0.750	1.200
	108.000	6.00%	−1.000	7.00%	+80 bp	−1.125	1.125
	107.625	6.50%	−1.625	7.50%	+65 bp	−1.500	0.923

Stability	110.250	5.00%	0.750	6.00%	+95 bp	0.750	1.000
	109.500	5.50%	-0.750	6.50%	+120 bp	-0.875	1.167
	110.250	5.00%	1.250	8.00%	+95 bp	1.750	1.400
	109.500	5.50%	-1.250	8.50%	+120 bp	-1.250	1.000
Recession	109.156	6.00%	-0.313	8.50%	+60 bp	-0.469	1.500
	109.969	5.50%	0.094	8.00%	+75 bp	-0.063	-0.667
	110.625	5.00%	0.406	7.50%	+90 bp	0.125	0.308
	111.000	4.50%	0.781	7.00%	+105 bp	0.125	0.160
	111.469	4.00%	1.375	6.50%	+120 bp	-0.156	-0.114
	109.156	6.00%	-0.250	8.50%	+80 bp	-0.375	1.500
	109.969	5.50%	0.063	8.00%	+70 bp	0.031	0.500
	110.625	5.00%	0.563	7.50%	+60 bp	0.375	0.667
	111.000	4.50%	1.125	7.00%	+55 bp	0.563	0.500
	111.469	4.00%	1.563	6.50%	+50 bp	0.938	0.600

futures contracts, you could buy 4.0 futures and account for the remaining 1.5% of the position via a forward rate agreement. The only difficulty in decision-making here is to figure when are you "close enough" that any additional hedging will not reduce the risk. This can be done by constructing a confidence interval for the hedge ratio. As I mentioned previously, some of the input numbers are "hard" and some are "soft." All of the soft-number inputs can be changed to include a margin for error. For example, in the duration model, instead of inputting the price of the cash security expected to prevail at the delivery date, you could input the expected price plus or minus 10%. In the basis point model, you could input a plus or minus factor for both of the dollar-value changes. This would result in a range of hedge ratios, but a fairly narrow range. See Figure 2.12 for an example using the basis point model. This tight range of hedge ratios can then be converted into an upper and lower value for the number of units of the hedge instrument needed to offset the risk. Any even number of units contained within this range can be considered a 100% hedge.

An aid to decision-making would be the ability to compare one hedge vehicle with another. For this we need to look at total commissions costs, the percentage of the risk position hedged, and the relative efficiency. Relative efficiency is the percentage of price variation that is reduced by implementing the hedge. However, this is not enough to stand alone, as it is only an estimate. I also believe that additional valuable information is provided by the percentage of upside potential sacrificed for each percentage of downside potential avoided. After all, implementing a hedge changes the probability distribution of outcomes. Some hedges are symmetric where the positive and negative possibilities are of the same magnitude, and some are asymmetric. See Figure 2.13 for some examples of symmetric and asymmetric strategies.

One last word of caution about hedging is required. When examining current and potential prices, it might help to remember that pricing is an art, not a science. As a result, projections of future price are best made by experts. Particularly when examining securities or portfolios with irregular cash flows, or when attempting to set a price assuming a large shift in supply/demand fundamentals, prices are apt to be a bit suspect. Remember an old programming adage: "Garbage In, Garbage Out." If your anticipated prices are too widely off the mark, the hedge is not likely to offer the protection you expect. There has been more than one case of investors feeling that they were protected

Figure 2.12.   The Basis Point Model: Practical Considerations

Since there is a large probability that some component of the hedge ratio will be measured incorrectly, it is occasionally useful to see exactly what range of hedge ratios has a random chance of occurring. This is done by adding in small error factors to the various components. For example, if we look at the hedge ratio derived using the basis point model in Figure 2.9, it takes on the following shape:

$$HR = (1.1468 \pm .15) \times (1.1334 \pm .05) \times (.70 \pm .2)$$

Any of the following combinations are correct

$(1.1468 + .15) \times (1.1334 + .05) \times (.7 + .2)$
$(1.1468 + .15) \times (1.1334 + .05) \times (.7)$
$(1.1468 + 1.5) \times (1.1334 + .05) \times (.7 - .2)$
$(1.1468 - .15) \times (1.1334) \times (.7 - .2)$

The upper value for the range of possible hedge ratios can be determined by adding all the error factors to the terms. Equally, the lower end of the range can be calculated by subtracting all the error factors from the terms.

$HR_H = (1.1468 + .15) \times (1.1334 + .05) \times (.7 + .2) = 1.6153$
$HR_L = (1.1468 - .15) \times (1.1334 - .05) \times (.7 - .2) = .5400$
So the range of values is $.5400 \leftrightarrow 1.615$

The value calculated in Figure 2.9 of .9098 is close to the middle of the range. Note that while the range for the hedge ratio seems fairly small, it does mean that the number of contracts needed to hedge the position can vary from 5 to 16 simply due to random events. So the hedge is less precise in reality than it appears on paper.

against some downside forecast, only to lose money on both the risk position and the hedge when the forecasted event came to pass.

TYPES OF HEDGE INSTRUMENTS

In all forms of commerce and industry, most ideas and innovations follow a similar path. Initially, a concept is created as a custom prod-

Figure 2.13.   Types of Hedge Strategies

Symmetric This type of strategy offsets *changes* in the market value of the underlying security, thus locking-in an effective price for the security

>   Buying or selling FRAs
>   Buying option straddles
>   Buying or selling futures contracts
>   Buying or selling swaps

Asymmetric This type of strategy offers protection against declines in the value of the underlying security, but allows participation in favorable market moves

>   Buying covered puts
>   Selling covered calls
>   Buying or selling caps
>   Buying or selling floors

---

uct, essentially "hand-made" and one-of-a-kind. Later, the concept becomes standardized, and comparison is possible because differences between products have become small. In a still later stage, there is an effort to customize the now standard product, so that once again it provides individualized capabilities. Like manufactured goods, this is the path of development taken by risk management products. Instruments based on underlying goods and securities are known as **derivatives.** First there were swaps and forwards, which evolved into standard futures products and forward exchange agreements. Only now are we approaching the last stage of development with **second-stage derivatives,** such as options, swaptions, caps and floors, and collars.

We will look at the various hedge instruments from a historical basis, progressing from forwards and swaps to futures and options. We will look at the newer and more innovative instruments in Chapter 3.

Forward Rate Agreements

Forward Rate Agreements are aptly named. These instruments refer to the interest rate forward in time. For instance, the three-month spot or current market rate that will apply three months from today is known as the three-month forward rate. A forward rate is quoted each day, but the dates covered will differ. There will always be a three-month forward rate available, but today's three-month forward is tomorrow's 89-day forward rate. We can determine the forward rate because a relationship exists between the three-month forward rate quoted today, today's three-month spot rate, and today's six-month spot rate. Since the two spot rates are given by the market, the third variable, the forward rate, can be calculated. See Figure 2.14 for the equation used to determine forward rates. The forward rate is the basis for a standardized contractual agreement known as a forward rate agreement or FRA. FRAs are specific individual contracts between two parties to enter into an investment at a particular time in the future at a particular interest rate. By employing a FRA, you exchange one type of risk for another. By fixing the interest rate in the future, you transfer interest-rate risk to the other party. At the same time, you assume a credit risk. That is, you assume that the other contractual party will be in business three months from now and will have the wherewithal to make the agreed-upon payments.

Because many similar contracts are written on an ongoing and regular basis, the growth of the FRA market has meant a standardized format for the contracts. The credit risk is generally thought to be minimal, as the major banks are the primary counterparties. However, this does raise credit constraints for particular maturities. When conditions are such that the maturities of the FRAs converge around a particular date, the conservative view is to "spread around" the contracts among a number of different counterparties. As a result, there may be occasions when the lowest bid cannot be accepted because there are already too many contracts done with that particular institution. Since the purpose of implementing an FRA program is to manage risk, it does no good to inadvertently assume more of another kind of risk. We often exchange a certain amount of one type of risk for some amount of another, more acceptable type. However, unless there is a particular reward for doing so, try to avoid unnecessary new risks.

The basics of the FRA are straightforward. The amount of funds upon which interest will be paid is called the **notional principal.** The interest is either paid or received depending on which way interest rates move. Buyers are looking for an insurance policy in case interest rates increase and attempt to lock in a maximum acceptable rate change. The contract specifies a **reference rate** and a **contractual rate.** Generally, the reference rate is LIBOR (London InterBank Offer Rate) or the rate on 90-day Treasury bills. However, the reference rate

Figure 2.14.   Forward Interest Rates

A *forward* interest rate is an interest rate quoted for a period of time begin-ning in the future and ending farther in the future. So to identify a forward rate both the beginning of the term for the interest rate, and the term length need to be specified. For example, if today is June first, the 3 × 6 forward rate is the interest rate for the 6-month period starting 3 months from today; i.e., the interest rate for the period from September first to December first. In comparison, the *spot* interest rate is the rate quoted for a period that starts today.

A forward rate can be calculated by looking at the spot rates of varying maturities. To illustrate, let's look at the following investment choice. If you have $1,000,000 to invest, then you can either invest your funds at today's date for six months (six months spot), or you can invest at today's date for three months and then re-invest three months in the future at the spot rate then prevailing for another three months. This latter combination involves a spot rate, and a forward rate.

The two investment choices should offer equal returns, or else supply would flow to the more attractive choice, thus driving down that return. So the forward interest rate can be derived by setting the two choices equal. If today's three month spot rate is 5.60% and today's six-month spot rate is 5.813%, then the three-month forward rate beginning three months in the future is:

$(1 + .056)\,(1 + R_{(3,6)}) = (1 + .05813)$
Generally, we can write
$(1 + r_{(o,t)})\,(1 + R_{(t,T)}) = (1 + r_{(o,T)})$

Where r = spot rate
      R = Forward rate
      0 = Today's date
      t = First Period End Date
      T = Second Period End Date

$R_{(3,6)} = .002 = .2\%$

Technically, this forward rate is the *implied* forward, since we do not know what rate will actually be the spot rate in the future. A more generic equation for determining different forward rates can be written. In the terminology, the first part of the subscript is the date for which the interest rate begins, and the second part is the length for which the interest rate is good. For instance,

Figure 2.14. Forward Interest Rates (*continued*)

all $r_{(t,6)}$ indicate interest rates with a six-month term, regardless of the date that the period begins or ends. That is, if the specific rate starts December first, it will end May thirty-first. If the term begins December second, it will end June first. In both examples the term is the same length.

The generic formula relating all spot and forward interest rates is as follows:

$$r_{(0,t)} = [(1 + r_{(0,1)}) (1 + R_{(1,2)}) (1 + R_{(2,3)}) \ldots (1 + R_{(t-1,t)})]$$

Again, R = Forward Rate
       r = Spot Rate

can be any mutually agreed upon rate such as the prime rate of the counterparty bank or the one-year rolling rates for Treasury bills. The contractual rate will be based on the forward rate equation, but will also reflect an expectation premium based on the buyer's view of the market and the economy. The notional principal amount is never actually transferred between the two parties, which is why the credit risk is so minimal. In fact, not even the full assumed interest payment is transferred. Rather, the payment is based on the difference between the reference rate and the contractual rate. The arithmetic to determine the payment is quite simple. The reference rate is determined in the contract itself and is the level of that rate on the starting date of the FRA. Then on the **settlement date,** the payment is calculated by taking the difference between the contractual and reference rates and multiplying it by the notional principal. At that point, this base figure is multiplied by the length of time the contract is to be in effect. This is called the **term** of the contract. This is done because the convention is to quote interest rates in annual terms. This makes contracts for slightly different numbers of days more easily comparable. The interest amount is then discounted to provide the present value of the interest payment. This discounting is necessary because forwards are paid at the beginning of the agreement on the settlement date, rather than at the end of the period. The rate used for discounting is the reference rate. It is this present value of the calculated interest amount that is actually exchanged between parties. Figure 2.15 represents this calculation.

Figure 2.15. Calculating FRA Payments

The general formula for calculating the exchange of monies between a buyer and a seller of a Forward Rate Agreement involves a *contractual rate*, a *reference rate*, the *notional principal*, and the *time period* for the agreement. Looking from the buyer's side, the formula can be written:

$$\text{Amount Received} = \frac{(RR - CR) \times NP \times \frac{ND}{DY}}{1 + \frac{(RR \times ND)}{DY}}$$

Where RR = Reference Rate
  CR = Contractual Rate
  NP = Notional Principal
  ND = Number of Days for Agreement
  DY = Number of Days Annually = Basis

We can amplify the example in the text by looking at an attempt to lock in a rate for the next three months on a $10 million loan. The amount of interest they pay on the loan is based on LIBOR, and they feel that the current rate of 8.35% may increase to an unfavorable level. They do not want to pay out more than a net rate of 8.75%. Suppose on settlement date LIBOR has increased to 9.00%. Then RR = 9.00%, CR = 8.75%, ND = 92 days, DY = 360, and NP = $10,000,000. The actual amount booked to offset the interest paid on the loan is the top part of the first formula, or:

$$\text{Offset} = (RR - CR) \times NP \times \frac{ND}{DY}$$

$$\text{Offset} = (9.00\% - 8.75\%) \times \$10 \text{ million} \times (92/360) = \$6,388.89$$

And the amount of money received =

$$\$6,388.89/[1 + (9.0 \times 92/360)] = \$6,245.25$$

So the full picture is composed of three parts: (1) Lending $10 million at LIBOR for 3 months means the company will pay out

$$\$10,000,000 \times 9.0\% \times 92/360 = \$230,000$$

Figure 2.15. Calculating FRA Payments *(continued)*

(2) The FRA hedge will take in $6,245.25 at the beginning of the period. (3) This amount will then be invested for the term at LIBOR to recoup the full $6,388.89.

The net cost of lending will be $230,000 − $6,388.89 = $223,611.11 at the end of the period. If we then calculate the net interest paid by working equation 1 in reverse, the net interest rate paid to borrow is 8.75%.

$$\text{Net Interest Rate} = \left(\frac{DY}{ND}\right) \times \left(\frac{NIP}{NP}\right)$$

Where NIP = Net Interest Paid

$$8.75\% = (360 / 92) \times \frac{\$223,611.11}{\$10 \text{ million}}$$

For example, assume that the reference rate is LIBOR and the contractual rate is 8.75%. If on settlement date LIBOR is at 9.00%, then the buyer will receive an interest payment based on the difference of 25 basis points. Had LIBOR at the time of settlement been 8.50%, the buyer would have paid out an interest amount based on the same 25 basis points.

Remember that all FRA terminology is based on the equation for determining forward rates. We can use today's spot rates to calculate forward rates that start at any date in the future and for any maturity period. Therefore, a six-month term contract might be a three by nine or a two by eight. That is, the six-month term might start in three months to end in nine months, or it might start in two months to end in eight months. The whole yield curve is available for trading in FRAs but some combinations are more common and see more active trading. For example, three by nines, six by twelves, and one by sevens are common.

Although FRAs are reasonably standard, their dates can be adjusted to cover weekends or to end early. This makes them more flexible than truly standardized products like exchange-traded futures and options. However, the number of players in the FRA universe is much smaller. This makes for wider bid/ask spreads, particularly in times of high interest rate volatility. In addition, there can be supply/demand crunches around particular settlement dates and for particular terms of contracts. When there are consensus views of market conditions, there may be great demand for six by nines, which will result in lower yields than would otherwise be expected. This is because the counterparty may hold the same view on rates that you do, and so is adding in a risk premium, or will feel the need to transfer the risk to another hedge vehicle such as the futures market. Therefore, the counterparty will need to include a cost for its commissions and the fact that there is not an exact match in transferring the risk. At times like these, it will be important to have a firm idea of exactly what price levels are acceptable. Otherwise, you may not be paid to transfer the risk.

See Figure 2.16 for an example of risk transferrals in flow chart form. Some of the intermediary risk-holders add extra required yield, or premium to their bid/offers to cover their own commissions and varying levels of desire for the particular risk exposure.

Forward Exchange Agreements

A new adjunct to the FRA market is the forward exchange agreement (FXA). Just as FRAs are used to lock in an interest rate for a specific time period starting at some point in the future, the FXA market exists to lock in exchange-rate differentials. So far, these are used more in Europe, with European banks being the major market makers. The FXA can be viewed as two FRAs in two different currencies combined into one financial instrument. For example, someone who wishes to

Figure 2.16.   Risk Transferrals

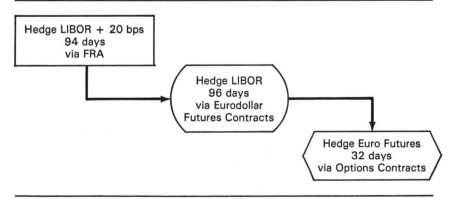

lock in an exchange rate based on dollar/mark levels from six months to one year might purchase an FXA. The mechanics differ slightly from FRAs, however. With the FXA there is an additional calculation date, which is a few days prior to the actual settlement date, so that the actual payment can be calculated and the figure agreed upon before the payment changes hands. Since executing an FXA requires knowledge of the domestic interest rate for the term, the foreign interest rate for the term, the spot exchange rate and the domestic forward rate for the term, calculating the payment due a few days in advance allows for easier settlement and decreases the processing costs.

Let's look at how this payment is actually calculated and where the uncertainty adds to the known risks. As with FRAs the notional principal is still the principal amount upon which the payment is based. The notional principal does not actually change hands. The purchaser of the FXA buys the near forward currency and also sells the far forward currency for a net transaction. That is, the purchaser buys the six-month forward marks and sells the one-year forward marks. The counterparty is selling six-month forward dollars and buying one-year forward dollars. The settlement day is the date that an FRA would settle for the near forward. In this case, the settlement date is at the beginning of the six-month term indicated as the near forward. If you look at the equation for calculating the payment in Figure 2.17, you will see that there are two "soft variables" that add uncertainty. First, we do not know what the spot exchange rate will be at the FXA settlement date (although, if we did, there would be no need for an FXA). Second, there is uncertainty as to the forward exchange rate at the settlement date for the next six months. That is, we do not know the forward rate that will exist on the settlement date, which is six months in the future. We can estimate a range of possible values for these variables based on history, and fundamental economic analysis should indicate any likelihood of currency appreciation or depreciation. However, since the FXA payment calculations are based on notional interest rates and exchange differentials, narrowing the range of potential levels is difficult. Therefore, most market makers will add an expectational or risk-adjusted component to the bid/offer of the FXA to cover their own costs. The possibility of sovereign risk (the chance that the country will default) or capital controls risk (that adverse taxes or other laws will be instituted) also adds to increased spreads. The recent addition of a new futures financial instrument might see

Figure 2.17.   An Example of Using a Forward Exchange Agreement

To calculate the forward exchange rate a certain number of periods from today, we need the following information: (1) the spot foreign exchange rate quoted in units of foreign currency per unit of domestic currency, (2) the domestic strip of forward interest rates, (3) the foreign strip of forward interest rates. These forward rate strips, or forward yield curves, can be calculated using the equations in Figure 2.14.

The equation for the forward exchange rate is:

$$FR_t = \frac{(1 + R_{(0,1)}) \times (1 + R_{(1,2)}) \ldots (1 + R_{(t-1,t)})}{(1 + R_{(0,1)}) \times (1 + R_{(1,2)}) \ldots (1 + R_{(t-1,t)})} \times FX_D$$

Where $R_{(a,b)}$ = Foreign interest rate for period $a \rightarrow b$

$R_{(a,b)}$ = Domestic interest rate for period $a \rightarrow b$

FX_D = Spot Foreign Exchange Rate

$$FR_t = \frac{\prod (1 + R_{(i-1,i)})}{\prod (1 + R_{(i-1,i)})} \times FX_D$$

$\prod$ = Multiplication function

This formula is needed to calculate the *Forward Points* for the contract when calculating the payment, or *settlement amount*. The settlement amount is the amount received by the contract purchaser if the number is positive, and the amount paid by the purchaser if the calculated amount is negative. There are a number of variables involved in doing this calculation. The notional principal (NP), the reference rate (RR), the number of days for the contract to run (ND), and the basis (DY), are all familiar from doing FRAs. As well, the spot exchange rate on settlement date is given by the market. There are three new variables involved: (1) the near-date forward exchange rate at the start of the contract (NFR), (2) the difference between the near and far-dated forward exchange rates at the time the contract is initiated, which is also known as the *Contract Forward Points* (CFP), and (3) the difference between the near-dated and far-dated forward exchange rates at settlement date, which is known as the *Settlement Forward Points* (SFP). The equation is as follows:

Settlement Amount =

$$NP \times \left[\frac{(NFR - FX_D) + (CFP - SFP)}{1 + \frac{(RR \times ND)}{(DY \times 100)}} - (NFR - FX_D) \right]$$

With all the required information now defined, let's look at an example. Suppose you are a pension fund manager for a multinational corporation. You need to make payments to retirees in Germany in one year and so are

Figure 2.17. An Example of Using a Forward Exchange Agreement (*continued*)

concerned about the volatility of exchange rates. So you are interested in buying these deutschemarks in the forward market to lock in the rate. As well, there are deutschemark funds coming due in six months, so these will be sold forward to lock in the total return as quoted in dollars. This combined series of cash flows becomes a six-month against twelve-month deutschemark for dollar FXA. If this transaction is entered into on June 1, then December 1 is the settlement date and possibly November 30 will be the calculation date. On calculation date, the forward rates quoted in the market will be used in the determination, and the reference rate is usually LIBOR. Since the difference between the near-date and the far-date is six months, the six-month U.S. dollar LIBOR rate will be the reference rate.

Thus, on the contract date of June 1, for settlement June 3, the spot exchange rate is .58248, the near-date forward (a valuation date of December 1) is .57412 and the far-date forward (valuation date of June 1 next year) is .56866. Then on November 30, the spot rate is obtained from the market at .5714 and the forward rate from settlement to the far-date is also obtained at .56258. This gives all the variables as:

NP = 10,000,000 deutschemarks
NFR = .57412
FX_D = .5714
CFP = .56866 − .57412 = − .00546
SFP = .56258 − .5714 = − .00882
RR = 6.1875%
ND = 185
DY = 360

So the settlement amount becomes:

Settlement Amount =

$$(10,000,000) \times \left[\frac{(.57412 - .5714) + (-.00546 - (-.00882))}{(1 + \frac{(6.1875 \times 185)}{(100 \times 360)})} - (.57412 - .571) \right]$$

$$(10,000,000) \times \left[\frac{(.00292 + .00336)}{1.0318} - .00292 \right]$$

$(10,000,000) \times .003166$

= \$31,664.51

Since this is a positive number, the pension fund manager receives it. If the manager did not have a natural position in deutschemarks, he would need to buy spot deutschemarks on June 1 and sell them forward for settlement December 1.

these expectational components decrease. A new product, the Diff futures contract, has recently been developed which specifically trades the difference between two currencies' interest rates. Currently the Diff futures contract is not very actively traded, but it is designed to offer an exchange-traded alternative for FXAs with a continually quoted market and so make it easier to transfer portions of risk to speculators.

It is sometimes difficult to visualize FRAs or FXAs because the buyer does not automatically pay out to the seller. Instead, payments are made or received depending on the size and direction of interest rate moves or exchange-rate differentials. However, try to keep in mind that FRAs and FXAs exist in order to simplify things. The FXA is designed to replicate the net cash flows of a series of different transactions. After all, if the FXA market did not exist, the person with the risk position would still need to look for a solution. Generally speaking, he would simply buy deutschemarks six months forward and promptly sell the same amount one year forward. By using the FXA market, the payment is based on the exchange differential, and the two payments are netted. As a result, there is an actual decrease in the level of risk, since the cash flows are smaller and are made with one party. Therefore, there is a much smaller chance of a credit default, creating a mismatched asset or liability. In addition, since spreads in the FXA market are only slightly higher than in the forward market, the commissions cost is likely to be a bit smaller although this may be a minor consideration.

Swaps

Swaps can be viewed as a series of forward rate agreements. They come in a variety of forms. The two main categories are interest-rate based and currency-based swaps.

The most common interest-rate swap is a fixed-for-floating rate swap, which is generally known as the "plain vanilla" swap. See Figure 2.18. In essence, this swap is designed to exchange cash flows rather than principal amounts. In asset/liability hedging, some liabilities are designated in floating rate terms, while the matching assets might be in fixed terms. The classic mortgage portfolio is a typical example. In this case, a bank may have issued floating-rate securities to lend the money on fixed-rate mortgages. With the capability of the swaps market, ei-

Figure 2.18.   A Simple Swap

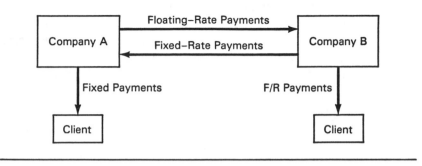

ther side could be converted to match the other type of rate structure. In this way, the fixed-rate liabilities will be matched to a stream of fixed-rate cash flows for the asset. Using this example for a base, it becomes intuitive to see that swaps can be fixed-to-floating, floating-to-floating, zero-coupon-to-floating, and the like. The floating-to-floating swap would occur where a liability cash stream is calculated based on 90-day Treasury rates, for instance, while the assets are calculated off LIBOR. This can happen frequently in a money center bank where short-term fundings and borrowings occur on an ongoing basis. In fact, a floating-to-floating swap is known as a *basis swap*.

The structure of a simple interest-rate swap is not complex. Again we encounter the concept of notional principal, which is not exchanged. Only the interest payments are exchanged. If the payments occur on the same date, then only the interest rate differential is actually exchanged. The calculation of payments is simple because it merely transfers cash flows from one place to another. For example, a company with a mortgage portfolio tranfers the interest portion of a principal-plus-interest mortgage payment it receives and in return gets a payment based on the same underlying interest rate to set against its floating borrowing costs.

In addition to matching cash streams, the swaps market can reduce financing costs between the two participants in the swap when conditions are right. For conditions to be right, the counterparties must be quite different in structure. There must be a comparative advantage for one in at least one type of interest rate for any costs to lessen. Admittedly, this does not occur often. Usually, one of the counterparties will be a money center bank. Should this bank spot a match-up of the type mentioned above, the bank can then offset the two swaps and retain the gains in the form of a wide bid/ask spread. See Figure 2.19 for a description of this process. This type of box diagram sees standard use in designing customized swaps. The plain vanilla swap can be adjusted by dates for settlement, or designed to reduce cash outflow, or other special criteria can be added. This is one of the most attractive features for use in hedging. Unlike an exchange-traded financial instrument, the over-the-counter market allows more customization and flexibility. Of course, this also makes two different swaps more difficult to compare.

Swaps are like FRAs in that they are quoted according to yield. However, payments are made over the course of the swap agreement, rather than at the beginning. In fact, the payments are usually exchanged at the end of the period rather than at the beginning. The cash flows are usually smaller, since they are differentials, so this timing shift is less important.

There are very few difficulties with doing interest-rate swaps. The credit risk is quite minimal for the stream of payments. The problem that recurs with this product is the need to spread out the various swaps among several brokers or dealers to keep the credit risk minimal. You must also keep an eye on the total payment streams due you from swaps as you could increase your risk accidently by having too many payments owed to you by the same dealer at the same time.

Currency swaps can be designated in the same currency, such as a plain vanilla swap denominated in pounds sterling, or can provide for

Figure 2.19.   Comparative Funding Swap

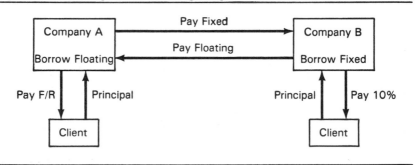

a transfer of payment streams denominated in two different currencies. The primary difference in the settlement process is that some of the notional principal is exchanged between the counterparties. This transferral of principal amounts is done at the spot exchange rate on calculation date, and the principal amounts are re-exchanged at that same exchange rate when the swap is terminated. The income stream transferred between counterparties contains the interest rate component as well as the currency component. For example, 8.0% U.S. dollar income may be paid and 7.25% yen income received. This increases the credit risk since the payments in full are exchanged, rather than just the differential. However, the currency swap is an excellent tool for importers and exporters, or for those with assets or liabilities denominated in other currencies, such as pension plan portfolio managers of multinational companies. This market also has seen a proliferation of broker/dealers, since otherwise finding the right counterparty can be difficult.

The currency swap comes in a variety of standard forms. Fixed-for-fixed, floating-for-floating, and fixed-for-floating are regular forms. The floating-for-floating currency swap works well when basis risk as well as currency risk needs to be managed. This swap contains the elements of transferring payments based on T-bill rates to LIBOR-based payments in addition to denominating the cash stream in the preferred currency. Since the notional principal is transferred and redeemed at the same exchange rate, no equity risk is incurred. Indeed, it is possible to lock in a return, as well. The times of the payment streams are determined in the contract. Therefore, if there is no pre-assigned need for the cash, the payment can be sold in the forward market. In that way most of the risk associated with playing in dual currencies can be transferred to other parties. The only risk assumed by selling forward is a small one. In case of a default by the swap counterparty, you would be left with an obligation in the forward market which would have to be redeemed at spot levels. See Figure 2.20 for a full example.

Futures

Interest-rate futures are based on the same concepts as forwards, but are a more standardized product. An interest-rate future is a standardized contract for delivery of a specific interest-rate security on a specific

Figure 2.20.   An Example of a Currency Swap

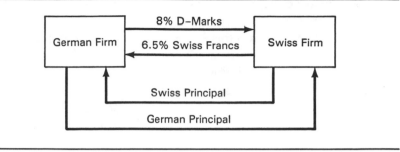

date in the future. For example, the June 1991 Treasury bond futures contract traded on the CBOT provides for delivery of an 8% coupon Treasury bond with a remaining maturity of at least fifteen years in June 1991. There are some specific adjustments for delivery of a similar but not exact security to ease supply constraints. They may be bought or sold, there are no special constraints to selling short in this market. Currency futures are similar. The contracts are standardized to specify how many U.S. dollars are to be delivered on what date. The contracts are then priced in the foreign currency, for example, how many deutschemarks are bid to receive the right to take delivery of $125,000. I will also discuss the advantage to a new type of futures contract, the diffs. Diffs are contracts that trade the difference between two different currency exchange-rates.

Futures have advantages, but also disadvantages as well. Standardization offers more liquidity, as investors transfer their risk to speculators. However standardization also provides more volatility in day-to-day trading. Futures also appear to have a more narrow bid/ask spread than forwards. However, this is hard to confirm, since forwards are not directly comparable unless dates, reference rates, and contractual rates are exact matches.

The first important difference between futures and forwards is in the way they are quoted. FRAs are quoted in yield, while futures are quoted by price. As a result, the person trying to manage interest-rate risk by protecting against an increase in rates will be a buyer of FRAs but a seller of futures. So, oddly enough, if you sell forwards, you would hedge this position by selling futures as well. The important thing to remember is to measure potential results the same way, using price or yield,* but not both.

A second important difference between futures and forwards is their form. Admittedly, both are contracts. But while a forward is between two specific parties, a futures contract is between the party looking for risk protection and the clearinghouse of a futures exchange, which matches up buyers and sellers.

A third important difference is duration. A forward is assumed to be held until the settlement date. Cancellations are rare and are usually offset if necessary by initiating another contract with a third party. This other contract may or may not match up exactly, so there is not a complete wash of the position. The futures market, on the other hand, makes reversing the exact position quite simple. In fact, it is so simple that a majority of contracts are reversed before their settlement date. This makes employing the futures market an excellent strategy for managing risk, as it has generally higher liquidity than the specific-sector FRA market.

A futures exchange is a forum for investors to transfer their undesired risk to speculators. The futures contract states that on a prespecified date in the future one party will buy from the other a certain fixed-income security at a certain fixed price. This contract is standardized by maturity date, face value of the security, delivery conditions, and the like. The only variable is the price, so the exchanges are based on that fluctuating variable. For financial risk management, there are a variety of products on a number of exchanges. In the United States, the two largest exchanges are the Chicago Board of Trade (CBOT) and the Chicago Mercantile Exchange (CME), of which the International Monetary Market (IMM) is a division.

Types of Futures Contracts. While there are a number of different contracts available, the most popular by volume are the 90-day Treasury bill contract, the 30-year Treasury bond contract, and the 90-day Eurodollar contract. The two short-term instruments are priced differently from the longer term instrument. This is based primarily on the

---

*This discussion will focus on the use of futures as a management tool, and so their valuation will be discussed only briefly in Chapter 5. Moreover, the question of valuation will be focused on how short-term mispricings can be used to decrease the costs of hedging.

differences between discount instruments and coupon-bearing instruments. When a position is taken in the bond contract, one agrees to either deliver or receive $100,000 face value of an 8% coupon Treasury bond with a maturity at least 15 years beyond the date of expiration of the contract. In actual fact, the bond delivered or received at the expiration of the contract can be a number of different cash instruments. For example, different coupon securities can be delivered with a yield adjustment. In the alternative, a security can have a call feature, so long as that call feature is at least 15 years past the expiration date of the contract. The yield adjustment is the conversion factor discussed earlier in the chapter. I refer you to the section on hedge ratio models.

The 90-day T-bill has a $1,000,000 face value, as does the 90-day Eurodollar contract. However, the Eurodollar is a cash settlement contract, while the T-bill requires delivery of a bill with 89 to 91 days to maturity from the date of delivery. The measure is from date of delivery, because delivery for the T-bill contract can be made over a number of days.

There are interest rate futures products for almost every sector of the yield curve, but the three mentioned above are the most popular and the most liquid. The ten-year note future is increasing in the volume traded, but is still substantially less liquid than either the bond, bill, or euro. Even less liquid are the five-year Treasury, the two-year Treasury, and the federal funds contract.

The contracts usually run in three-month cycles, with the term of the contract also set at three months. For example, the bond future has March, June, September, and December contracts, with the expiration dates set by the term delivery window at the Board of Trade. The contract with the most liquidity is referred to as the **front contract,** which is usually the contract with the nearest expiration date. However, when expiration approaches, the next current contract will become the front contract. This is because market participants will not want to take a position in futures with only a day or two left to expiration unless they intend to actually deliver or receive the bonds.

Futures contracts can simulate certain FRAs by running **strips.** For example, buying a three by six FRA can be replicated by purchasing a futures contract that expires in six months. If it is January 1 today, the FRA would settle March 1 to run until June 1. This is the same time period for the June Euro or T-bill contract. An FRA that is six by one year would be replicated in the futures market by purchasing or selling both a June and a September contract. This combination play of continuous futures contracts provides an alternative to some of the more liquid FRA time spans. See Figure 2.21. Since the futures are reasonably volatile and the contracts go out in a chain for three years or so, it also provides a chance to take advantage of short-term mispricings to lock in small arbitrage profits. Most usually these mispricings are slight, but no low-risk profit opportunity should be ignored.

Hedging. There are two basic types of futures hedges: a **strip hedge** and a **rolling hedge.** A strip hedge is described in the preceding paragraph. One would go either long or short a number of different contract months of a future at the same time, such as long the March, June, and September Eurodollar contracts. The combination of these contracts constitutes the hedge. By going long, the buyer receives the right to receive a 90-day instrument in March. This will mature in June at which point the buyer receives the next 90-day instrument from the June futures expiration. This one matures in September when the September contract expires and the last 90-day instrument is received. This expires in December. So by going long this strip hedge, the buyer has effectively locked in ownership of a short-term security from March to December—9 months. On the other hand, rolling a hedge is the process of keeping a hedge position on as the contract expiration approaches. For example, if you hedge by shorting the December 1990 T-bill contract, rolling the hedge involves buying back the December position and selling the March 1991 contract instead. Then, as the March contract approaches its expiration, you buy it back as well and sell the June 1991 contract. It is important to keep liquidity considerations in mind for both of these positions. If you are rolling a large hedge, waiting until just before delivery can give you the impression that price will converge toward the cash contract. However, the lack of liquidity can force a larger-than-expected price move in the contract away from the convergent price. In a strip hedge, the lack of liquidity in contracts nine months out or so can make placing a large position difficult.

There is also a practice known as **stacking,** which allows you to hedge a position that is farther out than any of the expiration dates of the futures contracts. In essence, this involves hedging the present value of the risk position in the nearby contract and, as the position is rolled, adding to the position. For example, this might entail buying

Figure 2.21.   Comparing FRAs to Futures Contracts Strips

An FRA contract guarantees a rate for a set period of time starting at some point in the future. A futures contract, on the other hand, assures a price lock-in for a specific security to be delivered at a specific date. However, the two can act as close replacements.

For example, on May 15, a 1 × 3 FRA rate based on LIBOR can be replicated by purchasing a June Eurodollar contract. If the futures price is .9395, then the yield for the three month security to be received on the delivery date in June is 6.05%. This is the same as locking in a yield for a 3-month security to start in one month.

Obviously, the matchup is closest on dates that fall exactly 30- 60-, or some even number of months before the futures contract delivery date. However, the difference is generally small even on other dates.

For longer dated FRAs, the process involves owning more than one futures contract, hence the terminology *strip*. For example, a 6 × 6 FRA priced on June 1 involves purchasing a December contract, and a March next year contract. This results in receiving a three-month security six-months from today that will provide a known yield, then when this security matures in March of next year, the receipt of another three-month security. Your principal will effectively mature in June of next year giving a net six-month investment that begins six-months from today. This is the same net cash flow as purchasing the FRA.

FRA Cash Flows
June 1—Purchase a 6 × 6 FRA to obtain an investment beginning December 1 and maturing June 1 next year. Rate = 6.48%

Futures Strip Cash Flows
June 1—Purchase a December Eurodollar contract at .9330 to yield 6.70%. Invest all monies owed except the margin required at the 6-month spot LIBOR rate of 6.20%. This security purchased via the futures contract will be delivered to you in December to mature in March of next year. Also purchase a March Eurodollar contract at .9315 to yield 6.85%. This security will be delivered to you in March of next year to mature in June of next year. To calculate the rate for the futures strip as a whole, the following equation is used:

Figure 2.21.   Comparing FRAs to Futures Contracts Strips *(continued)*

Equation 1:

$$(1 + SR_t) \times \frac{TD}{DY} =$$

$$\left[(1 + r_{(0, 1)}) \times \frac{ND_{(0, 1)}}{DY}\right] \times \left[(1 + R_{(1, 2)}) \times \frac{ND_{(1, 2)}}{DY}\right] \dots$$

$$\left[(1 + R_{(t-1, 5)}) \times \frac{ND_{(t-1, t)}}{DY}\right]$$

Where TD = Total Days
DY = Basis
SR_t = Strip Rate
$ND_{(a, b)}$ = Number of Days; Date A $\rightarrow$ Date B

This results in a strip rate of 6.476%. For the calculation, see Equation 2.

Equation 2:

$$(1 + SR_{12}) =$$
$$\left(\frac{360}{364}\right) \times \left[(1 + .062)\left(\frac{182}{360}\right) + (1 + .067)\ \left(\frac{91}{360}\right) + (1 + .0685)\left(\frac{91}{360}\right)\right]$$

50 December 1990 bond contracts, then before expiration selling 50 December and buying 55 March, then in February selling 55 March and buying 65 June, and so on. This takes advantage of short-term mispricings in the front month contract and fine-tunes the hedge as the anticipated risk comes closer in time.

Delivery. When you hold a short futures position until contract expiration, you need to deliver actual securities to a corresponding long-position holder designated by the Board of Trade. When making delivery, the long will be presented with an invoice for the cash securities actually presented. More than one cash security can be delivered for the bond contract at expiration. In that case, the invoice will be the product of the number of contracts held, the $100,000 face amount for the bond futures, the settlement price of the futures contract at expiration, and a conversion factor to adjust for yield differences. This way, the invoice price will be different if delivering a 10% coupon or an 8.50% coupon. See Figure 2.22 for the equation for the invoice and Figure 2.23 for the equation for the conversion factor.

This brings up the concept of **cheapest-to-deliver**. Because the U.S. government constantly issues debt, there are a number of government bonds that fit the delivery requirements at any given time. Since the cash market has some different criteria for valuation, we may see prices for these assorted bonds at prices above or below the yield-adjusted futures price. Therefore, there will be one bond at any given time for which the difference between the futures invoice price and the cash market price is most positive. This will be the bond that is "cheapest" to actually deliver in response to a futures obligation. The fact that the bond designated cheapest-to-deliver can change means that there is little predictability in knowing exactly which cash security will be delivered at expiration. Moreover, since delivery can take place over a number of days, market conditions and the shape of the yield curve will determine which day delivery is actually made. While these points may seem trivial, either can be a source of additional risk. It is up to the holder of the short position to instigate delivery. As a result, delivery

Figure 2.22.   Calculating a Futures Invoice

When receiving a security after purchasing a futures contract, the invoice price you pay will depend upon which of several securities are delivered. The *invoice price* is the product of the futures price at the time of purchase and the specific security's conversion factor at the time of delivery, or:

Invoice Price $= FP \times CF$

Where FP $=$ Futures Price
CF $=$ Conversion Factor

Then the total dollar amount paid to receive the security will be:

Total \$ paid $=$
$[(IP \times \text{Size of Contract}) + (\text{Accrued Interest})] \times C$

Where IP $=$ Invoice Price
C $=$ Number of Contracts Purchased

Figure 2.23. The Conversion Factor

The *Conversion Factor* is the price of a deliverable security that provides an effective specific yield. For example, the security specified for delivery in the bond futures contract has an effective 8% yield. The conversion factor adjusts the price of securities with non-8% coupons so that they may be used in the delivery process.

$$CF = \frac{\left(\sum \frac{CP}{(1.04)^t} + \frac{1,000}{(1.04)^n} \right)}{1,000}$$

Where CF = Conversion Factor
     CP = Semi-annual Coupon Payment
      n = number of periods until maturity
      t = number of periods until that payment is made

will be made under conditions most favorable to the short and least favorable to the long. For example, when the yield curve is very steep, the overnight financing costs are often less than the coupon of the cash security. In this case, delivery will be made as late as possible. On the other hand, if financing costs exceed the coupon in a flat or inverted yield curve, delivery will be made early.

Although it is easy to determine the cheapest-to-deliver security at the time the futures position is put in place, in times of high market volatility this can often change. This variation between the underlying cash security price and the futures price is known as the **basis.** This is yet another source of risk. However, as the expiration date of the futures contract approaches, the basis decreases as the cash and futures price converge. While convergence at expiration is relatively sure, difficulty arises because the price path of the basis is completely unknown. It is this uncertain price path that provides the market for floating-rate-to-floating-rate swaps, which are also known as basis swaps.

Yet one other source of risk in using bond and note futures is the **wild card delivery option.** This is currently a small risk, but it was fairly large a few years ago when M1 statistics were followed closely. The bond and note futures contract gives the short position holder the right to notify his intent to deliver up until 5 p.m. EDT. This is two hours after the futures market closes. Today, it is less likely that there will be large price moves in that two-hour period. However, when M1 was more popular, the current level would be announced at 3:30 or 4:00 p.m. EDT. An M1 or M2 that fell outside expectations could easily move the market by half to three-quarters of a point. This type of move could change the cheapest-to-deliver contract or otherwise give the short the opportunity to look for cheap securities, which he could then deliver against the 3:00 p.m. closing futures price. Again, this type of risk is relatively small, but you should be aware that it could occur in times of large price moves.

Valuation. Each futures contract has its own pricing convention, which must be understood before we can consider the hazards of the valuation process. The bond and note contract reflect the underlying security in that they are priced in 32nds. That is, each **tick** or minimal price move is 1/32 of a point. In cash terms, a tick equates to a minimal move of $31.25 per contract, with each point representing $1,000 per contract.

Bills and Euros also reflect the conventions of their underlying securities. They are priced in **basis points,** with the tick size set at 1 basis point. A basis point is .01% and equates to $25 per tick. The yield on these instruments is calculated as follows: if the December 1990 Eurodollar contract is trading at a price of 91.14, then we subtract the price from 100 to obtain a yield of 8.86%. This is in money-market terms, which is calculated based on 360 days per year. This is a potential source of risk when moving from short-term financial instruments to longer term instruments in that the longer term instruments calculate yield based on 365 days per year. However, this mismatch is so small that it can be ignored unless you are dealing with truly vast amounts of money, such as funds in excess of $500 million. This mismatch adds about 1.3% uncertainty to yield when moving from short-term funding to longer term instruments.

Most sources of price uncertainty are fairly small. This is because they generally net out to some degree, but they do have a cumulative effect on the distribution of possible prices for the security. As a result, they also reflect the mismatch in pricings between cash securities and the derivatives. These normally small risks are much of the source of error in correlations of price moves between the cash and derivatives markets. See Figures 2.24A and B for a price distribution chart and a graph of the effects of pricing correlations. In Figure 2.24A the first distribution is the naked, or unhedged position (white bars), and distribution (black bars) the second is the position once a hedge has been implemented. The third distribution (white bars in Figure 2.24B) takes the hedged position and adds in the effects of potential price correlation risks. Note that the naked position and the final distribution are quite similar.

There are a number of valuation models used for pricing futures contracts. The most common one involves calculating a *cost of carry* to determine whether it is cheaper to fund a desired position in the cash market or in one of the derivative markets. This is most commonly used in reference to futures. Note that the price of the futures contract will vary from this cost-of-carry price. However, the cost-of-carry model provides a boundary so that price will not vary far.

The cost-of-carry model for financial futures involves a calculation of how much it costs to finance the transaction. The basic assumption is that the funds used to establish a position do not sit idle, but are currently in an alternative investment. This model then calculates an "opportunity cost" for establishing the position in one market rather than the other. See Figure 2.25.

For a simple example, assume that you wish to open a position in long bonds, that is, to go long either cash securities of a certain maturity or long bond futures contracts, which will allow the position to be established at a later time with a lesser price risk. Since futures are a margin security, you will need $3,000 per contract for initial margin to establish a position equal to an exposure of $100,000 in cash securities. To match this position in the cash market, you must borrow the full $100,000. Ignoring commissions to brokers or possible payments of accrued interest at purchase for the cash item, the difference in cost for establishing the positions is (1) the basis, or the variance of price between the cash and futures markets, and (2) the added financing costs for the cash position. The cost to establish a position in the cash market will not vary that much from the futures market due to the presence of arbitrageurs. Therefore, when treated as an equality it provides a useful gauge of anticipated financing levels. By assuming the net costs of futures and cash are the same, then the rate of financing required to make the two equal is called the implied repo rate. This term is used because the repurchase agreement market (or repo) is the market most often used by institutions to fund short-term government securities positions or to invest excess cash for short terms. It is an over-

Figure 2.24.   Price Distributions

(A) Theoretical Effect of a Hedge

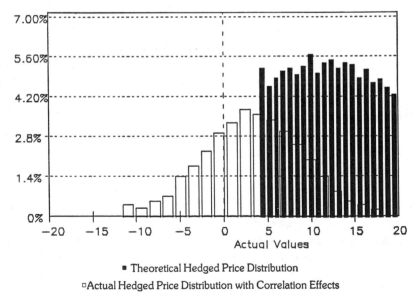

□ Unhedged Price Distribution   ■ Theoretical Hedged Price Distribution

(B) Theoretical vs. Actual Price Distribution of a Hedge (including correlation effects)

■ Theoretical Hedged Price Distribution
□Actual Hedged Price Distribution with Correlation Effects

Figure 2.25.   The Cost-of-Carry Model for Futures Pricing

This model attaches an opportunity cost to investment. That is, there is an assumption that the money could be used elsewhere if not used for futures. The cost attached to investing is the risk-free rate for lending it elsewhere. So the valuation for a futures contract becomes:

$$FP_t \approx CP + (CP \times r \times t)$$

where FP_t = Futures Price at time t
$\quad\quad CP$ = Cash Price
$\quad\quad\quad t$ = Time Period
$\quad\quad\quad r$ = Monthly risk-free interest rate

night interest rate. Since this market is where most of the financing would take place, the implied repo rate calculated by the cost-of-carry model should approximate this. The only difference between implied and actual financing costs will be an expectational factor. When the two costs are equal we can infer that the implied repo rate is considered fair by a consensus of market participants. A higher implied repo rate indicates that the market thinks financing costs should increase. That is, either short-term rates should increase or there is an anticipated future supply problem. On the other hand, a lower implied rate indicates a lack of demand for funds or a perception that short-term rates are too high.

This examination of funding costs is critical to placing a hedge because it looks at the consensus opinion of whether costs are fair or not. As a result, if you have access to better than average financing, you can place a hedge with a better than average return. This slight additional return helps cover commissions costs and makes up for price correlation risk in the hedge.

The cost-of-carry valuation model works best for Treasury bills and for bond positions that are not expected to be held long. It must be modified for bonds held for a longer time, because an opportunity cost is associated with futures. That is, not only is the income from the cash securities lost, but the interest-on-interest component is lost as well. Essentially, the futures price for bonds has to include a discounted income figure for the life of the contract. The uncertainty in this figure comes from the discount rate assumed and the equal uncertainty in the reinvestment rate for the coupons received. These levels will vary over time as real interest rates change and as the shape of the yield curve changes. Again, the presence of arbitrageurs in the market means that variances will probably not be tremendous, but it again is part of the cumulative effect of risk as far as potential prices are concerned. There is a net effect for expected price, but a gross effect for potential price.

The Eurodollar contract is fungible with the Singapore International Monetary Exchange (SIMEX). This means that a futures position taken in Chicago on the CME can be mutually offset on SIMEX, which allows for round-the-clock management opportunities. Although the bond and Euro contract on the London International Financial Futures Exchange (LIFFE) are not fungible, they are sufficiently similar that positions can be used to replicate CBOT positions. However, since they are not fungible, these positions must be closed out separately. As the commissions costs and the margin costs are almost double to keep an account open on both exchanges, it is worthwhile only if your risk position is such that managing it in the extra time zone is important.

Currency Futures. Currency futures are closely linked with interest-rate futures in hedging forward exchange agreements and, in general, hedging both fixed-income and equity obligations denominated in other currencies. A currency futures contract permits a separation of the currency risk from the financial risk. In combination with interest-rate futures or equity futures contracts it is a powerful risk-management tool. Of course, the currency futures contract can also be used for hedging cash currency exposures for cash flows denominated in currencies other than the dollar.

The IMM, SIMEX, PHLX, and LIFFE all offer futures contracts for currencies other than the U.S. dollar. The Chicago and Philadelphia markets are the most active, with LIFFE falling far behind. The size of the contract varies from currency to currency. For the pound sterling, it is $25,000. For the deutschemark, $125,000 and for the yen it is $12 million. There are also contracts for the Swiss franc, French franc, and Canadian dollar. There is also a contract for a dollar-denominated market basket of currencies—a sort of dollar index. In cash terms, the minimum price fluctuation is generally $12.50 per tick or $.001 per unit of currency. The exceptions are the Canadian dollar at $10.00 per tick and the pound sterling at $2.50. The yen is $.0001 per unit of currency because of the magnitude of the mismatch between the yen and the dollar base unit.

The valuation techniques for currency futures is simple because no cash flows are involved. The currency futures reflect the underlying spot market in each currency. However, the trading price is inverted from the spot to futures markets. The spot or cash market for currencies is denominated in terms of currency/dollar. For example, when the French franc is quoted at 5.85, it means 5.85 francs for each U. S. dollar. So the franc is worth about 17 cents each. On the other hand, the futures markets are priced by the amount of U.S. dollars bid for a unit of currency. For example, the December 1990 deutschemark contract trades at .6568 dollars for each deutschemark.

The prices of spot and futures are not exactly equal except as the expiration date of the contract approaches, because futures have a forward point spread built in. This is because the spot market will settle the next day while purchasing futures implies a settlement date at the expiration of the contract. While the forward points include an expectational component, it usually acts as a discount factor because the futures contracts yield the current spot position starting some time in the future. To clarify this, think of the currency futures position as follows: buying the currency spot, investing the currency at rate **r** for the term of the futures contract, and locking in the price of the transaction by selling the spot currency plus the currrency earned by investing at price **F**. This discount component must be added into the futures price or an opportunity for risk-free profits would exist. See Figure 2.26 for an example. This possible arbitrage limits the potential price range of the futures. However, the forward/spot price ratio is a component of this exercise, and this will fluctuate in response to changes in respective nominal rates and in response to anticipated changes in respective nominal rates. As usual, the expectational factor adds to the uncertainty of price.

Diffs. A third category of futures is called Diffs, Euro-rate differential contracts. This is a futures contract based on interest-rate differentials between two countries' 90-day Euro deposits. Currently, there are U.S./sterling, U.S./yen, and U.S./deutschemark. The price of a Diff

Figure 2.26.   Currency Forward Points
_____

The Forward point spread is the difference between the spot currency rate and the applicable forward rate. Including this factor in pricing futures contracts eliminates the opportunity for risk-free profits.

$$CFP = FX_{(0,t)} - FX_{(0,0)}$$

Where CFP = Contract Forward Points
$FX_{(0,t)}$ = Exchange Rate today for a transaction starting time t
$FX_{(0,0)}$ = Spot exchange rate
_____

contract is derived from subtracting the difference between the 90-day dollar-denominated LIBOR rate and the 90-day non-dollar LIBOR rate from 100. Like Eurodollar contract, they are priced in basis points and are available through the CME.

An example of the calculation is as follows: if the 90-day Euroyen is at 6.90% and the 90-day LIBOR in dollar terms is at 8.00%, the differential is 1.10. Therefore, the price of the U.S./yen Diff contract will be around 98.90 (100 − 1.10). The price cannot be calculated precisely because there is a current lack of liquidity in this contract, although the volume traded may grow if they work in practice as they do in theory. In addition, price is influenced by the usual expectational component and a very small discount factor. Since we are pricing the differential for delivery in three months, a discount factor must be incorporated to calculate the present value of the differential. While this factor is small, it will fluctuate as the yield curve moves. See Chapter 4 for an example of how Diffs can be used.

In the future the Diff contracts may succeed, but they may also die a natural death since there already are a number of well developed futures and options exchanges around the world. The TIFFE (Tokyo International Financial Futures Exchange) offers a fairly liquid forum for yen-denominated futures and options for both equity and fixed-income. Both Frankfurt and Paris have exchanges, and the exchange in Vienna is attractive to Eastern European countries in need of financing. The products and their depth varies from country to country and exchange to exchange. However, for multinationals or companies with two-country exposure, it may be easier to look to these markets rather than to use Diffs.

Options

Having looked at the so-called first stage derivatives, I now want to examine second stage derivatives. These are derivative financial products where the underlying instrument is not the cash market, but rather another derivative market. The first one we will look at is the interest-rate options market.

An interest-rate option is a contract that provides the purchaser with a right, but not an obligation to buy or sell a security or a basket of securities at a particular price. Interest-rate options come in two specific versions, European and American. European options can execute the terms of the contract only at the expiration date. This is called **exercising** the option. In American options, the right can be exercised at any time the contract is in effect. As a result, the valuation procedure is much simpler with the European options, but the American options are more flexible and, therefore, are more common in the market.

The seller of the contract is called the **writer.** This terminology comes from the time before options were traded on exchanges when the person interested in selling a right to buy or sell a security would actually write a contract. In today's environment, be careful using exchange-traded options in hedging cash positions. The underlying security for these interest-rate options is futures contracts, so there is the chance of additional price correlation risk.

There are two types of options. The right to purchase a security is a **call** and the right to sell is a **put.** The price of the underlying security should the option be exercised is the **strike price.** An option buyer can purchase either a call or a put, just as an options seller can write either a call or a put. While the ability to put on a position in either direction is equally easy, the risk exposures can be very different. The buyer of an option pays a **premium** to the seller, which is the price of the option. Thus writing covered calls, that is selling to someone else the right to purchase from you a security you already own at an agreed price, is a method of yield enhancement for a portfolio when historical costs are below the market.

Options are also classified by the position of the exercise price in relation to the market. Options are **in-the-money** when the exercise price versus the market price provides a profit opportunity. Options are **at-the-money** when the exercise price is close to the market price, and are **out-of-the-money** when there is no current profit or break-even opportunity.

When the underlying security is already owned by the option writer, the resulting position is **covered.** If the underlying security is not owned, the position is **naked.** The risk profiles for naked versus covered positions are also dramatically different. For example, if you write a put on a security that you currently own (writing a covered put), then there is a limited reward—the premium received—and a limited risk—the need to sell the security at the pre-arranged price. However, if you write a naked call, you are agreeing to sell a security at a certain price that you do not currently own. If the price of the security moves sharply higher than the exercise price, you must buy it at market rates and sell it at a loss to the purchaser of the call. Therefore, the writer of a naked call has unlimited risk and a limited reward amounting to the premium received. The purchaser of a naked call however, has a limited risk—the premium paid out—and an unlimited reward potential. See Figures 2.27A and B for the risk profiles for various options positions.

Valuation. There are two ways to price interest-rate options: in points or in dollars. The preferred methods usually use points for interest-rate options and dollars for currency options. Bond options trade in points and 64ths (half of 32nds). The option premium in points multiplied by the dollar per point gives the total dollar value of the option premium. Likewise, the dollar value for the option premium multiplied by the number of units in each futures contract gives the dollar value of the option premium.

The price of the option, or the premium, is made up of two factors: the **intrinsic value** and the **time value.** The intrinsic value is the difference between the market price and the expiration price. Since the intrinsic value cannot be negative, the intrinsic value falls to zero if the strike price is below the market price for a put, and the strike price is above the market price for a call. The time factor, or **theta,** depends on a few variables. Theta increases as the length of time to expiration increases. The magnitude will also depend on whether the option is in-, out-, or at-the-money, with theta being largest for at-the-money options. In addition, the level of interest rates has a small effect, but it is sufficiently small and ambiguous that it usually can be neglected with safety. Finally, a major factor influencing theta is market volatility. Re-

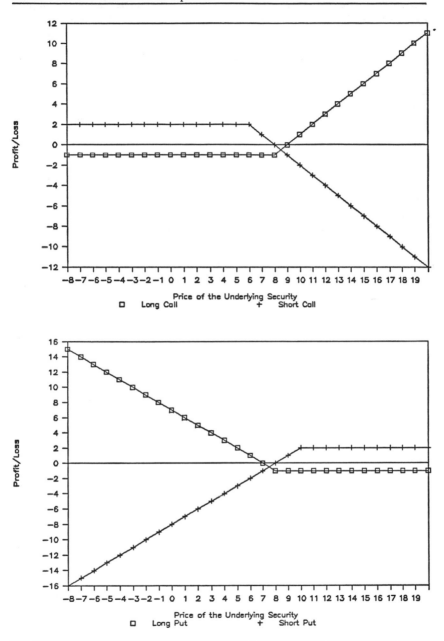

gardless of how it is measured, the value of theta increases as the perception of volatility increases. After all, if prices are changing rapidly, then an out-of-the-money option has a greater chance of becoming an in-the-money option. Of course, this is true only if you believe that prices are random or within a tight range.

Theta is an example of how straight-line pricing systems work best for at-the-money options. See Figure 2.28 for a graph of theta and its relationship to the strike price. As you can see, it drops off sharply as the time to expiration approaches, but increases quite slowly for time periods of six months and longer to expiration.

Because of the different risk profiles inherent to certain positions, some options prices will vary significantly from the price calculated by an options-pricing model. However most of the valuation work has been done on calls. Moreover, since there is not a symmetric price relationship between puts and calls, there is an added risk in using options. That is, there is a risk involved in not knowing whether a perceived mispricing is due to an error in the model, or whether risk premiums have changed, or whether supply/demand conditions have

Figure 2.28.   Theta over Time: Effect of Time Decay on Option Values

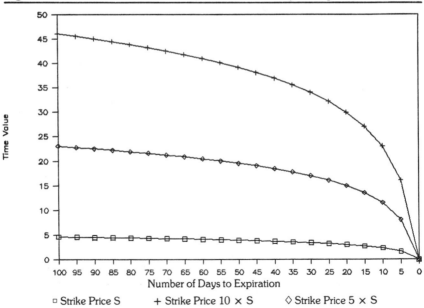

□ Strike Price S   + Strike Price 10 × S   ◇ Strike Price 5 × S

changed. It is important to know the assumptions that underlie the pricing mechanism you use. No model currently in use accurately reflects real-world pricing decisions, nor do they have a very flexible view of the direction of interest rates. Most pricing models involve the concept of "random walk," which implies that price movement has no discernable trend. Certainly this is the case in some market conditions, but it does not always hold true. There is also an added correlation risk. The exchange-traded options are designed to closely follow price moves in the underlying financial futures. However, there is a small mismatch between the option and the future and an additional mismatch between the future and the cash market. On occasion, this can add to a significant pricing difference.

A second source of risk lies in the pricing model design. Most models are designed for "straight-line" price movements. However, it is commonly accepted that price moves are non-linear. This means that the option model works best under conditions of small price moves where the exercise price is close to the market price. As the exercise price moves away from the market price, sources of pricing error increase at an exponential rate.

Some other concepts that affect options prices are delta, gamma, and kappa. Delta is also known as the neutral hedge ratio, and is another way of weighting risk-management positions. **Delta** is defined as the change in the price of the option for a given one-unit change in the price of the underlying futures contract. For instance, if a one-point move in the bond contract results in a change in the price of the 92-00 calls of $.75, the delta is .75. Delta is a way of measuring risk exposure, since it calculates the number of options contracts it takes to equal the risk of one futures contract. However, this is also a non-linear measurement, so this measure is also more accurate for small prices changes. See Figure 2.29 for a graph of delta as the option moves from out-of-the-money to at-the-money and then to in-the-money for different volatility assumptions. The acceleration, or rate of change of delta increases quickly as the magnitude of price changes increases.

The behavior of delta is subject to some general rules. For example, delta is low when the option is out-of-the-money. This makes sense, because theta flattens out for out-of-the-money options, and a price move would have to be large to get an out-of-the-money option back to at- or in-the-money. When the option is in-the-money, deltas are higher but are still less than one. This is true for in-the-money options

Figure 2.29.   Changes in Delta: From Out-of-the-Money to In-the-Money

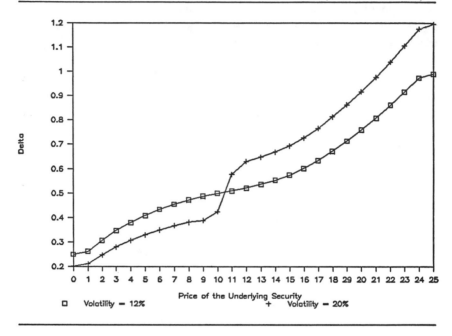

because a one unit change in the price of the underlying future is primarily intrinsic value and translates almost entirely to the option. However, there is a negative expectational premium for theta, so delta will remain less than one. If the option is at-the-money, delta will hover near .50. This reflects the concept of random price moves and implies a 50/50 chance of price moves in the underlying security moving the at-the-money option either into or out of the money. Lastly, if the option is already out-of-the-money, then the value of delta will be in direct relationship to the length of time to expiration. This is because, as the length of time increases, there is a higher probability that market volatility will "help out" the option by moving more into-the-money from its current position. As a direct corollary to this, delta decreases in inverse relationship to the time remaining to expiration if the option is in-the-money. Basically, there is a higher chance that market volatility will wipe out any current profits.

One of the reasons we look at delta is to establish positions with minimal risk. A general goal in options risk management is to be "delta neutral." To be delta neutral means that the options position will exactly offset small price moves in the underlying futures contract, leaving a position that is neutral to price moves. That is, you are not taking a view on the market, and you are indifferent to small upward or downward moves in price. The delta is employed to measure how much of the underlying future must be bought or sold to establish this so-called riskless position. For instance, the delta of .75 calculated in the previous example would work in the following manner: Buy 100 92-00 puts with a contract delta of .75. The delta position for this exposure is .75 × − 100 = − 75, so we need to buy 75 futures contracts, each futures contract having a delta of 1, to get an opposite delta position of 75 × 1 = + 75. The net delta position is zero, so the hedge is deemed riskless. To maintain a "riskless" hedge in times of market volatility can sharply increase expected commission costs. Buying and selling the appropriate number of futures or options can also be expensive in manpower costs.

Gamma, the second influence on options prices, is the measure of the rate of change of delta. In mathematical terms, this is the second derivative for price movements. A more straightforward description is the curvature of an option. Gamma is measured as the number of deltas gained or lost for each unit change in the underlying future. Gamma is additive, that is, you take the current delta and add or subtract the gamma to calculate the new delta for the option when dealing with both calls and puts, the shape of the delta curve is almost the same. The shape of the gamma curve is then also the same for puts and calls, since we are looking at change in the delta curve. The rate of gamma reaches a maximum when the option is at-the-money, but the magnitude of change in gamma slowly decreases as the strike price increases. Figure 2.30 shows graphs of gamma versus the price of the underlying for different volatility levers. Figure 2.31 is a diagram of gamma over time. This latter graph indicates the large effect theta has on price.

Depending on the strike and the time to expiration of the option, the level for gamma can range from zero to twenty or so. It becomes more constant as the time to expiration increases. This raises another hazard of playing with derivatives. By ignoring the options position after it is initiated, the level of risk exposure can move tremendously. Gamma is also very sensitive to changes in volatility. At low levels of volatility, from zero to 12%, gamma can also see a wide range of values.

Figure 2.30.   Changes in Gamma: From Out-of-the-Money to
In-the-Money

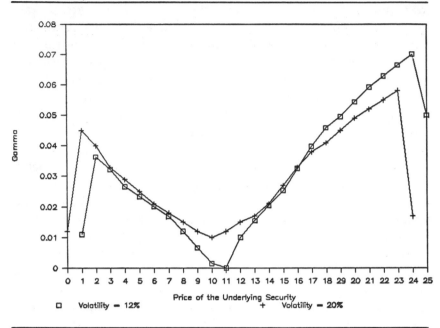

It is not until annual volatility increases above this level that gamma
settles into a range. Since 12% is generally considered average volatility for the current environment, this means that gamma needs careful
watching when markets start range-trading.

The third influence on options prices is **kappa**, also referred to as
vega, zeta, and **sigma prime**. This factor gauges volatility. Specifically, kappa is the option's change in price for a given change in market
volatility. This is heavily dependent on the strike price and how far in-
or out-of-the-money it is. Kappa has a direct but non-linear relationship with the time remaining to expiration. Absolute levels of kappa
change for a given volatility, but not in a parallel manner.

A fourth factor, **rho,** should be mentioned, although it is rarely
used. Rho is the change in the option's price for a given change in
interest rates. Since the future contracts price has yield as a major component, this measure seems to be redundant. Moreover, rho works

Figure 2.31. Gamma Over Time

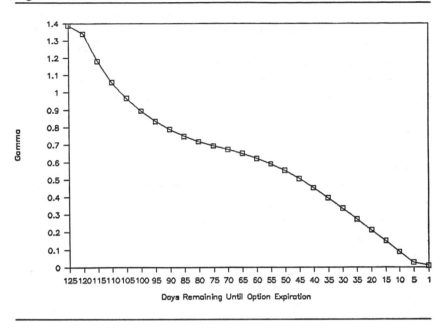

best for parallel moves along the yield curve, but they almost never occur.

For an example, when the futures December 1990 bond contract is trading at 90–10, and the December bond put with a strike of 92–00 is trading at 1–63, it will cost 1 and 63/64 points to purchase the right to sell bonds at a price of 92–00 when the current market price is 90–10. The intrinsic value of the option is 1 and 22/32 points, which can also be expressed as 1 and 44/64 points. The additional 19/64 is the theta. Combined, the intrinsic value and the theta make up the market price.

Options Pricing Models. There are a number of options pricing models on the market. Most of them are some variation of models by Fisher Black & Myron Scholes or J. Cox & S. Rubenstein. In actuality, these two models are not conceptually that different. A third model is the Binomial Options Pricing Model (BOPM). All of these models use statistics and probability theory, and all assume random price moves. With interest-rate models it becomes more complicated. After all, yield movements are not usually parallel along the curve, and re-investment rates fluctuate over time. A factor in the fundamental valuation is the right to own a future stream of payments at a fixed level. The present value of this future cash flow is subject to variations and actually can increase risk by widening out the price potentials for a securities position. Most of the original work was done on equities, for which the cash flows are a much smaller percentage of the security's price.

Options valuations models will provide an indication of where the options will trade. However, the market will see faster changing assumptions in volatility and expectational components and will usually vary from the theoretical price. If the market price and the theoretical model-generated price are different, it does not mean that the option is incorrectly priced. Usually, this means that the model does not correctly describe the way the market makes decisions or that the market consensus on the level of volatility differs significantly from the model's assumptions of volatility.

There is a more detailed discussion of options pricing model in Chapter 6.

Put/Call Parity. There is one advantage to the options market in pricing, the principal of put/call parity, which puts limitations on the price movement of the premium. This parity principal is also the basis for synthetic securities. The assumption is that the market does not allow riskless opportunities to exist for very long. Certain relationships exist that allow such riskless opportunities if the relationships are violated, so they work well as price boundaries. If you watch these boundaries, you will not have to depend on your pricing model to any great extent.

Some of these boundaries are simplistic. For example, the price of an option must be non-negative, that is, the lowest price of an option is zero. The right to place a trade at a predetermined price can never detract from profits by more than the premium paid. In fact, the minimum price of an American option has to be at least the intrinsic value, since it can be exercised at any time. There is also a relationship between the value of the option and its strike price at any given time. For example, the price of a call option with a lower strike price will be worth more than the price of a call option with a higher strike price at the same time. This is the opposite for a put. There is also a possible ranking of options value in accordance with time left to expiration. If two calls or puts are identical except for the time left to expiration, the one with the longer maturity will be at least as valuable as the one with the shorter maturity. The option with the longer maturity will be at least as valuable because theta will not necessarily change significantly from one option to the other if both are sufficiently out-of-the-money.

Another price boundary is that the American version of an option will always be greater than or equal to the value of an otherwise identical European option. This is true for both puts and calls because of the ability to exercise the American option before expiration. Theta can only add value, not subtract it. Looking wider, we can say that the probability distribution of an option is defined by the price of the security on the one hand and zero on the other. The upper boundary is obvious because there is no need to buy the option if the price of the option exceeds the price of the security. In fact, for American-style put options the upper boundary of value is the strike price, since the put will reach a maximum price when the underlying security is worth little or nothing. When the underlying asset is worthless, the right to sell the security at a price above the market will be valued equal to the strike price.

For securities that have cash flows, essentially bonds or notes, these boundaries must be adjusted by the amount of the present value of the cash flows. For example, even if the bond itself has no value outside its cash flows, it still retains those cash flows until the U.S. government goes bankrupt. Therefore, it is necessary to adjust the value of the put/call by that amount. For bonds, the cash flows are known and the credit risk is nil. There is a small capital controls risk, since the U.S. government could potentially change the rules of the game if pressed, but this is quite unlikely.

This relationship is also the basis for putting together **synthetic securities**. For example, suppose you would like to go long a futures contract. You could instead buy a call and sell a put to achieve the same cash flows. In this case, purchasing a Eurodollar December 1990 future at a price of .9200 ensures that at expiration you can receive cash settlement equal to a price of .9200 for that security. Buying a call for the same expiration date means that you are paying a premium to have the right to buy this Euro position at a price of .9200 on or before expiration. Selling the put means that you are receiving a premium for a possible obligation to sell the Euro at a price of .9200 at expiration. If at settlement the price of the Euro is .9210, then the future gains 10 ticks. For the synthetic security, the put expires unexercised and the call gains an intrinsic value of 10 ticks. Since the premiums should nearly or exactly cancel out, the two positions are equivalent. Equally, if the price at settlement is .9190, the future loses 10 ticks. The call expires worthless. The put is exercised, requiring the holder to buy in the cash market at .9190 and sell to the holder of the option at .9100, which results in a loss of 10 ticks. See Figure 2.32 for a list of synthetic equivalent positions. Note that each of the synthetics has a delta close to the delta of the equivalent cash-only position. Thus, the effort involved to monitor the synthetic position should not be much different from managing the cash position. Synthetics provide an alternative that is sometimes more attractive, as part of the position might already be part of the portfolio. It also allows you to change your mind with somewhat more ease.

Currency Options. There also exists a good market for currency options. They are traded on the IMM and also on the Philadelphia Stock Exchange, where they originated. The size of the contract varies for each currency, as they are denominated in U.S. cents per unit of foreign currency. The actual dollar value of the put or call is the premium quotation multiplied by the size of the contract. A large part of the universe of market participants in currency options are importer/exporters. Again, since liability is limited in options, the downside is zero. In general, the price of an American foreign currency call will be bound by the soft price of the currency on the upside and zero on the downside, with an approximate price being calculated by using the

Figure 2.32.   Synthetic Positions

1. Long Positions:
    Long the underlying security = long call + short put
    Long call option = long underlying security + long put
    Long put option = short underlying security + long call
2. Short Positions:
    Short the underlying security = short call + long put
    Short call option = short underlying security + short put
    Short put option = long underlying security + short call

value of the investment in the foreign currency minus the present value of the strike price. For puts, this is the reverse, that is, the present value of the strike minus the value of an investment in the foreign currency.

There is also a put/call parity for foreign options. The premium for the put will equal the premium for the call minus the investment in the currency plus the present value of the strike price. In general, the price of the call plus the strike price minus the investment in the currency will be greater than or equal to the price of the put, which will be greater than or equal to the price of the call plus the present value of the strike minus the spot price.

This concludes the brief introduction to the basic tools of interest-rate risk management. Knowing the critical variables affecting the market price and how the price of the derivative relates to the cash securities market can allow below average costs hedge programs to be implemented.

CHAPTER 3

New and Developing Products

Risk management is not a static field. New products and financial instruments are continuingly being developed to meet new needs. While most risks can be managed with the traditional hedge instruments discussed in Chapter 2, there is still room for improvement. A number of risk management choices require close monitoring or fairly high commission costs, and many do not reduce risk in the way desired. Therefore, there is a demand for new strategies to manage risk.

For the most part, these new products build on the standardized products discussed in Chapter 2. Financial risk management tools are seeing less standardized innovations than previously. This offers a new version of customized product.

It is necessary to add in a substantial liquidity premium for new product use, but they offer the chance of protection that is much more complicated when replicated by some of the more standard products. Note that I stress that they *can* be replicated, but that the management and effort involved to do so can tip the balance from making risk management attractive in price to unattractive.

Among the many new and developing products are caps, floors, collars, corridors, compound options (including swaptions, captions and floortions), dual-currency options, path-dependent options and option-linked loans. These products are relatively new. Therefore, their commission costs tend to be higher than average and there is not a long history to show how their prices actually move in extreme conditions. In addition, they are much less liquid than other instruments. However, they have attracted an audience because they are tailored to meet specific needs.

CAPS

A **cap** is a contract between two parties that sets a maximum level for the purchaser's funding rate. That is, if you are borrowing money by issuing a floating-rate security, a cap sets the maximum interest rate that you will have to pay out.

Under certain conditions a cap is similiar to a swap, but can be viewed more clearly as a customized option. The advantage to this type of hedge over a swap is that you are still able to take advantage of a drop in rates. On the other hand, if you are the owner of a floating rate security, you might be inclined to sell a cap to get some additional yield through the receipt of a premium. For example, if your view is for a limited upward move in rates and you own $200 million of a floating-rate security, then the additional risk of selling a cap might be acceptable. See Figures 3.1 and 3.2 for the payoff diagrams associated with buying and selling caps.

There is some basic terminology used in the construction of a cap. First, there must be an **underlying interest-rate index** to act as the representative of general market rates. The most common choice is LIBOR, but a cap can be sufficiently customized to use other indices, such as the prime lending rate or commercial paper rates. The **strike rate** acts like the strike price of an option. At yields greater than the strike rate, the purchaser of the cap owns interest-rate risk protection. At levels below the strike rate, the purchaser bears the risk. While there is generally an inverse relationship between the proximity of the strike rate to the current market and the price paid for the cap, or *premium*, it is not a proportional relationship. Starting at the current market rate, each additional point added to the strike rate will decrease the premium, but not by the same amount. The premium will decrease by an increasing amount for each additional point until we

Figure 3.1. Hedged vs. Unhedged Funding Rates: How a Cap Sets a Maximum Cost

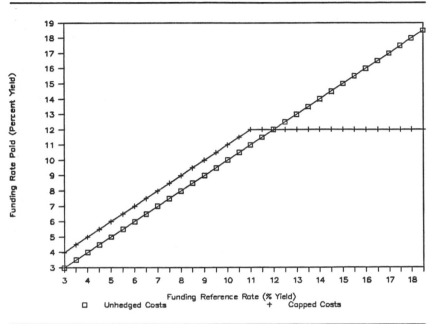

reach a level high enough above the market where the premiums are sufficiently low that they stabilize. This level above the current market is dependent on the term of the contract. The **term** of the contract is the length of time that the contract is in effect and is comparable to the maturity of a security. The **settlement frequency** is how many times annually the cash flows will be exchanged. By making all of these choices, a synthetic security is created. Rather than relying on the marketplace to provide a sufficiently representative security in the size needed to hedge your position, one can be artificially constructed. The **notional principal** is the amount that is established as the base for determining the cash flows. Although there are amortizing caps, the notional principal is usually fixed. Again, **premium** is the fee paid by the buyer to the seller for the interest-rate risk protection. It is paid upfront. The size of the premium is affected by the strike rate, the term, the volatility of the underlying index, the shape of the yield curve, the credit rating of the counterparty, and other factors. Since a

Figure 3.2.   Selling a Cap: Yield Enhancement for Lower Rates

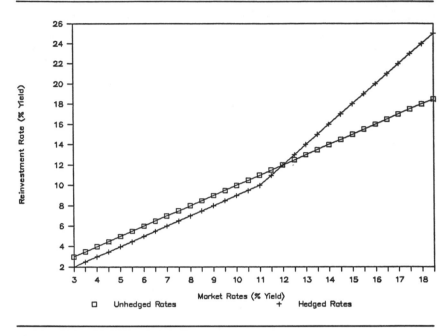

cap is most closely related to options, its pricing theory is derived from options pricing theory. However, caps are more like European than American options, since the payments are determined by the settlement frequency rather than being exercised at the holder's choice. As a result, a cap with a less frequent settlement will have a lower premium attached. For example, if two caps are exactly the same except for settlement frequency, a cap with an annual settlement will have a lower premium than a cap with a quarterly settlement. Settlement is usually determined on an actual/360 basis, but this is a contractual term than can vary. See Figure 3.3 for a list of variables that affect the price of a cap.

A simple example will explain the mechanics. Suppose you are issuing a five-year floating-rate note (FRN) with a minimum coupon of 8.50% and an annual reset. The reset rate is determined as one-year LIBOR plus 2.75%. As the issuer, you do not anticipate that rates will move substantially higher that the present levels. This is logical, since you would borrow at a fixed rate if you thought general interest rates

Figure 3.3.   Variables Affecting the Price of a Cap

Items that Increase the Premium:

    Strike Rate At-the-Money
    High Settlement Frequency
    Long Term of Contract
    Highly Volatile Reference Index
    Lower Credit Rating of Counterparty
    Steep Yield Curve

Items that Lower the Premium:

    Out-of-the-Money Strike Rate
    Low Settlement Frequency
    Short Term to Contract
    Reference Index with Lag or Lower Volatility
    High Credit Rating
    Flat or Inverted Yield Curve

would increase substantially. You are willing to accept the risk of a wrong forecast up to paying a rate of 13.50%. This rate is determined usually by a spread over the current fixed-rate borrowing levels. Suppose at today's rates you can borrow on a floating-rate basis for the period with a 8.50% coupon for the first year, but borrow fixed-rate for five years at 11%. By borrowing floating (if you are correct in your interest rate outlook) you can save 2.50% the first year alone. Twice this savings or 5% is usually the maximum extra you are willing to pay for being wrong, and usually only a symmetric level of error is acceptable. This 13.50% (8.50% + 5%) is then the strike rate. The notional amount or notional principal is based on the amount issued. If the note issue, the underlying position, is $200 million, then you can hedge all or part of the issue. Certainly, buying a cap with a $200 million notional amount is not particularly unusual or difficult to execute. An index is then chosen that has a high degree of correlation with the underlying note issue. In this case, with a one-year rest, the twelve-month LIBOR is acceptable. However, a cap using one-year LIBOR is non-standard and thus would raise the price. You could alternatively use six-month LIBOR or, since the issue is a corporate, some of the credit spread risk might be hedged by using one-year commercial paper rates or prime, instead. The term of the cap will be for the five-year life of the note. The settlement frequency will also be annual, just as the note rate resets. Usually, the date is chosen to closely correspond with this reset date. As mentioned above, the cap is a European option variant, as is the FRN. Since both are subject to exercise only on a specific date, the hedge needs to be very close to the same reset date or a timing risk (also known as reset lag risk) occurs. The contract is then drawn up between the two counterparties, often of a standard contract form. The premium of this cap is small because the strike rate is so far away from current market rates. Let's look at .50% or 50 basis points. On $200 million, the premium will be $1 million, which must be paid upfront.

If prime is at 9% when the first reset appears, and LIBOR is at 7-3/16% no cash flows are exchanged on the cap because the funding cost is below the strike rate. Your funding costs on the note are one-year LIBOR plus 2.75%, or 7-3/16% plus the margin to get 9.9375%. However, to calculate the total funding cost, add in the amount of the premium amortized over the life of the note, or .20%. Therefore, the total funding cost is 10.1375%. However, if prime is at 14% when the second reset occurs you will be entitled to 1/2% protection due to changes in interest rates. Therefore, you will receive prime minus strike multiplied by (days in settlement period/360) multiplied by notional principal, or $1 million. The cost of funding this year when one-year LIBOR is at 12%, is 14.75% to the coupon holders plus .20% annual amortized premium minus 1/2% receipt from the cap, or 14.45%. This will be the maximum annual funding cost. From this level, any increases in the coupon payments to note holders will be offset by receipts from the cap counterparty.

Caps were designed to meet the need of clients who desire to reduce interest-rate risk, such as the risk of asset/liability cash-flow mismatches, but who have no need to completely eliminate the risk. Interest-rate caps limit borrowing costs when rates increase, but do allow some participation if rates fall. The participation in favorable market moves is only minimized by the amount of the premium spent to buy the cap, amortized over the length of the contract. In addition, there is a two-way market in caps, that you might resell the cap to the same institutional counterparty or transfer it to another to recover some of the initial premium paid if your outlook on rates changes. Unless the market moves are favorable, it is unlikely that the premium paid to sell the cap will be greater, as there is a time-decay aspect associated with its value. The longer the term of the contract, the more likely it is that the owner of the cap will receive a payment. As the length of the contract decreases, the premium required will also decrease, since there is an increasingly smaller likelihood that a payment will be made to the holder. The cap premium will also depend on consensus outlooks for volatility in the market you choose. Unless conditions are unusual, the premium will be at a maximum when it is at-the-money, that is, when the cap is at near-market rates.

Despite all the variations in index and settlement frequency, the basic cap is a 90-day LIBOR cap. Generally, these are used to offset loans made or resetting for the same period. The match of dates must be as exact as possible. The coverage period runs from the start date of the term, but it excludes the end date. Convention has designated the payment date as generally two business days after the end of the period. Remember that expectations for rates will help you decide whether to use a cap or a swap for hedging. If the strike price of the cap is at 9.5% and LIBOR is above that on the reset date, there will be no difference in costs between a cap and a floating-to-fixed swap with a rate at 9.5%. However, should LIBOR be reset at 9.5% or below, the swap cost would exceed the cost of the cap.

While the basic cap uses three-month LIBOR as the index, it can be used even for semi-annual or annual resets. However, we encounter a problem with rate correlation when a 90-day index is used to hedge an annual or semi-annual rate. You should try to keep the index as close as possible to the underlying unless it will dramatically alter the premium paid to own the cap. Negotiating with the counterparty will usually result in a compromise between correlation and the amount of the premium. Using cap terminology to be precise, we might speak of a three-year 9.5% three-month LIBOR cap. This would have 11 separate resets. An example of the customization capable in a cap is that each term can have both a different strike price and a different notional amount. This would allow stacking as time progresses without having to use future or forwards in combination. When the index is something other than LIBOR, the cap will often be written as an average rather than the spot rate. This is particularly true for prime or commercial paper caps.

For pricing purposes, the 90-day LIBOR cap is like a strip of three-month European options. Thus, the same factors used to price interest-rate options are used to price caps. A cap can be viewed as offering contingent ownership rights to an artificially constructed security. This view makes a cap comparable to a call. The differences lie in customization. A cap provides contingent rights to specific cash flows, designed to match a particular underlying position, and exercisable only on specific dates. To replicate a cap might involve the purchase of assorted different calls in odd sizes, or even be impossible due to the choice of reset dates. This similarity, though, means that caps are priced like calls. So there is a similar risk of mispricing and the same mismatch of risks for naked positions in the instruments. One of the primary sources of error is the present-value calculation and the reinvestment assumptions as we go forward in time. As a practical matter, there are a number of boundaries for caps pricing, just as there are for options. First, there is an increasing monotonic relationship between the cap and the future interest rate. That is, the price of the cap increases as the future interest rate increases. Therefore, you should build a forward yield curve using the futures and swaps quotes. The problem is to decide as you go forward how much liquidity premium has been built into the rates and how much they will change over time. This curve will explain why some caps are priced so differently, even though they are otherwise identical except for their start time. This curve also gives us the second parameter to pricing: the price of the cap will increase as perceptions of market volatility increase. The price is based on implied volatility levels. As these levels increase, so do the chances of a payoff, and the price will increase as well. Third, the value of the fixing will decrease as the strike price increases. This has often been compared to the deductible on insurance premiums, as it behaves the same way. Therefore, each increase of 100 basis points in the strike price, the price of the cap will drop increasingly. Finally, as time increases, the price of the cap will increase. This is partly due to an increased risk premium by the counterparty and partly due to the value of the additional reset period, since each additional reset is the same as buying another European option.

FLOORS

A **floor** is the mirror image of a cap that sets a minimum rate for an asset or liability. If you issue a floating-rate note with a minimum coupon, it is the same as selling a floor to the security holder. (See Figure 3.4 for the payoff diagram for selling a floor.) For the receipt of an up-front premium payment, you give up full participation in a favorable move in rates. However, the premium lowers your average cost of funding if the floor is not exercised. From the other point of view, the buyer of a floor locks in a minimum investment rate by sacrificing some of the upside by making the premium payment. (See Figure 3.5 for the payoff diagram for purchasing a floor.) Other than holders of securities with a minimum coupon, the buyers of floors are often pension program portfolio managers looking to minimize their asset reinvestment rates. For lenders in any market sector, buying a floor is attractive. Should rates move below the strike rate, you will receive additional payments to increase your return; should rates rally, there is upside participation when volatility is to your advantage. The floor can also be sold so that a company with floating-rate receivables can see some yield enhancement via the premium without much addi-

Figure 3.4.   Payoff Diagram: Selling a Floor with a 7.5% Strike

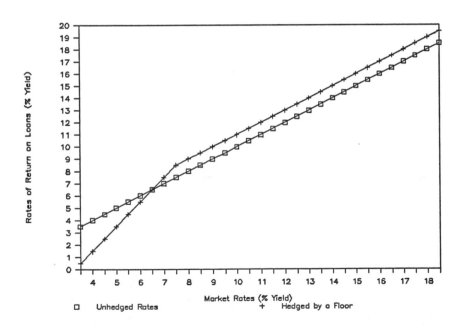

Figure 3.5.   Payoff Diagram: Purchasing a Floor with a 7.5% Strike

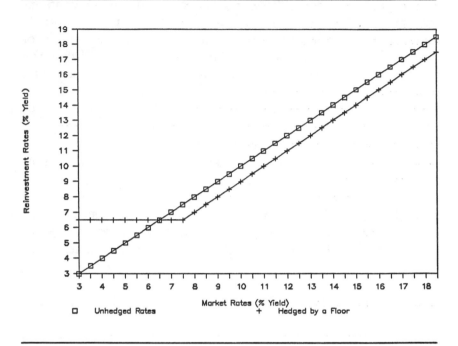

tional risk. As with caps, there is a two-way market, so the floor can be bought back if you view of interest rates changes.

A floor contract is similar to a cap contract, and it includes the same terminology. There is a strike rate, term of contract, underlying index, settlement frequency, day count, and notional amount. The mechanics are also similar. Suppose that you are the treasurer of a company with $50 million in floating-rate loans on the books. All of the interest rates are set to float off the 90-day Treasury bill rate with quarterly resets. This combination of loans is a sufficiently high percentage of your investment assets that you are concerned about its risk posture. Since these assets are also tied to an annually floating borrowing, you want to assure a certain minimum return on the investment. You are already exposed to a timing risk in the asset/liability match, since the quarterly reset may prove more volatile than the annual resets. With this in mind, you decide to purchase a floor. Suppose the market has 90-day LIBOR at 7.10% when you decide to purchase the floor. Given economic fundamentals, you feel that a minimum return of 9% on your commercial loans is the desired protection. This is LIBOR plus 1.90%, which you will use as the index. Instead of 90-day LIBOR itself, you will use LIBOR plus 1.90% for the index to match the strike. This allows a minimum asset spread of 1.50%, since the median commercial loan is reset off LIBOR plus 3.25%. Therefore, the index is 90-day LIBOR plus 190 basis points, and the strike is 9%. The settlement frequency is quarterly. The notional amount is $50 million. You might set the term of the contract equal to the duration of the loans, although this is not an absolute rule, and there are many alternatives. If the loans are callable or have early termination clauses, you might set the term of the contract equal to the average life of the loan portion of the portfolio, or you might choose to hedge for the length of time that it takes for two-thirds of the principal of the loans to be repaid. If we choose the term to match a 100% principal repayment of the loans, it would be four years. That is, if all of the cash flows from the loans were devoted to paying back the principal lent, this would be done in four years. Note that this floor is close to being at-the-money, that is, near market rates. Also note that the notional amount is a bit on the small side for a floor and that the settlement is quarterly. Therefore, the premium will be correspondingly high, at 2½%, or $1,250,000.

In this example, as market rates increase for the first reset, LIBOR is 7.1385%, so the index is calculated at 9.0385%. Since this is above the floor strike rate, no cash changes hands. The assets are earning a median amount of LIBOR plus 3.25%, or 10.3885%. However, when we subtract the annual amortized premium, which is .625% each year for the four years of the contract, the actual annualized earnings on the assets will be 10.3885 minus .625, or 9.7635%. If rates have fallen at the next quarterly reset a three-month LIBOR is at 7.00% exactly, the index will be calculated at 8.90%. The owner of the floor will then receive the difference between 9.00 and 8.90 multiplied by 92 days/360 multiplied by $50,000,000, or $12,777.78. His return on assets for this second quarter is 10.25% (7.00 plus 3.25% margin) annualized or 2.619% for the period. Subtracting the quarterly amortized premium of .15972% and adding this payment of $12,777.78 in percentage terms results in .0256%, which gives you a periodic return of 2.485% or 9.7234% return annually. Note in this example that the payment received at the money (.0256% for the period) is overwhelmed by the premium paid (.15625%). Typically, the **break-even** rate is the index minus the premium paid. In this case, with a premium of 2.5% of the capital and a strike rate of 9.0%, the index must fall to 8.375% before the payment received equals or exceeds the amortized amount of the premium, which is .625% each year. Calculating the break-even yield is often a good way to tell if the protection is desired at that price. Lowering the floor will decrease the premium quickly.

COLLARS

The devices known as the collar and the reverse collar are combinations of a cap and a floor. A collar is the purchase of a cap and the sale of a floor. A reverse collar is the purchase of a floor and the sale of a cap.

In the case of the collar, the cost of upside protection is minimized by giving up some of the advantages of a downside move. This works best when the view is for the interest rates to remain stable or move significantly higher. The primary reason for a broker to offer such a product is to earn the fee, but he also can disaggregate the collar and hedge his own assets and liabilities. A bank or brokerage might also choose to offset all or part of the exposure to another counterparty. Think of the bank as an options trader, but in a customized fashion, selling a call and buying a put on interest rates. Selling a call on interest rates means that the bank is selling to someone else the right to buy a security from the bank when interest rates are higher than the strike rate. This equates to the customer having the right to buy the asset below the set strike and to sell the asset at the strike to the bank, as if the bank sold to the client the right to average down his cost of owning the asset as it falls under a set limit. For the floor, the bank is purchasing the right from the client to receive payments on the interest rate differential as the base rate falls under a specific level. That is, the bank owns the right to average up the cost of the asset after it hits a pre-specified level. Thus, purchasing a naked collar is a mildly bullish position, and selling a naked collar is a mildly bearish position. However, from a hedging position, owning a collar is a hedge on floating-rate liabilities, because it limits the level you will pay; selling a collar is a hedge on fixed liabilities, because it allows participation in the move if rates decline. The cap and floor rates can even be set so that there is no initial payment, and the two premiums will net out. Again, as rates move above the strike rate of the cap, the counterparty pays to the client the difference between the market rate and the cap rate. However, as rates fall below the floor, the client pays to the counterparty bank the difference between the market rate and the floor. Therefore, there is essentially an unhedged position within the band of the two strike rates See Figures 3.6A and B for the structure and payoff diagram of a collar.

The reverse collar is simply a hedge for the asset side. The client buys a floor as the primary unit and sells the cap to minimize his hedging costs. Buying the floor provides the client with a series of payments when rates fall below a specified level. As a naked position, it is mildly bearish. However, as a hedge it protects floating-rate assets. Selling a reverse collar acts as a way of participating in an upward move in rates while owning fixed assets.

Although the primary market today sees clients purchasing collars, they can be sold as well. That is, selling a cap and buying a floor has uses in the financial world. A growing sector is pension plans with long-term liabilities and conservative reinvestment assumptions. For them, a reverse collar can be a way to enhance yield. In the currency market environment, many actuarial reinvestment assumptions are well below what the current yield curve implies, so the pension fund must invest more money today to assure that the long-term liability will be met with the pessimistic assumptions. By purchasing a floor, the pension plan will receive payments of the interest rate differential when and if rates move below the floor rate. In this way, the pension fund receives payments that lock in a reinvestment rate higher than the actuarial assumption. Selling the corresponding cap, with the same maturity and same notional principal, provides an offset to the premium paid for the floor. The pension fund will make payments on the differential between spot and current rates only when spot exceeds the cap rate. Therefore, the reinvestment rate can reach a maximum level. This is a good, conservative strategy. Moreover, when a "stacking" effect is added by increasing the notional principal at each reset period to account for additional monies needing to be hedged, the reverse collar can be fine-tuned. This stacking effect is called "stepping-up" in swaps parlance.

This more complex arrangement can be reduced to fundamental building blocks. As the band of the cap and floor narrows and approaches the same strike, the arrangement can be looked at as a swap

Figure 3.6. (A) Interest-Rate Collar; and (B) Interest-Rate Collar Payoff
Diagram: 11% Strike Cap and 7.5% Strike Floor

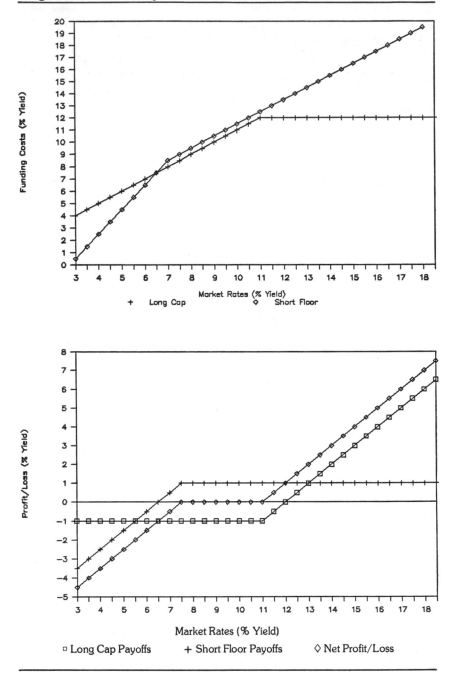

in which the purchaser of a basic collar is paying floating and receiving fixed. Likewise, a swap is really a series of forward contracts. With so many products acting as near-substitutes, a class of computer-assisted arbitrageurs has evolved that searches for minor mispricings. This has aided the liquidity of these new products and lowered the average cost by providing a constantly quoted market. Ultimately, all fixed-income securities and their derivatives can be viewed as a stream of cash flows. Let me mention here that the mispricings are normally due to relative supply/demand which varies from sector to sector.

Corridors

The universe for participants in collars is somewhat smaller than for forwards. The credit check must be good for both counterparties, since either could end up with the credit risk. As a result, the market has developed a slight variation to the collar. Known as a **corridor,** this variation consists of buying a cap with one strike rate and selling an identical cap with another, higher strike rate. Instead of offering unlimited protection above the strike price, there is instead a "corridor" of protection. See Figures 3.7A and B. For a reduced premium, the client receives payments from the counterparty bank when the market rate exceeds the strike rate for the lower cap, but the protection ends when the market rate moves above the strike rate for the upper cap. For example, suppose you have bought a corridor by purchasing a cap with a strike of 8% and selling a cap with a strike of 10%. The index is three-month LIBOR, which is at $7\frac{1}{16}$% at the time of purchase. As LIBOR moves to 8.25%, you receive a payment calculated as index rate minus strike multiplied by number of days/360 multiplied by the notional amount. Thus, for a $200 million notional principal, a quarterly settlement payment might be 8.25% minus 8.0% multiplied by 92/360 multiplied by $200 million, which equals $127,777.78. If the corridor is to fund a floating-rate liability, your cost of funding might be 8.25% (the floating rate of the liabilities) minus the payment received of .25% plus the annual amortized premium.

The premium for a corridor is usually much less, because chance of payoff is reduced. However, if the consensus outlook on rates is for a limited upwards move, or if the settlement frequency is high, or if the upper cap strike rate is significantly out of the money while the lower strike rate is near to at-the-money, then a corridor might cost as much

Figure 3.7. (A) Interest-Rate Corridor; and (B) Interest-Rate Corridor
Payoff Diagram: Buy 11% Cap and Sell 14% Cap

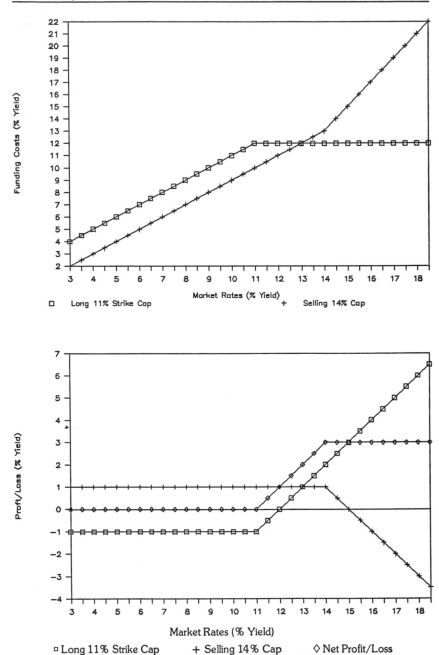

as a straight cap while giving a less truncated risk profile. On the other hand, if this is a naked, mildly speculative position or if the liabilities you are hedging are floating-rate but callable, then a corridor works very well.

Participating Caps and Floors

A less common type of collar is called a **participating interest-rate cap.** This is both conceptually and structurally closer to a swap than either the cap, floor, or collar. The cap and floor have the same strike price, so there is no band where the risk is unhedged. However, the payout structure is slightly different. When rates move above the cap strike rate, the client will receive the full expected payment. However, should rates move lower, the client pays out less than 100% of the expected differential. The amount of payment offset, or the percentage of expected payment made, is the **participation rate.** See Figure 3.8. The goal is to set the participation rate so that the value of the client's part of the floor equals the value of the cap. As the strike price of the cap moves lower, the percentage of expected payments made increases. If the cap moves sufficiently low, near to at-the money, the participation rate is 100% and the participating interest-rate cap becomes a swap.

In fact, we can look at the participating cap as a type of asymmetric swap. The buyer of the standard swap receives fixed and pays floating. Therefore, as interest rates increase above the strike rate, the owner of the cap pays 9% (the strike) but receives 11% (the market rate) for a net cash flow to the owner. As rates move lower, the cap owner still pays 8% (the strike), but receives only 6% (the market rate) for a net cash outflow. By contrast, in a participating swap the owner of the cap still pays 9% and receives 11% on the total notional amount. However, as rates decline, he "participates" by paying the 9% and receiving 6%, only on a percentage of the notional amount, as if he were buying a cap for 100% of the notional principal but selling a floor at the same strike rate on only a percentage of the notional amount. This is economically viable for the seller of the participating cap primarily because the strike rate is not at-the-money. When the strike is near to at-the-money, there is no premium exchanged, because the premium is the difference between at-the-money and nearly at-the-money. A participating cap requires no premium because there is less of a chance

Figure 3.8.   Participating Cap vs. Regular Cap: 11% Strike

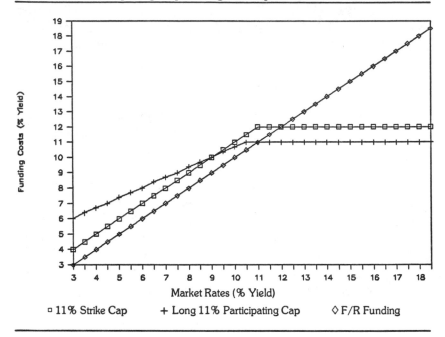

that any outflows will be made by the seller as the strike rate moves out-of-the-money.

The participation rate is determined by calculating present values for the cash flows. After all, the seller of the cap is committing to pay a series of cash flows on a periodic basis, which is the same as selling an annuity. The rate of the annuity is the market rate minus the strike rate for all values where the difference is greater than zero. At the same time, the seller of the participating cap is contracting to buy a series of cash flows in which the rate is the strike rate minus the market rate for all values where the difference is greater than zero. Setting the two annuities equal does not give the percentage of favorable participation, because we are missing a piece of the equation. Basically, the convention is that the cap annuity stream is represented by the premium it costs to own it. This premium is based on the present value of the annuity, but it has additional factors as well. To set the present value of the floor annuity stream equal to the cap premium, we must multiply each side by the percentage of relative participation. Therefore, the cap premium must be multiplied by the percentage of participation where the present value of the floor annuity is multiplied by 1 minus the percentage of participation. Thus, for near-market strike prices, you get almost 0% in favorable moves when no up-front premium is paid. However, as the strike rate moves out-of-the-money, the percentage of participation increases.

This leads to the conclusion that a participating cap will not be attractive all of the time. If interest rates increase, a floating-rate liability will have higher costs under a participating cap than it would under a pay-fixed/receive-floating swap. The upward protection for the cap starts only after a significant move, while the swap will give you a known rate of fixed rate minus the amortized commission. However, if rates fall, the costs of the swap do not move lower, as they will for the participating cap owner.

A **participating floor** provides a locked in reinvestment rate and a limited upside "participation" for further increases in interest rates. By adjusting the participation ratio and the floor level, this hedge can also be done with no upfront costs. See Figure 3.9 for a comparison of regular to participating floors. Just as the general risk-manager is more likely to purchase a cap than a floor, the use of participating floors is less common than the use of participating caps. There is a degree of unfamiliarity that makes pension fund managers more inclined to use other products. Also, IRS policy has historically seemed to treat an option as a speculative investment until proven otherwise. This does not encourage the initial use of new products. However, as the future economic scenarios grow more tentative, acceptance is likely to occur because there are few alternative products available to meet the need of guaranteeing minimum reinvestment rates.

SWAPTIONS

Swaptions are options to purchase or sell swaps. Almost exclusively, their current use sees clients buying swaptions. They are non-standard instruments in that every deal is customized between the two parties. If one can speak of a usual swaption, it is to pay or receive fixed and receive or pay three-month LIBOR with the start date usually within the month. Typical usage is to buy a swaption that gives the right to execute a swap within a certain period of time. Although there are

Figure 3.9.   Types of Floors: Regular vs. Participating 7.5% Strike

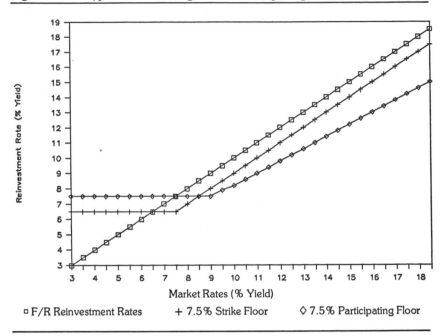

□ F/R Reinvestment Rates   + 7.5% Strike Floor   ◊ 7.5% Participating Floor

American options that can be exercised at any time within the period, the bulk of the business is currently in European window exercise, since these are much easier to value. There are also swaptions that give the purchaser the right to terminate an existing swap with the counterparty and even one instance of a swaption designed to transfer a swap extant with another counterparty to a new bank counterparty. Swaptions are used when a hedge must be placed on a contingent asset or liability, or when current interest rates have a possibility of dramatic change but not the probability of doing so. For example, suppose you are the issuer of a floating-rate note that is nearing unacceptably high rates of payout. As the next reset date approaches, you would like to be hedged if rates increase. However, if you wait until the reset happens, the hedge rate either will rise or will cost more. As a solution, you may work out the details of a desirable swap and approach your bank to see if it would write a swaption. Depending on the bank's interest-rate outlook for the near term and the way its book is positioned, you may be able to negotiate a swaption at an attractive level. Another solution with callable debt is to create a swaption that effectively calls the debt. This is known as a **synthetic call.** For example, an issuer of floating-rate debt may wish to call the issue if rates move a certain degree out-of-the-money. The issuer's obligations to holders can be transferred to a second party if the issuer receives floating, which he then flows through to the security holders, and pays the principal to the second party. Rather than paying a lump sum amount, the principal can be transferred in fixed amounts over the remaining length of the debt. Alternatively, an issuer of floating-rate debt might stabilize his funding costs by entering a swap to pay fixed and receive floating. To have a chance to take advantage of a downward move in rates and lower the average cost of funds, the issuer might buy a swaption to either terminate the original swap or buy one with the option to buy a new swap that pays floating and receives fixed at the same strike as the original swap. In this case, the fixed payments would offset each other.

A final common use of swaptions is an example of the contingent asset/liability case. Before an issue has been placed and before the indication rate has been set, the issuer may know that he will hedge it with a swap after the issuance is completed. If he waits to buy the swap until after the debt is issued, he risks that there will be an increase in volatility over the last day or so. By purchasing an option to enter this swap on the day the debt is sold, he locks in a known fixed-rate funding cost. Instead, if rates move favorably, so that a more attractive swap can be purchased, then the swaption is allowed to expire worthless. The premium of the swaption is amortized over the life of the debt and does add to the funding costs, but the reduction in risk is generally worth the cost in this type of case.

The European option structure for a swaption is usually cheaper than the American form because it reduces the chance of a payout. However, for our type of example, a European option is fine. The term of expiration can be set for the same date as the reset, or it can be set a day or two afterward if that is preferred. However, if the swaption is to be used to arbitrage between callable bonds and swaptions, then the American structure is preferred. The concept underlying such arbitrage is that the call option attached to corporate securities has previously been underpriced. The arbitrage is done by issuers, who then write a swaption and lower the overall costs by the amount of premium received. As the universe of options participants increases and the level of sophistication increases at all levels, the arbitrage profit will disappear. Indeed, there may be a higher hidden cost to this type of arbitrage in terms of manpower hours, systems, and general administration than can be justified by profit.

Swaptions, as one of the newer products, are not yet as standardized as caps, floor, collars, and so on. There is no standard terminology yet in use, so if comparing alternatives among brokers, be very clear about the reset dates, cash flow rights, and other important issues. However, it is still an affordable product, despite the customization. And in type of short-term protection offered, it has no equal. Swaption pricing terminology is also not as standardized as the system for caps, floors, swaps, or forwards. Swaptions provide the advantages of swaps: smaller cash flows and reduced exposure to interest rate volatility.

CAPTIONS AND FLOORTIONS

Captions and **floortions** are rights to buy caps and floors under certain pre-specified circumstances. The client will define the underlying cap by setting the maturity or expiration date, the strike price, and the exercise price in dollars. While American options are becoming the standard in the business, captions and floortions are still available in both American and European forms. There is also an exercise alternative called "American window." American and American window differ in that the former sets the term of the cap and the latter sets the maturity of the cap. Thus, in the American form, the exercise can be at any date within a range; regardless of the date of exercise, the length of the cap will be the same. For the American window, the exercise can be at any date within a range, but the maturity date for the cap is fixed. Because the end date is set, the counterparty to an American window caption has much less risk to transfer. Therefore, the American window version tends to be cheaper.

COMPOUND OPTIONS

Swaptions, captions, and floortions are types of **compound options,** or options on options. You can buy an option to buy or sell almost any other type of option. Compound calls and puts are not common, but they do exist. As the market participants become more sophisticated, this sector should be one of the fastest growing.

The construction of options with another option as the underlying security is subject to a good deal of price risk. This is because the volatility effects are squared, not merely doubled. When the graphs for delta and gamma of a typical compound option are drawn, the curvature is much more pronounced. See Figure 3.10 for the changes in delta and Figure 3.11 for gamma over time. The value of the compound option will vary sharply as the value of the underlying changes, and that will vary as its underlying security moves. Therefore, compound options are really best for hedging or substituting the respective option, but not the security holding up this pyramid. A compound option is also a good choice if there is a substantial amount of uncertainty in exactly how much protection will be needed or if the time horizon starts to extend past five years. Cash flows become increasingly uncertain as the forecasting horizon increases, and small errors can cause large differences in cash flows over a longer time period. However, compound options can sufficiently truncate the probability

Figure 3.10. Changes in Delta: Standard Option vs. Compound Option

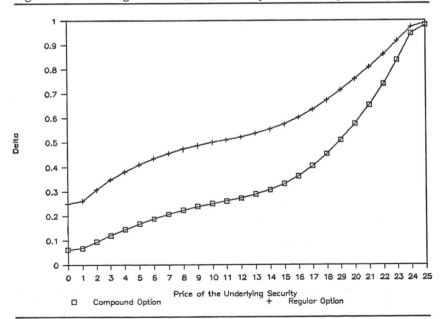

Figure 3.11.   Gamma over Time

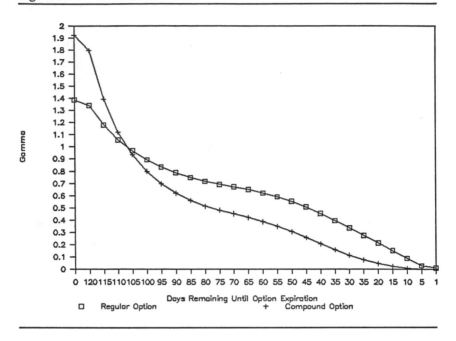

distribution and make the probable-to-potential price ratio improve, that a relatively small cash outlay can be worthwhile in special circumstances.

Compound options have also been known as split-fee options, although this term is less common. This name refers to the fact that the compound-option premium is paid upfront. Then, if the option is exercised, the premium for the underlying option is paid at the end of the compound-option period. In effect, it appears that the total premium on the position is "split" for the option and compound option.

Use of a compound option subjects the purchaser to a steeply curved delta which requires regular observation and adjustment. Also, due to the excessive volatility, there is a lower price correlation with the underlying than is normally expected. However, use of a compound option can also provide additional leverage, allowing you the choice of altering the strategic profile of a position as a reasonable cost. Since the various derivative products can all be viewed in terms of rights to own versus right to sell, we can look at a basic compound option in terms of puts and calls. For example, the profit and loss profile for owning a call shows that the price increases interest rates decline over the strike price of the call, the owner of the call will see a profit of market price minus strike price minus premium paid. As interest rates rally and price declines below the strike price, the owner of the call will see a maximum loss equal to the premium paid. For a compound call option, the premium is smaller, since it invokes a short-term contingent obligation on the part of the seller. Therefore, as price declines, the maximum loss is this smaller compound premium. However, as price increases (interest rates decline) above the strike price, the total gains are less, because the profit is calculated as market price minus strike price minus compound premium minus call premium. The same is true for a compound put option. Owning the right to sell an asset at a given strike price implies a profit as price declines of strike price minus market price minus premium. As price rallies above the strike price, the maximum loss is the premium paid. Since the compound put has a smaller premium, the loss if price rallies is smaller. However, the profit as price drops is also smaller, calculated as strike price minus market price minus compound premium minus put premium. Therefore, a compound option imparts more skew to the risk profile than a regular option.

In theory, buying an option to sell a call would be an attractive strategy, but it appears that this has not yet been done. When selling a call option, the maximum profit is the premium received. If you purchased a right to sell a call, the maximum loss would be the compound premium paid as price increased above the strike price. If price dropped and you exercised the short call position, the maximum profit would also be less, as it would consist of the premium received for the sale of the call minus the premium paid for the compound option. However, as a yield-enhancement strategy, your asset continues to participate in an upward move in price, but the net premium received works to offset a decline in price. Owning the right to sell a put can be equally attractive. Admittedly, as the price of the asset increases, the short put position gets exercised and receives a premium. If a compound short put position is owned, this maximum profit is offset by the compound premium paid. However, the risk that price will decline and that you will be forced to buy the asset at above-market prices is minimized, because the compound option is simply not exercised if that happens. This sets your maximum loss as the upfront premium paid on the compound option. See Figures 3.12A and B for profit/loss diagrams comparing standard options and compound options.

DUAL-CURRENCY OPTIONS

General foreign exchange options are complex because they involve at least two currencies. Buying a dollar call is the same as buying a put on the accompanying currency. For example, buying a call at 1.5400 dollar/mark is actually two options. You own the right to buy dollars and the right to sell marks. This means that with a little manipulation all sorts of offsets are possible by using put/call parity and a reasonably liquid market.

The standard currency option involves two currencies, but the payoff currency is set. The so-called dual-currency option allows the contingent obligation to be paid off in one of two possible currencies. For instance, a dual-currency call provides for the sale of dollars and the receipt of either marks or yen if exercised. The choice of which currency to deliver usually, but not always, rests with the option contract writer. For fund managers with diversified international portfolios, the currency received may not matter, and the premium is often a bit lower since the time frame is usually short. This type of option arose as the number and size of international funds increased. It offers risk protection to fund managers and manufacturers whose total return depends in part on the relationship in value between different currencies. As an example, we can look at a computer manufacturer. His home office is in the United States, but he buys parts in Japan and Germany, and has sales in the United Kingdom as well as at home. If both the yen and the pound sterling move in the same direction, he is not affected. However, if the yen appreciates so that his yen-denominated payments increase, and the pound sterling depreciates so that his sterling-denominated revenues fall, then his profit margins are squeezed. Other than using forwards, he might find it attractive to buy a dual-currency put. This involves the right to sell either pounds or yen if certain absolute exchange-rates occur or if the relationship between the yen and the pound, known as a **cross-rate,** reaches certain levels. He will receive dollars in return.

Since there are a number of products with which the broker or counterparty can hedge the undesired risk, I expect this market to in-

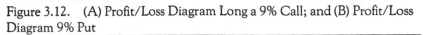

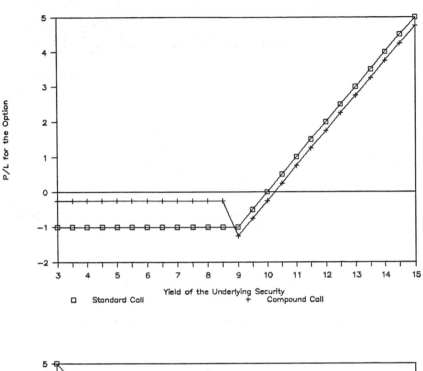

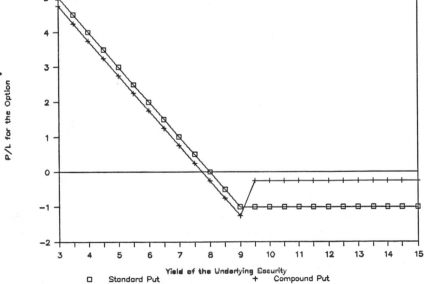

crease. However, it may do so rather slowly since the manufacturer may choose to hedge with Diff futures contracts or simply hedge by using the forward exchange market. In addition, given the large market in currency forwards, the currency options offer a right, but not an obligation, to hedge an offsetting obligation. Owning an offsetting currency obligation for a currency-forward commitment does allow participation as currency prices move favorably, but it locks in the maximum rate paid.

The **path-dependent option** is strictly a foreign exchange option at the moment. However, the structure is such that it should develop in domestic markets in the future. This modification on the basic currency option has a European structure with a strike price that is based on the average exchange rate over a period of time, so that the actual strike price is not determined until the exercise date. In actual practice, the average is taken from the start date of the option to a pre-agreed setting date. For instance, importers could buy a path-dependent option structured as a put to sell currency for dollars at the average rate due to expire at year end. With this option their foreign-currency revenues could be translated into dollars at the average exchange rate for the year if they exercised the option. If their transactions over the year resulted in a lower average for accounting translation, then the option would expire worthless. However, if they had the bad fortune to buy at the high end and sell at the low end of the annual range, they could exercise the call. Specifically, if the average is below the current market, they could exercise the option and sell it spot or forward to book a profit.

The design of an annual average is so that multinational corporations that are in the market on a regular basis can hedge their accounting translation methods. Current accounting methodologies provide for foreign currency transactions to be translated at either the spot rate when the transaction was done or the spot rate for the date of the balance sheet. Any variations of this can be flowed through into income. If a path-dependent call is purchased, then the option can be exercised if the balance sheet rate is greater than the strike rate. This results in the appearance of additional income. The additional income is calculated by multiplying the nominal amount by the difference between the strike rate and the current spot rate and subtracting from this product the amount of premium paid.

Returning to our example, by purchasing an at-the-money currency-call option with an American structure as well as the path-dependent dollar call, the importers obtain a low-risk speculative position. They pay a small premium for the chance of a short-term, below average rate mispricing, and already have this position sold for the average exchange rate at year end. Equally, selling at-the-money American-style puts on the currency lets the importers receive a premium. The position is low-risk because they are already naturally long dollars. Again, the average rate is locked in because of the path-dependent option. The actual difficulty is in determining the amount of currency to hedge. If revenues in the currency are sharply outside expectations, either above or below, then there will be one of two possible results: either the amount hedged will be greater than the revenues, in which case the importers will be long excess dollars at the average rate, or they will be underhedged with a need to translate excess revenues at spot rates. The overhedge and the underhedge expose the importers to spot rate exposure, but this can be remedied by stacking with futures contracts of FXAs as a combination to the path-dependent option. As revenues exceed the protection the option gives, the excess currency could be sold in either the futures or forward market or a currency swap could be purchased. Alternatively, an additional fee, the amount of the path-dependent option could be adjusted. However, there is risk because this market is new and not liquid.

A bank can offer this type of option because its natural exposure in everyday spot dealings leaves it with an average exchange rate on the books. By selling a path-dependent option, the bank offsets the average rate for a certain amount of currency. The premium received allows for yield enhancement by reducing funding costs or dropping the bank's average exchange rate. In addition, the bank stands to make management fees and commission costs in other fields as part of this option, so it is worth the risk that sport rates will be well above the average at the time the path-dependent option expires. Moreover, the bank can pursue its own hedging program by monitoring the average over the year. This is done by the moving-average method. Under this method an average for a given period of time is calculated each day. For each calculation, the earliest date is removed from the calculation and the most recent date is inserted. When the spot exceeds the current average rate, the bank can sell the currency, since the path-dependent option obligates the bank to buy the currency at the average rate if it is exercised. In this way, small arbitrage profits can be locked in. This method requires management by the bank, but it receives a corresponding premium for this product. Short-term dips below the current average can be used as opportunities to sell the currency, so the bank receives a premium for a chance to hedge its short-term speculative risk. This risk can be substantial, so any chance to reduce it is attractive.

There is also a **look-back option.** In this case, a hedged bank would receive a large premium for giving the client the right to buy the lowest or sell the highest rate of an asset for the duration of the option contract. Just as in the path-dependent option, the actual strike price is uncertain at the time of execution. The look-back option comes in both call and put variations. That is, you can purchase the right to buy the lowest price or the right to sell the highest price. The look-back option applies to all markets, but the foreign-exchange market has seen the most interest so far, due primarily to accounting conventions for transactions in other currencies. Current accounting standards require a company to pick a functional currency, which may or may not be U.S. dollars. The functional currency is distinct from the reporting currency, which is U.S. dollars. The currency in which the transaction is done is exchanged into the functional currency and then re-exchanged into dollars, if necessary. All of this translation from currency to currency can show phantom profits, upon which taxes must be paid, or indicate equally phantom losses that offer a tax write-off. So the rate at which the currency translations are done has great importance.

While the premium for the look-back option is large, the purchase of this option can be attractive if the client assesses costs on a transaction basis but accounts for all foreign exchange transactions at the average rate. This is particularly true when the range of price for the asset or currency is wide. For example, a company may need to buy computer parts from Japan. The price is fixed and higher than the world average, but the parts are the only ones available that fit the company's requirements. To make the transaction attractive, the bank buys a look-back call to purchase yen at the lowest rate, which makes the net dollar cost of the transaction more in line. If the transaction were done April 15, 1991, the cost would be calculated as 129.07 $/yen times the 1,000,000 yen purchase, which gives a dollar cost for the transaction of $129,070,000. However, when it comes to year-end accounting, this transaction is added with all the other purchases and generally is translated at the average exchange rate, which might be 132.00 $/yen. The additional exchange rate difference can flow through to the income sheet and the company will appear slightly more profitable. Equally, the bank is hedged over a different time period and so may have an opportunity to receive a large premium for a position that is already covered. In this way, it can reduce its average exchange rate or funding costs. The seller of the option buys currency as the rate increases and sells the currency as the rate decreases, this process can be thought of as currency portfolio insurance.

OPTION-LINKED LOANS

The next product is the **option-linked loan,** which is similar to the option-linked bond. However the more general word "loan" is used because more than one currency is involved.* Option-linked loans are included in this chapter, although strictly speaking they are not derivatives but rather hybrid securities. However, they are an increasingly common item on corporation balance sheets, and behave much like dual-currency options under certain circumstances. An option-linked loan involves the addition of contingent rights that allow changes in the payoff currency for specific contractual loans between two parties. Their most common use so far has been in equity swaps between companies.

Generally, when a company needs to borrow a currency for an effective date in the future, it is because it is guaranteed to be receiving a certain dollar amount and will need to convert these dollars into the currency at that time. The option-linked loan allows the company to do this forward loan more cheaply. The counterparty bank will lend the currency, while the client company sells dollar puts and currency calls. The company then receives a premium for the option that is dependent on the volatility of the respective exchange rate. Should the dollar fall below the strike price, the option will be exercised and the company's currency debt will be re-denominated into dollars. However, the company's receivables are already dollar denominated, so

---

* An example of this type of structure is described in the discussion of callable bonds in Chapter 4.

there is a natural hedge. But if the dollar then rallies back above the strike price by the loan redemption date, the company gets below-market rates for the loan, including the premium. The risk here is that the final currency for the loan is somewhat uncertain, so multinationals or companies with ongoing business in the two currencies find their risk the lowest. The advantage is the flexibility of the structure for the most part and the way that it requires little management. Most of the care for the loan is done by the needing to repay the loan.

Option-Linked Bonds

As a variation on this theme, there is the increasingly common option-linked bond. **Option-linked bonds** are bonds with early call dates. They are discussed here because they incorporate second stage derivatives. A bond with a series of puts and calls attached can be viewed in many ways. We might look at a bond with early call provisions as a bond with an attached swaption. An issuer can sell the swaption attached to the bond at a discount, because historically the attached options provisions have been underpriced by the market. The buyer gets a swaption at less than 100% of face value, and the issuer gets the premium that gives him an effective lower coupon for the bond. The swaption is exercised only if rates move sufficiently so that the bond is not called. In that case, the holder of the swaption makes a profit on the swaption, and the issuer is hedged by the swap itself against needing to make the contingent liabilities of the payments after the call date. Often the issuer might own a swap from issue date to call date in any case to fix the funding costs, particularly if there is a mismatch in cash flow from the liability to the asset side.

An example will help to clarify the complexity of the bond structure. On January 2, 1985, the client issues a bond with a ten-year maturity, callable in five years, with the coupon fixed at 10%. The issuer looks at the yield curve and decides to enter a ten-year fixed-to-floating swap. This gives him the opportunity to sell a swaption (generally to the swap counterparty) to deliver fixed from years five to ten. The swap counterparty will pay a higher fixed rate to receive this right. If rates fall, the swap counterparty exercises the swaption, which then nets out the ten-year swap and leaves the issuer free to call his bonds. He will then refinance at the new lower rate.

You should be aware that many bonds contain specific clauses limiting the circumstances under which issue can be called and how refinancing can be done. It would be a good idea to review the covenants of the bond issue before entering this type of deal.

Dual-Currency Bonds

A mix of option-linked bond and dual-currency option is the **dual-currency bond.** The plain vanilla form pays the interest coupon in a currency other than the principal. Such an investment is very attractive to pension funds of multinational companies, since they need to fund their liabilities in assorted currencies. For example, if a pension fund needs to make 6% of its retirement payments in lira, then owning bonds paying coupon in lira is a way to match the asset cash flow to the liability cash flow. However, if the principal is in a foreign currency, then the bond subjects the parent company's account to additional risks, since the bond can fluctuate in price both on its own and due to foreign exchange variations. If the principal is in the company's home currency, then this added risk can be avoided. The issuer can find this structure attractive under varying circumstances as well. If a multinational has a series of regular but relatively small cash flows in a foreign currency, perhaps due to sales of its goods in another country, then the issuing corporation can divert these flows to the bond holders. The borrowing can still be done in the home currency and invested there. In this way, the issuer does not need to find a home-currency cash stream to match the liability.

Dual-currency bonds have so far been issued more in Europe than in the United States. There are several issues that have principal denominated in marks but that pay coupons in Swiss francs or Dutch guilders. However, there has been recent interest by United States issuers, and we may see more of them in the future.

CHAPTER 4

Examples of Common High-Risk Situations

With the building blocks in place, we can look at some examples of how the decision-making process works in specific situations. Several strategies will be proposed for each Case, and not all of the suggestions will fit your circumstances. However, they will demonstrate the risk-management products that are currently most common and available and will guide you in making your risk-management decisions.

CASE 1. ISSUING FLOATING-RATE SECURITIES WITH A LOCKED-IN MINIMUM COUPON

Few new securities are issued today without some form of floating rate. These securities vary in the way that they float and in the frequency of the reset, but all have similar features. For Case 1, we will use a floating-rate certificate of deposit (CD). The methods used to hedge Case 1 are also applicable to corporates or mortgage-backed securities.

Recently, with fears of inflation built into the ordinary investor's mentality, commercial banks and savings and loan associations have started to issue a new type of CD. This CD has a minimum coupon payable to the investor, and it also includes reset dates on which the coupon can increase if market conditions so warrant. The coupon of the CD is usually set to a particular spread, with 90-day Treasury bills being most common base rate. For example, a CD with a maturity of two years issued when Treasury bills are at 7.00% may have a minimum coupon initially set at 7.25%. If rates drop in the next 90 days, the coupon will remain at 7.25%. However, if rates increase, the CD contract may increase the coupon payment to 7.50%.

This exposes the issuing institution to a risk of interest-rate mismatch. The issuing institution makes its money by borrowing at one rate and lending the borrowed funds at another rate. The difference between the two rates is known as the spread, which must cover any costs the bank incurs for doing the deal and also build in a risk premium and a profit margin. If the funds borrowed by the bank are reinvested at a fixed-rate, any increases in the coupon paid on the CD will eat into this profit margin. See Figure 4.1. If the bank invests in a floating rate security or loan, a lag between the two rates may be introduced. If rates fall, the profit margin might be reduced, since the amount paid in by the new floating-rate investment would also fall, but the amount paid out on the CD would stay at the fixed minimum.

There are several basic strategies that can be used to hedge a floating-rate certificate of deposit. The advantages and disadvantages of each are compared in Table 4.1, which appears at the end of Case 1.

Strategy 1—Invest in a Matched Instrument

The bank could invest its borrowed funds in a vehicle that floats off the same index as the CD. In this way, a particular spread would be locked in. For example, the bank could pay a CD with a quarterly reset after one year fixed and invest in an instrument or a loan with a quarterly reset after one year fixed. The holders of the CD might have a one-year fixed rate at 7.25% and would receive the higher of 7.25% or 25 basis points over 90-day T-bills. If the T-bill rate is 7.00% or lower after one year, the holder would continue to receive 7.25%. However, if the T-bill rate goes to 8.50%, the holder would receive 8.75%. On the other side, the bank might receive 9.75% for its investment for one year and then receive the higher of 9.75% or 275 basis points over 90-day T-bills. In this way, the bank is assured of always

Figure 4.1.   Issuing Floating Rate CDs

This figure indicates the interest rate paid and received under various base-rate scenarios. We are examining a case where the CD pays the higher of 7.25% or the base-rate plus 25 basis points. The floating-rate security in the table pays the base-rate plus 275 basis points. You can see that a fixed-rate investment of the borrowed funds is more profitable in a falling rate environment, and a floating-rate investment is more profitable in an increasing-rate environment.

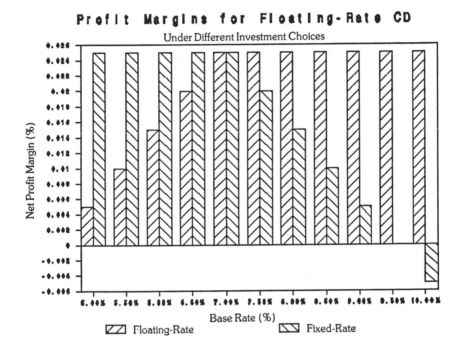

Base Rate	Interest Paid on CD	Interest Received Fixed-Rate	Interest Received Floating-Rate
5.00%	7.25%	9.75%	7.75%
5.50%	7.25%	9.75%	8.25%
6.00%	7.25%	9.75%	8.75%
6.50%	7.25%	9.75%	9.25%
7.00%	7.25%	9.75%	9.75%
7.50%	7.25%	9.75%	10.25%

making a profit. See Figure 4.2 for a probability distribution of profits. At a T-bill rate of 7.00% or lower at the end of the first year, the bank would continue to receive 9.75%. Its profit would be 250 basis points, which is the difference between the 9.75% earned by the bank and the 7.25% paid to the holder. If the T-bill rate rallies to 8.50% after the first year, the bank would receive 11.25% and its profit would be the difference between 11.25% and 8.75%, or 250 basis points. See Figure 4.3 for the probability distribution chart of profits for this strategy.

However, this solution raises several problems. First, finding such a match of terms and length of investment is not easy. Even when such an investment is found, it generally will be of a lesser credit quality. As a result, when rates increase the bank may find itself with an obligation to pay 25 basis points over 90-day T-bills but not receive anything on its own investment. Also, the institution issuing the CD will generally offer the same CD structure for a period of time, so there will be a stream of funds coming in. As well, banks traditionally borrow short-term and lend longer term. This causes a maturity mismatch to these

Figure 4.2.   Probability Distribution of Profits for the Unhedged CD

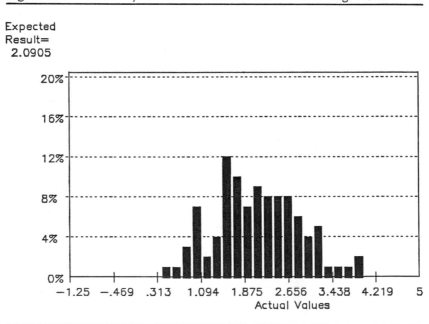

Figure 4.3.   Probability Distribution of Profits for Strategy 1

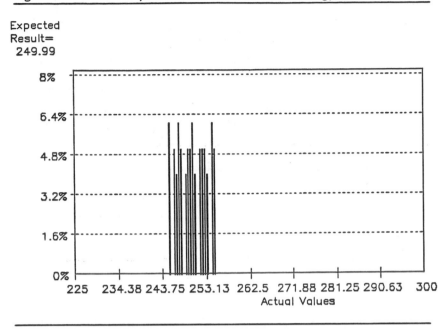

offsetting investments. These problems can be eliminated by alternative strategies.

Strategy 2—Purchase a Callable Swap

By investing the borrowed funds fixed for the entire term of the CD, the bank's first-year profits will be assured. However, the bank has a risk in the second year. It needs to have some participation if an upward move in rates should occur and protect itself against a downward move. To achieve this, the bank might participate in a callable swap. See Figure 4.4 for a diagram of the structure. In the second year, the bank could enter such a swap, paying fixed and receiving floating. The plain-vanilla swap structure discussed in Chapter 2 helps for an upward move in interest rates, but it offers no protection in case of a decline in rates. However, if the bank owned a swap with an added call attached or an early termination clause, the swap counterparty could narrow the spread paid to the bank while giving the bank its downside

Figure 4.4.   Payment Structure for a Callable Swap

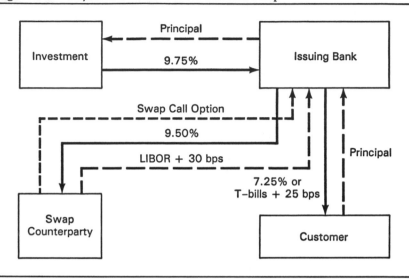

protection. Such a modified swap will be more expensive, so the bank would have to see how much the higher fixed-rate paid and the termination fee cut into its profits. Remember, it is worth buying the protection only if the risk is unacceptable. Note that this strategy is not the same as purchasing a swaption.

By participating in a swap, the bank could arrange for customized maturities and size to take advantage of the uncertainties in the amounts borrowed. After all, the notional principal does not have to be an even amount, nor does the length of the swap need to be exactly 360 days. However, there will be disadvantages. In this type of swap arrangement, the bank would make whatever investment appeared consistent with its credit requirements and looked most attractive. This investment of the borrowed funds could be either fixed rate or floating rate. However, since the bank would pay out floating rates to the customers, it would want to receive floating rates, so that it would pay out the type of cash streams that the swap is paying in. In a typical situation this would entail paying fixed and receiving floating but might also pay one floating-rate and receive another. A plain-vanilla swap would offer protection in the case of increasing rates, but if rates fell the bank would remain at a disadvantage Returning to the basic example, if the floating rate index fell to 7.00%, the bank would pay 7.25% on the CD, receive 9.75% on the investment, pay out 9.50% fixed in the swap, and receive only 7.00%. The bank would experience a net loss of 25 basis points plus commissions. See Figure 4.5 for a table of the cash flows for this hedge strategy. To obtain downside protection, the bank might choose to add an early termination clause to the swap in the form of a general call option that would give the bank the right to buy back the swap at its discretion. This callable swap is a fairly common modification. After all, if rates decline and the bank is invested at a fixed rate, the situation becomes hedging a fixed-rate liability. There is already a fixed spread to the investment and no additional downside hedge is needed. See Figure 4.6 for the probability distribution of profits for this strategy.

Strategy 3—Buy an FRA

A forward rate agreement would be particularly useful if anticipated interest-rate movements were expected to be short-term, although a higher degree of management would be required. Remember, an FRA is a way to lock in a rate for a future cash stream, and a series of FRAs is a swap. The FRA is merely a contract to purchase a specific asset at a specific date in the future for a specific price. This eliminates much of the uncertainty, but it introduces the cost of not being able to participate in a favorable interest-rate move. Given that the forward interest rate is determined by the current level of rates, its purchase is a way to profit from an increase in interest rates, since the price of assets will then decline. For example, suppose the bank is concerned about an increase in interest rates that will result in a corresponding increase in the payments made to the owner of the CD in the next period. If the payment period is quarterly and will start next quarter, the bank can purchase a 3 × 6 FRA. See Figure 4.7 for an example. There is a large OTC market, so the bank offering the CD would probably go to a commercial bank for the quotes. At the setting date, which is usually two days before the settlement date in one month, the difference between the investment rate and the borrowed rate, which are prespecified in the FRA contract, is present valued for the three months. This dollar amount is paid on the settlement date. If rates have indeed increased, then the bank will receive money, which will widen the spread between the investment and the borrowings. If rates are un-

Figure 4.5.   Payment Flows for a Callable Swap Hedge

The underlying security is a CD with a minimum coupon of 7.25% and a floating rate of 25 basis points over the 90-day Treasury bill. The rate is fixed at 7.25% for the first year, and afterwards re-sets quarterly. The funds borrowed in this method are invested for two years at a fixed-rate of 9.75%.

In a scenario of stable or increasing rates, the swap protects the bank's profits as follows:

	Pay	Receive	Net	Swap Flows		Net Return
Q1	− 7.25%	+9.75%	2.50%	0		+2.50%
Q2	− 7.25%	+9.75%	2.50%	0		+2.50%
Q3	− 7.25%	+9.75%	2.50%	0		+2.50%
Q4	− 7.25%	+9.75%	2.50%	0		+2.50%
Q5	− 8.00%	+9.75%	1.75%	−9.50% +	8.25%	+0.50%
Q6	− 8.25%	+9.75%	1.50%	−9.50% +	8.50%	+0.50%
Q7	− 9.00%	+9.75%	0.75%	−9.50% +	9.30%	+0.55%
Q8	−10.00%	+9.75%	−0.25%	−9.50% +	10.50%	+0.75%
AVE	− 8.03%	+9.75%	1.72%	−9.50% +	9.14%	+1.54%

Note, however, that rates need to increase quite dramatically before the protection is needed. In this particular example, entering the hedge lowers the average return on investment although it successfully avoids booking a loss.

The next table demonstrates the importance of the call option on the swap in a declining rate environment. If the call option on the swap were not available, the average returns would fall from +2.50% to +1.23%. This type of option is more important for a longer maturity security.

	Pay	Receive	Net	Swap Flows	Net Return
Q1	−7.25%	+9.75%	2.50%	0	+2.50%
Q2	−7.25%	+9.75%	2.50%	0	+2.50%
Q3	−7.25%	+9.75%	2.50%	0	+2.50%
Q4	−7.25%	+9.75%	2.50%	0	+2.50%
Q5	−7.25%	+9.75%	2.50%	−9.50% +7.50%	+0.50%
Q6	−7.25%	+9.75%	2.50%	−9.50% +7.00%	+0.00%
Q7	−7.25%	+9.75%	2.50%	−9.50% +6.80%	−0.20%
Q8	−7.25%	+9.75%	2.50%	−9.50% +6.50%	−0.50%
AVE	−7.25%	+9.75%	2.50%	−9.50% +6.95%	1.23%

Figure 4.6. Probability Distribution of Returns for Strategy 2—Call Option Exercised at − 1.00% Return

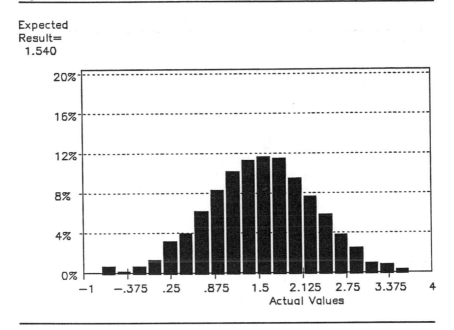

Expected
Result=
1.540

Figure 4.7. Buying an FRA to Hedge Specific Cash Flows

If the floating-rate CD is unhedged, and rates have been trending higher, then the purchase of a Forward Rate Agreement to hedge only specific cash-flows might be an alternative. This type of hedge is contingent on the assumption that you believe this rate move is temporary, or the CD is near to maturity.

See the following table for an example of a scenario where the purchase of an FRA reduces risk.

	Pay	Receive	Net	FRA Flows	Net
Q1	−7.25%	+9.75%	2.50	0	2.50
Q2	−7.25%	+9.75%	2.50	0	2.50
Q3	−7.25%	+9.75%	2.50	0	2.50
Q4	−7.25%	+9.75%	2.50	0	2.50
Q5	−8.00%	+9.75%	1.75	0	1.75
Q6	−8.25%	+9.75%	1.50	0	1.50
Q7est	−8.75%	+9.75%	1.00	0	1.00

Figure 4.7.   Buying an FRA to Hedge Specific Cash Flows (*continued*)

Based on the anticipated seventh quarter's rates, the bank decides to purchase an FRA. The rate period to be covered will start in three months and last for three months. So they will investigate rates on 3 × 6 FRAs. Using LIBOR as the reference rate to keep the FRA commission as low as possible, the contract rate for this period is set at 8.80%.

At settlement, the reference rate is 8.90% and Treasury bills are at 8.60%. So the payout to the CD owners will be 8.85%. However the FRA payment will be:

$$\text{FRA Payment} =$$
$$(8.90\% - 8.80\%) \times \$1,000,000 \times 91/360$$
$$= .10\% \times \$1,000,000 \times .25278$$
$$= \$252.78 \text{ per } \$1 \text{ million principal}$$

So for the seventh quarter, the rate paid to CD owners will be 8.85%, the rate received on the investment will be 9.75%, and the payment on the FRA will cash an inflow of .02528% for a net of +.92528, rather than the +.90 if the flow was not hedged. However, suppose that the forecasted move in interest rates was incorrect. Suppose the rate of Treasury bill was 8.25% and the reference rate was 8.40%. The outflow from the FRA would be:

$$\text{FRA Payment} =$$
$$(8.40\% - 8.80\%) \times \$1,000,000 \times \frac{91}{360}$$
$$= (-.40\%) \times \$1,000,000 \times .2528$$
$$= -\$1,011.20$$

In this case, if the cash flow had been unhedged, the payout rate would be −8.50%, and the inflow +9.75% for a net of +1.25. Since it was hedged, there is a reduction of .101% in the net for a return of +1.149.

changed, the bank will lose the commission on the FRA. However, if rates decrease, the FRA loss will eat into the profit margin expected by the bank. This still may prove attractive as a hedge, since the "worst-case" can be locked in. In addition, the FRA will be active for only one reset of the CD, so losses from adverse interest-rate moves will be minimal. The cash flows will be smaller, since only the difference between the rates will be paid or received. See Figure 4.8 for probability distribution of returns.

However, if this anticipated short-term move in rates is prolonged, then purchasing the next FRA to cover the next three months will be more expensive. Moreover, while this strategy requires little management for the term of the reset, it will require much more management over the life of the CD. In this event, interest rates must be forecasted quarterly and bid/asked on the appropriate FRA quoted, and the entire decision-making process must be run through each quarter or half-year.

Strategy 4—Sell Futures Contracts

The bank might choose instead a more mobile hedge. For instance, the bank could sell T-bill futures contracts to participate in the upside move in rates, as the price of the futures will fall as the interest rate increases, and invest the borrowed funds at a fixed rate. The profit

Figure 4.8.   Probability Distribution of Returns Using FRAs as the Hedge Instrument

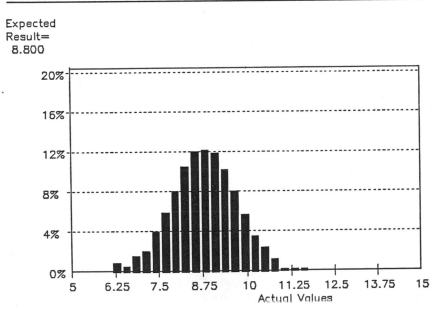

made from an increase in rates will make up for the short-fall in the spread between the floating interest payments and the fixed receivables. See Figure 4.9 for an example. Instituting a buy-stop would limit any large losses from the futures position if interest rates fall. The dis-

Figure 4.9.   Hedging by Selling T-bill Futures Contracts

The first table shows this hedge strategy in a favorable light, as the scenario is one of increasing interest rates. Since Treasury-bill futures contracts have a life of three months and the re-set period in the example is three months, we can sell each upcoming contract to offset each approaching cash flow. For example, if the front month contract is June, then the June, September, December, and next March contracts will approximate the four cash flows we wish to hedge the second year.

	Pay	Receive	Net	Futures Flows	Net
Q1	−7.25%	+9.75%	2.50%	0	2.50%
Q2	−7.25%	+9.75%	2.50%	0	2.50%
Q3	−7.25%	+9.75%	2.50%	0	2.50%
Q4	−7.25%	+9.75%	2.50%	0	2.50%
Q5	−8.00%	+9.75%	1.75%	+ .40	2.15%
Q6	−8.50%	+9.75%	1.25%	+1.10	2.35%
Q7	−9.00%	+9.75%	.75%	+1.35	2.10%
Q8	−10.00%	+9.75%	−.25%	+2.40	2.15%

If your forecast of interest rates is correct, this hedge acts to preserve the rate of return at a cost of some additional volatility. However, to see how it appears when rates decline, see the next table:

	Pay	Receive	Net	Futures Flows	Net
Q1	−7.25%	+9.75%	2.50%	0	2.50%
Q2	−7.25%	+9.75%	2.50%	0	2.50%
Q3	−7.25%	+9.75%	2.50%	0	2.50%
Q4	−7.25%	+9.75%	2.50%	0	2.50%
Q5	−7.25%	+9.75%	2.50%	− .40%	2.10%
Q6	−7.25%	+9.75%	2.50%	−1.10%	1.40%
Q7	−7.25%	+9.75%	2.50%	−1.65%	0.85%
Q8	−7.25%	+9.75%	2.50%	−2.00%	0.50%

Note that the average return decreases by a significant amount, from 2.50 to 1.86. In the case of a range, the hedge actually reduces the volatility of returns though.

advantage to this type of hedge is that there is a high degree of price volatility to the futures markets. There also may not be an exact correlation between the futures price, which includes an expectational component, and the index from which the CD payments are derived. In addition, the futures market hedge would require more monitoring and possibly would require additional upfront monies due to margin requirements. Finally, due to the volatility of the futures market, the stop may be triggered without truly indicating a decrease in interest rates. This means that the expenses of hedging will have been incurred without actually providing the protection.

The number of futures contracts to be sold is determined by using the hedge ratio. The number of contracts is calculated by dividing the dollar value of the futures contract into the face value of the CD and multiplying by the hedge ratio. The hedge ratio can be calculated a number of ways, but using the conversion factor method is often the easiest. Since in the basic example the CD has a maturity of two years, the bank may choose to use the two-year note futures contract rather than the treasury-bill contract. However, this points out some of the difficulties in using this type of hedge. The conversion factor is determined for government notes that are deliverable at the expiration of the futures contract. While the coupon and maturity of the CD may be close substitutes for one of these deliverables, there is a difference in liquidity and in credit quality. Both of these issues will cause the price of the CD to vary from the price of the deliverable note. Thus, these two securities will not have a perfect correlation in price, and the hedge will not be perfect, either.[1]

Another difficulty is that the two-year futures contract is not particularly well traded. While there is a market made on a regular and ongoing basis, there might be difficulty in placing or unwinding large positions. True, hedging a CD would probably not move price that much, since the management of such a hedge would involve only a few contracts per million dollars of CD issued. The conversion factor for the hedge ratio at the time the CDs in the basic example are issued will be close to 1.0. and 1,000,000 (face value of the CD) divided by 100,000 (face value of the contract) is equal to 10. As price changes and the conversion factor changes, then the number of contracts will vary

---

[1] By the way, if the CD does not match up with any of the deliverable notes, then you could construct a conversion factor using the formula given in Chapter 2.

by a couple, but will always be near ten for each million dollars issued. This hedge will require management. Overall, it will not be very expensive, but it may cost more in personnel management and transaction fees than is desirable. See Figure 4.10 for a probability distribution of returns using this strategy.

Strategy 5—Hedge Separate Re-Sets

Using a variation on Strategy 4, the bank might choose to hedge each reset of the coupon separately. This is fairly similar to using FRAs. There would be no initial hedge, as the spread is locked-in for the first year, but the bank would then hedge each reset as it approached using the front-month T-bill or Eurodollar contract. The Eurodollar contract might be preferable in this case since it would better approximate the same type of credit risk as the CD. At one time there was a specific CD futures contract, but it never achieved a wide audience of traders and is now inactive.

Figure 4.10.   Probability Distribution Using a Short-Futures Strategy

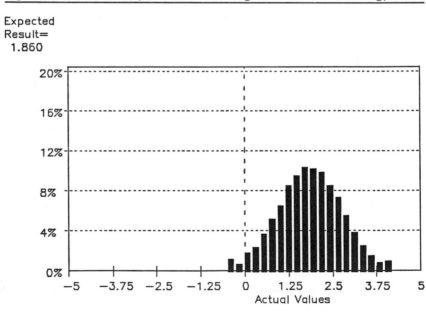

Strategy 6—Buy a Put on the Investment

As an alternative, the bank might choose to invest the funds in either a fixed-income or equity security, and purchase a *protective put* on the investment to minimize a downside move. This put would probably be purchased on the OTC market to allow for customization of size and maturity. The investment would have to be a security or a portfolio of securities, since there is no market for puts on commercial loans. This strategy buys the right to sell the investment at a cost below the current market rate, since the value of an investment at a fixed rate will fall as market rates rally. Should the value of the fixed-rate investment decrease below a pre-specified amount, the put will be triggered and the investment sold. The funds generated by selling this initial investment can be used to re-invest at a higher rate and again widen the spread between the rate at which funds are paid versus the rate at which funds are received. See Figure 4.11 for an example, and Figure 4.12 for the probability distribution of results.

Common practice is for the bank to lend the funds generated by its CD on a commercial basis. However, since there is not an options market specifically geared to this type of loan, the bank might instead purchase a put on a stock from its investment portfolio with the same value as the loan. Quite often, in fact, such a commercial loan requires equity collateral, so owning the put on this equity can be a possible alternative. This is a case where there are no hard and fast rules. The goal is to own a put on a security that has a high price correlation with the underlying investment. If the investment is of a commercial nature, then its price may act more like a representative equity than a fixed-income alternative. For example, construction loans are typically better represented by stocks than bonds. However, if the investment is mortgage-related in some fashion, puts can be purchased on GNMAs.

The basic difficulty with this strategy is that the costs of such a customized put can be high. In addition, such an instrument is not very liquid, which causes problems if the investment is repaid early. The put also must be marked-to-market over time, which may cause some accounting problems; the options market is volatile, and the price of a customized option is difficult to ascertain. There are also tax questions when options are used in a portfolio; the price volatility can lead to the appearance of profits on which taxes must be paid, but the

Figure 4.11.   Hedging Using a Protective Put

The principle behind this strategy is to sell the asset if rates increase suffi-ciently and use the funds to re-invest at the new, higher yields. The drawback is the premium paid for the put must be amortized over the life of the security, so the average return is reduced if the hedge is not triggered. See the table for a scenario with higher rates.

	Pay	Receiver	Net	Put Premium	Net
Q1	−7.25%	+9.75%	2.50%	−.25%	2.25%
Q2	−7.25%	+9.75%	2.50%	−.25%	2.25%
Q3	−7.25%	+9.75%	2.50%	−.25%	2.25%
Q4	−7.25%	+9.75%	2.50%	−.25%	2.25%
Q5	−8.00%	+9.75%	1.75%	−.25%	1.50%
Q6	−8.50%	+9.75%	1.25%	−.25%	1.00%

The put is exercised, and the funds invested for the remaining six months at 10.50%. However, the total invested is less, so the percentage earned based on the original principal is 10.35%

	Pay	Receiver	Net	Put Premium	Net
Q7	−9.00%	+10.35%	1.35%	−.25%	1.10%
Q8	−8.50%	+10.35%	1.85%	−.25%	1.60%
AVE	−7.875%	+9.90%	2.025%	−.25%	1.775%

In this case, the put allows the average return to remain fairly high, at 1.775%. Note, however, that this case is typical. The cost is so high that the unhedged average return would have been better than the hedging case. Un-hedged, the average return is 1.875%. However, the .1% return is often deemed an adequate payment for the reduced volatility.

apparent profits may quickly disappear. Since losses do not allow a rebate on taxes paid, but rather act only as an offset to other profits, this may offer a potential disadvantage to the bank.

Strategy 7—Buy Calls on the CD

Another way of looking at the CD in the basic example is that the bank is issuing a fixed-rate CD with an attached series of European floating-rate call options with different exercise dates. That is, the holder of the CD can on certain dates choose to exercise his option to receive more interest. For example, the total CD package sold by the bank consists of many pieces: (1) a fixed-rate CD with a yield of 7.25%

Figure 4.12.   Probability Distribution of Returns Using a Protective Put

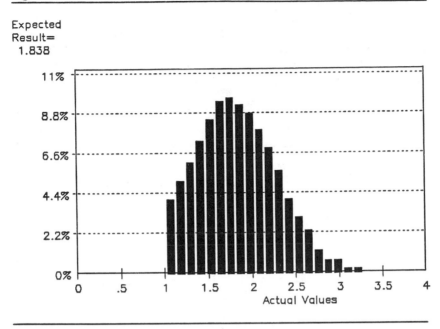

Expected
Result=
1.838

and a two-year maturity, (2) a call option to buy a CD of the same size with a maturity of 3 months and a rate calculated as the excess over 7.25% of 90-day Treasury bills plus 25 basis points, (3) a call option to buy a CD of the same size with a maturity of 3-months and the rate again calculated at the excess over 7.25% of 90-day Treasury bills plus 25 basis points. The exercise date for this call option is in 15 months. (4) Still another call option with the coupon and size remaining the same but with an expiration date 18 months in the future. (5) The last call option resembles the others but the expiration date is 21 months from the date of issue. Therefore, the bank needs to hedge the attached call options. Since it has, in effect, sold a series of call options on the CD yield at staggered dates, the bank needs to offset the short-call position. See Figure 4.13 for an example of valuing the attached call option.

A short call can be offset buy purchasing another call. While the bank will have sold the right to buy to a second party, leaving it with a contingent obligation to sell, it also owns the right to buy from a

Figure 4.13   The Attached CD Call Option

Evaluating the attached call option portion of the CD is fairly simple because it is a short-term instrument with a maximum life of 90 days. So theta and gamma have small effects and present valuing the potential cash flows will have little compounding effects. So the simplified equation used to price the option portion of the Certificate of Deposit is:

$$V_c = \frac{[(B+S) - I] \times P}{M} \geq 0$$

Where V_c = Price of Call Option
   B = Base Interest Rate
   S = Number of Basis Points Used for Calculating
      the New Coupon
   I = Minimum CD Coupon Rate
   P = Face Value of CD
   M = Number of Reset Periods Annually

As an example, if the base rate = 9.00%, then in the basic case example, the value of the call option is calculated

$$V_c = \frac{[(.09 + .0025) - .0725] \times 1,000,000}{4} = \$5,000$$

but if the base rate is 6.00%, then the value is

$$V_c = \frac{[(.06 + .0025) - .0725] \times 1,000,000}{4} = -\$2,500$$

However, the option value cannot be negative since it offers rights but no obligations. So the price of the call option in this case is zero.

By offering the adjustable-rate type of CD, the issuer is selling an item with a possible value of $5,000, or .5%. The issuer would consider this type of issuance attractive if he can offer rates .5% or more *under* the equivalent fixed-rate CD and still attract interest.

---

third party. In effect, the bank will have passed along its contingent obligation. However, this second call does not need to be purchased outright. Some of the previous strategies have used put-call parity as a substitute. Therefore, the second call can be in the form of owning and underlying security and a put, while borrowing the present value of the effective strike price of the call. In practice, this is done by borrowing funds via the CD, investing them in a floating-rate vehicle, and buying a put on that investment. This is similar to the protective put strategy. However, a true synthetic requires that the borrowed funds be invested in an instrument that floats off the same index as the CD, while the protective put is more generalized. In addition, the protective put is purchased out-of-the-money, while the synthetic is usually at-the-money. See Figure 4.14.

Additional Strategies

The bank could simply buy a strip of call options for the face value of the CD with expiration dates matching the reset dates. The strike price could be either fixed at the bank's level of pain or tied to the same floating-rate index as the CD. Since a naked short call position has unlimited risk if it is not hedged, adjusting the probability distribution of returns is probably worthwhile unless the price is deemed excessive. See Figure 4.15 and Figure 4.16.

The bank could also choose between strategies that provide slightly less protection. Since the CD represents a series of cash flows, the bank could hedge each flow separately. For instance, it might choose to sell some of the back-month T-bill futures, thereby hedging only the payments owed in the second and third quarters of the second year. Second, the bank might wait until there is a perception that rates actually will increase and at that time enter a swap to receive floating-rate payments. However, this choice will leave less protection if the perception turns out to be incorrect. Third, purchasing a swaption might offer enough protection if the bank feels strongly that rates will remain sideways to lower. In this case, the bank and the counterparty must agree to the terms of the swap, just as if it were going to be executed. This is a type of American option, in that it can be exercised at any time during the guarantee period.

Finally, in a more volatile rate environment, using a cap or caption would provide good upside protection. When interest rates on the index move above 8.00%, for example, the counterparty in the cap

Figure 4.14   Alternatives to Off-Set a Short-Call Position

1. Buy another call with a similar exposure.
2. Buy the underlying security, buy a put on the underlying security, and invest the present value of the strike price of the put.

Figure 4.15   Hedging the CD with a Strip of Call Options

First, let's look at the time-table for the strategy.

January 1, 19xx
    Floating-Rate CD is issued with a minimum coupon rate of 7.25%. The funds are invested in a fixed-rate instrument with a coupon of 9.75%.

January 1, the next year
    The floating-rate option on the CD goes into effect. As a hedge, the bank purchases March, June, and September call options on Eurodollar futures contracts. The choice to use Eurodollar rather than Treasury-bill options is due to the credit spread between the CD and Treasury-bills. The risk of lower price correlation between the instruments has been noted. This hedges the next three re-set periods.

March 1, the same year
    Purchase Eurodollar call options with a December expiration to hedge the last re-set period.

    Now let's look at how all these cash flows net out. For simplicity's sake, I will confine the calculations to the second year in the life of the CD.
    In this example, the hedge reduced the average returns from 2.47% to 1.79%, primarily because rates moved moderately higher. Had rates stayed low or the maturity for the hedge been longer, the monies earned would have offset the premium paid. This strategy is one of the few that allows the bank to gain when rates move below their minimum re-set level.

	Pay	Receive	Amortized Premium on Calls	Gain/Loss on Calls	Net
Q5	−8.25%	+9.75%	−.50%	0	+1.00%

At the start of the next period, the June calls are exercised, and the bank receives Eurodollar contracts which it then sells at the market at a yield of 6.60%, and pays 7.25%. This adds $4,000 per contract in dollar terms.

	Pay	Receive			
Q6	−7.25%	+9.75%	−.50	+.65	+2.65%
Q7	−8.00%	+9.75%	−.50	0	+1.25%

Again, the December call options are exercised due to a decrease in rates (increase in prices). The bank receives Eurodollar contracts at 7.00% and pays 7.25%.

	Pay	Receive			
Q8	−7.25%	+9.75%	−.50	+.25	+2.25%
AVE	−7.69%	+9.75%	−.50	+.23	+1.79%

Figure 4.16. Probability Distribution of Returns Using a Strip of Call Options

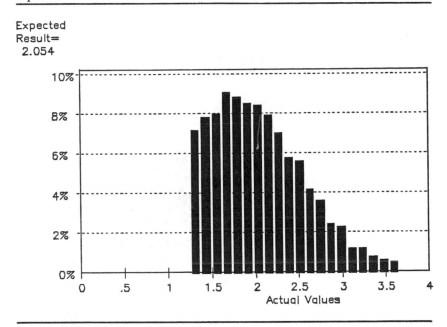

Expected
Result=
2.054

would make payments to the bank, although the bank would have to pay a premium for this type of protection. To recover some of the costs, the bank might choose to sell a floor, which would turn the strategy into a collar. By selling a floor with a 6% strike price, for example, the bank would make payments to the counterparty when the index fell below that rate. Selling a floor in this case may not be a wise strategy. After all, when rates decline, the bank will own a fixed-rate obligation to match a fixed-rate asset. There is no increase in the spread, since the CD rate cannot fall below a minimum. By trying to recover some of the costs of purchasing a cap, the bank opens itself to the risk of narrowing or negative spreads in an interest-rate decline. See Figures 4.17 and 4.18 to compare the probability distributions of return. When a severe decline in rates corresponds with the chance that the credit quality of the asset may also decline, there is a higher chance of default and greater risk. And there seems to be no sense in adding to risk while trying to manage risk. In the case of the caption, all the terms of the cap are agreed to, and the bank can choose to

Figure 4.17.   Probability Distribution of Returns Using a Cap Hedge

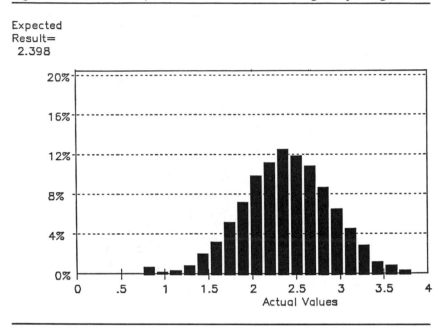

exercise it over a period of time or let it expire. Note that the price of a caption increases greatly with the length of time until expiration.

Choosing a Strategy

Any of these strategies will minimize the possibility that the bank will lose money by issuing a floating-rate CD. To choose the one best suited to your preferences and circumstances, weigh the following considerations:

A. Which strategy changes the probability distribution of profits to maximize the probable/possible ratio? This will generally be a strategy that matches the interest rates of the asset side to the liability side. For an example, see Strategy 1.

B. Which strategy has the lowest commission costs? As a general rule, exchange-traded instruments are both the lowest in commission and the most liquid. Specifically, exchange-traded options are the cheapest because of the leverage effect. Futures are next in cost, followed by spot items, which will vary widely. Here look to Strategy 7 and Strategy 3.

Figure 4.18.   Probability Distribution of Returns Using a Collar Hedge

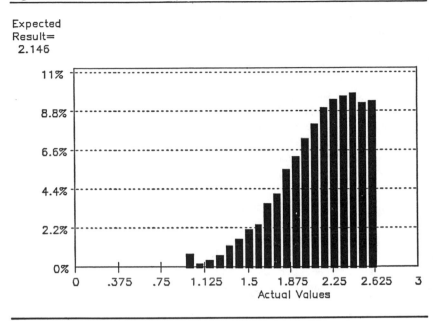

C. Which strategy requires the least amount of upkeep? Fixed maturity-date solutions and customized solutions are often less liquid but offer less market volatility in pricing and generally are designed to lock in a specific return or maximum loss figure. See Strategy 1 and Strategy 2.

D. Which strategy offers the best trade-off between maximum downside protection and a minimum of lost upside opportunity? This trade-off is called measuring the skew. Options strategies are known to impart skew to probability distributions. For example, the put strategies all truncate a certain amount of the downside distribution. Selling call options assumes an unlimited downside risk unless the underlying security is owned, but it provides only limited and known gains. Simply owning various combinations of securities can change the relative shape of the probability distribution curve but will not truncate it. See Strategy 6, Strategy 8, and the cap strategy.

E. Which strategy will work best under extreme conditions? Certain strategies work for smaller changes in interest rates but offer little help for larger moves, which is when it will be needed most. For an example, look for Strategy 1, 2, and the collar strategy.

Table 4.1.   Hedging Alternatives for a Floating-Rate CD

Strategy 1.	Asset/Liability Match
Advantages	zero commission costs
	zero management costs
Disadvantages	few acceptable securities available
	possible addition of credit risk
	decreased liquidity for investment
Strategy 2.	Entering a Swap (Pay Fixed/Receive Floating)
Advantages	lower up-front fees
	choice of underlying investment
	low management costs
	good credit quality
Disadvantages	potential liquidity problems
	added costs to reverse the trade
	moderately high total commissions
Strategy 3.	Purchasing an FRA
Advantages	participation in upside interest-rate moves
Disadvantages	needs periodic management
	higher transaction costs
	loss if rates fall
Strategy 4. & 5.	Selling Futures Contracts
Advantages	lower per-unit brokerage fees
	good leverage
	good liquidity
	easily reversed
Disadvantages	high volatility
	high total commissions costs
	inexact price correlation
	possible additional required cash-flows
	much higher management costs
Strategy 6.	Owning a Protective Put
Advantages	customization
	no additional management
	no additional cash-flows
Disadvantages	low liqudity
	higher per-unit brokerage fees
	questionable tax status
	guaranteed loss in adverse rate moves

(continued)

Table 4.1.   Hedging Alternatives for a Floating-Rate CD (*continued*)

Strategy 7.	Synthetic call strategy
Advantages	little management needed
	no additional cash needs
	customized size
	good leverage
Disadvantages	questionable liquidity
	higher transaction costs
	limited investment opportunities
Strategy 8.	Purchasing a strip of calls
Advantages	customized size and dates
	little ongoing management required
	no additional cash needs
	good leverage
Disadvantages	questionable liquidity
	higher transaction costs
	limited investment alternatives

CASE 2. MATCHING CASH FLOWS—ASSET/LIABILITY MANAGEMENT

Consider the pension fund for the municipality of Everywhere, which paid out $210,600 monthly in benefits in 1990. The plan includes a cost-of-living adjustment that is tied to the annual inflation rate. This is an example of potentially skewed cash flows, as benefits can readily go up but can move lower only with difficulty. This effect is called "sticky price action." The pension fund has a balance initially between assets and liabilities, but this is not a static condition. If 15 people retire in the next year and the inflation rate increases to 6.25%, there will be an increase in principal as funds are moved from capital growth to the fixed-income area, but outgoing amounts will also increase. There might also be a time gap in incoming monies from the fixed-income portfolio. For instance, the payments to pensioners may need to be disbursed on March 31, but the bulk of the interest payments for the portfolio may not arrive until June 15.

Strategy 1—Dedication

A common pension plan portfolio strategy is called dedication. It involves assigning an outgoing "home" for each incoming cash flow.

That is, the plan manager "*dedicates*" the asset stream to the liability stream.

As an example, suppose the pension fund manager calculates that he will need to disburse a minimum of $150,000 each month on the fifteenth of the month for retirement benefits. To assure that the cash is available for these known payments, he may structure his portfolio in the following manner:

(1) Buy a fixed-income security with $18,600,000 principal and a coupon of 9.75% that pays January and July 15. This will secure a coupon payment for those dates of $151,125. Any excess amounts will be re-invested.

(2) Buy another fixed-income security with $20,000,000 principal and a coupon of 9% that pays February and August 15. This will meet the minimum sum of $150,000 exactly.

(3) Buy another fixed-income security with $20,500,000 and a coupon of 8.80%. This one pays March and September 15 with a coupon payment of $150,333.33.

These securities are being purchased as much for their payment dates as their credit quality and coupon.

It can be difficult to find securities that match the outgoing stream of the pension liabilities. First, such payments may be made monthly and in odd amounts, while most fixed-income securities pay semi-annually and in round lots. It is a waste of the time value of money to receive an interest payment in June, for example, and simply hold it as the pension payments are made each month thereafter. Second, there is a degree of uncertainty as to how many employees will choose to retire and at what payment levels they will be when they do. These factors will affect how much is to be paid out in benefits. The purchase of a security today will not necessarily mean that pension benefits are assured a match a year from now, even disregarding any credit mismatch. Fortunately, derivatives are perfect for adjusting differences in cash flows.

Strategy 2—Duration Matching

The theory of immunization or duration matching attempts to minimize the differences in interest-rate sensitivity between assets and liabilities. For example, if the assets are very rate sensitive and the liabilities are less so, which is the usual case, the present value of the assets will change more than the present value of the liabilities for every small change in interest rates. This implies more frequent movements of principal to assure that liability payments can be made, and it also implies a greater risk. If this interest-rate sensitivity is reduced, however, the risk is reduced, as the relative values should move together.

Another way of looking at this is an attempt to assure a certain minimum value to the asset side regardless of how rates move. To do this, we first calculate the duration of the liabilities, then calculate the duration of the assets. We then set the two durations equal by buying (to lengthen the duration) or selling (to shorten the duration) either futures or forwards. Typically, the adjustment is done on the asset side. Manipulation of the assets to assure a cash flow capable of making those payments is essential. Remember that the duration is the weighted-average time to maturity of the cash flows of a security. Duration has an additive property, in that the duration of a sum of cash flows is equal to the sum of the durations of the separate cash flows. By adding together the duration of the individual assets, we arrive at the duration of the portfolio. When the duration of the assets and the duration of the liabilities are set equal, then the average time of the incoming cash flows and the outgoing cash flows are equal. In this way, we avoid the problems of dedication caused by specifically matching asset A to liability A, which limits the investment alternatives. By matching durations, instead, we can match portfolio of assets A to portfolio of liabilities A. The arithmetic is lengthy, but not complicated, and there are several computer programs that will do the calculations.

The duration-matching methodology raises several problems, however. First, there is a good deal of management involved, since the duration of each security will change as interest rates change and as time to maturity changes. Second, duration is only an approximate measure of a security's interest-rate sensitivity. As an approximation, it is most accurate for small changes in interest rates. When a large change occurs—when you need the most protection—duration matching is unfortunately most inaccurate. The reason for this inaccuracy is the desire for simplicity. Duration is calculated in a straight-line method. That is, it acts as though there is a one-to-one relationship between changes in price and changes in interest rates. Unfortunately, this is not so. Because of the approximate nature of duration matching, some secondary conditions should be met: (1) the present value of the assets—which is equal to the market price when using a yield-to-maturity measurement—must be greater than the present value of the liabilities and (2) the dispersion of the assets must be greater than the dispersion of the liabilities. The dispersion is a measure of the fluctuation of the security's payments around its duration. For instance, while a bond's duration may be 8 or 10 years, the maturity is 20 years, and the fluctuation of the payments around this duration might be 12 to 65 years-squared. See Figure 4.19 for the formula and calculation. Current usage considers deviation to be a measure of the variance of the coupon payments where the duration is the mean of the cash flows. However, for theoretical reasons and intuitive understanding, you might use the square-root of the dispersion (SRD), instead. In this way, the measurement is in years and it becomes a type of standard-deviation measure. This also provides the ability to choose assets with a lower SRD when the asset has a higher credit risk. See Figure 4.20.

A third problem inherent in duration matching is that duration assumes that price action is the same whether interest rates increase or decrease. However, most securities exhibit some form of sticky price action. Using a straight-line method makes the arithmetic more simple and we are able to add durations of different securities. In actuality, however, the relationship between price changes and interest-rate changes is non-linear; it moves along a curved line. The line of each security will be more or less curved depending on its specific interest-rate sensitivity; the more sensitive it is, the greater will be its degree of curvature. In financial analysis, we have arrived at a methodology that separates out the linear portion—the duration—and calls the curved portion by another name: convexity. See Figure 4.21. This means that the actual price of a security may be under or over the price calculated by using duration, and the change in actual price versus calculated price will differ more greatly as the level of interest rates change. This difference is important because, if the price calculated using duration is wrong, then the implication is that the duration of the portfolio is also wrong. Therefore, while the duration-matching strategy appears to offer the potential for exactness, it has hidden flaws and will be most inaccurate under extreme conditions. That is not to say it has no use, merely that you should be aware of the possibility for incomplete protection when there are large shifts in interest rates.

A fourth problem is that duration does not take into account interim price reactions. That is, when the market experiences volatility

Figure 4.19.   Measuring a Portfolio Dispersion

A portfolio's duration is the weighted average of all the individual securities' durations. So two portfolios with the same duration can be comprised of very different types of securities.

Portfolio A

$10,000,000	Security 1	Duration = 5.4 years
$100,000,000	Security 2	Duration = 3.1 years
$50,000,000	Security 3	Duration = 7.8 years

Duration Portfolio A = 4.71 years

Portfolio B

$25,000,000	Security 4	Duration = 4.72 years
$25,000,000	Security 5	Duration = 5.00 years
$25,000,000	Security 6	Duration = 4.41 years

Duration Portfolio B = 4.71 years

Dispersion is related to the idea of variance, in fact we might look at dispersion as the variance of duration in a portfolio. The equation for calculating it is:

$$\text{Dispersion} = \text{Dis} = \Sigma \frac{(D_i - \bar{D})^2}{N}$$

where D_i = Duration for Security i
$\bar{D}$ = Portfolio Duration
N = Total Number of Securities

The dispersion calculations for Portfolios A and B are as follows:

$$\text{Dis}_A = \frac{(5.4-4.71)^2 + (3.1-4.71)^2 + (7.8-4.71)^2}{3}$$

$$\frac{(.476 + 2.59 + 9.55)}{3}$$

$$= 4.205 \text{ years-squared}$$

$$\text{Dis}_B = \frac{(4.72-4.71)^2 + (5.00-4.71)^2 + (4.41-4.71)^2}{3}$$

$$\frac{(.0001) + (.0841) + (.09)}{3}$$

$$= .058 \text{ years-squared}$$

Since the securities in Portfolio B are more homogeneous, its price behavior is more readily predictable than that of Portfolio A where the securities are more diverse.

Figure 4.20.   Measuring the Square-Root Dispersion

This concept is related to dispersion in the same way standard deviation is related to variance. It is designed purely to make the units of measurement more intuitive. As we refer back to Figure 4.19, the SRD of Portfolio A is 2.05 years. So we may infer that the duration of the securities in Portfolio A cluster around 4.71 years, give or take 2.05 years.

$$\text{SRD}_A = \sqrt{4.205} = 2.05 \text{ years}$$

For Portfolio B, the SRD is only .24 years, or not quite three months. We can safely infer that the duration of the securities in this portfolio may be treated as being 4.71 years.

$$\text{SRD}_B = \sqrt{.058} = .24 \text{ years}$$

---

such that there is a swing downward in rates followed by a correction, prices do not necessarily return to their previous levels. This is an example of both the expectations component to price and the sticky price action. There is no way currently to quantify this type of price behavior, so it is useless to expect a truly exact hedge.

A fifth problem is that duration matching contains an underlying assumption that all interest-rate changes are parallel for the entire yield curve, while the duration measure itself assumes a flat yield curve. Unfortunately, that is not the case. Due to both the greater sensitivity of short-term rates and the changes in supply/demand for distinct maturity sectors of the curve, few changes in interest rates are equal along the yield curve. In addition actual experience shows that a flat yield curve is not "normal" for the United States at this time. The more usual appearance of the curve is a slightly upward sloping line.

Despite these problems, the duration-matching strategy is used in various ways. Although it offers only an approximation, the approximation is good most of the time. Nonetheless, it is wise to be aware of the circumstances that might cause a risk-protection strategy to fail. We will discuss hedging this type of event risk where risk is greatest for large price moves in Case 13.

Buying and selling derivatives is an easy way to keep the durations of assets and liabilities equal. We can use the futures markets, buying

Figure 4.21.   Measuring Convexity

Convexity is measured in years, as is duration. The price change in a security due to convexity, added to the price change due to duration, gives a more accurate estimation of actual price changes that will occur should interest rates change.

$$\Delta P_c = \text{Price Change due to Convexity} = \frac{1}{2} \times C \times (\Delta Y)^2 \times 100$$

where $C = \text{Convexity}$
$\Delta Y = \text{Yield Change}$

and convexity itself is measured:

$$\text{Convexity} = C = \frac{1}{\left(1 + \frac{y}{k}\right)^2} \; \Sigma \; \frac{t \times (t + 1) \, \text{PVCF}}{k \times k \times \text{PVTCF}}$$

where $y = \text{Annualized Yield}$
$k = \text{Number of Payments Annually}$
$t = \text{Time period of cash flow receipt}$
$\text{PVCF}_t = \text{Present Value of the Period } t \text{ Cash Flow}$
$\text{PVTCF} = \text{Price of the Security}$

For an example, suppose a security with a 6.75% coupon is maturing in two years and has a price of 96.70. If the yield increases 1.50% (+ .015), what percentage of the price change is due to convexity?

In this example, the effect is rather small due to the short maturity of the security.

$$C =$$

$$\frac{1}{\left(1 + \frac{.0675}{2}\right)^2} \times$$

$$\left[\frac{(.5 \times 1.5 \times 32.63)}{(2 \times 2 \times 96.70)} + \frac{(1 \times 2 \times 31.54)}{(2 \times 2 \times 96.70)} + \frac{(1.5 \times 2.5 \times 30.49)}{(2 \times 2 \times 96.70)} + \right.$$

$$\left. \frac{(2 \times 3 \times 29.48)}{(2 \times 2 \times 96.70)} \right]$$

$$= (.9673) \times [(.0633) + (.1631) + (.2956) + (.4573)]$$

$$= (.9673) \times (.9793)$$

$$= .9473$$

$$\Delta p_c = \frac{1}{2} \times (.9473) \times (.015)^2 \times 100 = .0107\%$$

contracts to increase duration and selling contracts to decrease it. This also keeps the process of adjustment convenient for floating rate liabilities. We can also purchase contracts in various maturities to adjust duration. Again, duration is a weighted average of cash flows. Since T-bill futures would increase the total dollar amount of cash flows while adding only slightly to the average time to maturity, the purchase of the short-term instruments can shorten a portfolio's duration. For example, a portfolio with a duration of seven years can buy T-bill futures in large amounts and decrease duration slightly that way. A Treasury bill contract expiring in three months has an approximate duration of three months. After all, it is effectively a zero coupon instrument and so will have a duration equal to the expiration date of the contract. Since duration is additive, buying 10 front-month T-bill contracts adds a face value of ten million dollars to the portfolio with an average duration per million of only 74 days or so. Thus, the total portfolio would see the average duration decrease. In addition, since futures require a margin of only $1,500 per contract, we can purchase quite a few contracts before reaching a significant additional investment for the portfolio. Depending on the internal regulations for managing the portfolio, this can be preferred to selling bond futures.

If you do sell a bond futures contract, you can achieve negative numbers in the cash flow stream, which also will shorten duration. Subtracting $100,000 per bond contract sold from the portfolio face value, and subtracting around 10 years duration per contract as well, will quickly lower the duration of the portfolio. Equally, buying bond futures or note futures can lengthen duration.

Duration matching helps to reduce the risk of timing mismatches. An example of a timing mismatch is when both the asset and the liability reset off T-bills, but the assets resets on March 2 and the liability resets on March 11. The nine days in between can see the index move and also expose the investor to basis risk, as the cash security and the index may also vary during that week. At the very least, a timing mismatch introduces a lag into the portfolio. There will be a period when the assets have reset and the liabilities have not, or vice versa. If there is a lag of 10 days for a reset period during a fiscal quarter, then there is a mismatch in rates for 10 days out of 90, or 11% of the time. These added risks are the reason that duration matching is such a widely practiced method of portfolio management.

Options can also be used in duration management. A combined

cash and options position can change the possible cash flows, which will change the duration of the portfolio. However, this requires a good software program to implement, so it is not used often. The numbers get complicated so see Figure 4.22 for a simplistic example. The numbers are "fudged" a bit to keep the calculations simple. Real life will seldom be so accommodating.

Equally, entering or terminating a swap will change the duration of a portfolio. However, since swaps are not as flexible as futures or options and since duration changes quickly, a swap will usually be a part of the portfolio and the futures contracts will be the tool for matching it. In other words, a swap will fix particular cash flows, probably for the near term of a year or two. The futures contracts will then be used to fine-tune the week-by-week position. After all, duration matching works best for small interest-rate adjustments. By actively managing the hedge, the larger interest rate moves are broken down into a number of smaller ones. The only disadvantage to active management is

---

Figure 4.22.   Using Cash, Futures, and Options in Duration Matching
_____

Let's use the case where the portfolio of liabilities is currently at 7.50 years, and the portfolio of assets is only 5.2 years. There are many ways to increase the duration of the assets, but I would like to look at a method using futures and options contracts.

Suppose the portfolio of assets has a principal value of $125,000,000. Then $125,000,000 multiplied by the desired 7.95 years is equal to 993,750,000. Currently assets multiplied by duration is equal to only 650,000,000. By purchasing bond futures contracts with a duration of 8.1 years, we can increase duration. The purchase of 4000 contracts increases the total size of the portfolio to $525,000,000. This increases duration to 7.41 years. Then the purchase of at-the-money bond puts can change the size of the portfolio base by assuming that a certain percentage of options will be exercised and decrease the size of the asset base. However, since owning the option is a contingent right rather than an obligation, it does not affect the cash flows. To reach the 7.50 years duration, we must decrease the asset portfolio size to $518,666.67. Assuming that .33 of the at-the-money puts will be exercised, we purchase options with a face value three times the difference between the current asset portfolio size and the desired portfolio asset size, that is: (525,000,000 − 518,666.67) × 3 = $19,000 000.

So the last adjustment to the portfolio is 190 bond call options contracts with an at-the-money strike price.
_____

the higher transaction fees associated with regular adjustment. Depending on the size of the portfolio, a less exact hedge and fewer fine-tunings might be worth the savings in brokerage fees.

You will also need to decide which type of duration measure to use. There are two common versions: Macaulay's and modified. The modified version incorporates a yield-to-maturity factor. It is most commonly used today because it is easier to use in calculating the expected change in price for a given change in interest rates. When using the Macaulay's version, the yield factor is treated as a separate part of the equation. Modified duration will act more as a measure of the interest-rate sensitivity of the portfolio's duration. Macaulay's is better used when forecasting interest-rates using a mulit-scenario method.

Strategy 3—Stacking

In the case of the pension plan, where the liabilities are uncertain because both the interest-rate levels and the number and pay scale of retirees is uncertain, a stacking strategy of duration matching may be preferred. For instance, the plan manager could purchase a series of forward contracts based on the floating index and, as time goes on, additional amounts could be added to or subtracted from the closest-to-maturity or front-month contract. The manager could also use the stacking strategy in the futures market. For instance, the manager could buy two futures contracts in the near or front-month. When these contracts are near expiration, he could sell the two contracts to close out that position and buy three of the next contract instead of just two. Remember, present value increases as the time of the payment approaches. The number of contracts needed to hedge the pension plan's liabilities will depend on which method the manager used to determine the hedge ratio. If the liabilities remain stable, the position would be rolled and the same number of contracts purchased. This allows hedging of the "base" liability, but still offers an opportunity to fine-tune it as time progresses. A series of forwards could be adjusted in the same way. This strategy offers general protection to payments owed farther in the future, but permits more exact protection for payments owed soon.

The major differences between using forward contracts and using futures contracts have to do with liquidity, volatility, the exactness of the hedge, and credit risk. The futures contracts offer a greater liquidity because they are traded on an exchange. Forward contracts, on the other hand, are made with a specific counterparty, so they lack liquidity. However, the futures contracts are also more volatile, and they require marking-to-market on a regular basis as an accounting procedure. The forwards allow a specific match of maturity or reset date, while the futures contracts have mixed maturity dates. The futures are sometimes preferred because there is less of a credit risk; indeed, futures are often perceived as having no credit risk. However, since there is the slight chance that an exchange could enter bankruptcy, there is a credit risk to futures, although it is a small one. The primary reason to choose one instrument over the other would be the exactness of the hedge. Calculating the hedge ratio often results in an overly precise figure that cannot be matched by an even number of futures contracts. Thus, the position would be underhedged or overhedged, but it would not be exact. Instead of rounding to the nearest whole number, forwards could be used to place an exact hedge. The forwards would also compensate for the time lags between the liability resets and the futures expiration dates.

Strategy 4—Mixed Solutions

The pension plan's risk can be managed with some familiar solutions: (1) buy a swap to fix the rate of the liabilities by receiving floating and paying fixed, (2) invest floating and buy futures for the time frame of the reset to protect against a downturn in rates, (3) invest fixed and purchase a protective put on the assets, or (4) selectively hedge only a portion of the asset-liability matches, perhaps those with lesser credit quality or those due soon.

These suggestions are something of a compromise between the dedication and immunization strategies. For example, buying a swap to receive floating and pay fixed means that the pension plan is actually transforming the floating and contingent liabilities into a fixed liability. This is an improvement because it is simpler to match the cash flows of a fixed liability. However, this swap will be more expensive than a plain-vanilla swap because of the contingent obligations that may result from increased retirements or the cost-of-living increase. Therefore, the pension plan would need a right to a stepped-up notional amount or reverse amortization of the notional principal. That can be thought of as the receiver of floating owning a call on a swap that is exactly the same except for an additional principal amount. That type of call would be exercised if the pension liabilities increased due to greater-than-expected retirements or higher-than-expected pay scales. An advantage to the swap strategy is that the monies paid or delivered will be relatively small, as they will be calculated on the base differential. However, matching the asset side to the now-fixed liabilities still means that attractive investment alternatives may be sacrificed.

An investment in instruments that have the same index as the liabilities will take advantage of the possibility for an increase in rates. This is a less exact but more flexible hedge. It should be used in combination with buying futures with a sell-stop in case rates decline. With this strategy, when rates increase, the cash flows from the assets will increase to meet the added obligations of the liabilities. However, when rates decline, the profits from the long futures position will offset the decreased income on the asset side and allow the pension to make its minimum payment.

Depending on the pension fund's investment criteria and the outlook for rates, it may be able to invest in fixed instruments and then own protective puts on the asset side. In this case, when interest rates decline, the incoming payments would be unchanged and would allow the plan's minimum liability to be paid. However, as rates increase, the price of the fixed assets would drop and the put would be exercised to free up funds to be invested at higher rates. Unfortunately, this strategy has rather high transaction costs and needs a substantial amount of management time to find and purchase puts on the securities. In addition, replacement investments must be found if the securities are put. On the other hand, this strategy allows an opportunity to manage the credit risk of the portfolio as the options are exercised.

For the pension plan to "selectively hedge" the asset side, it must analyze the portfolio on a cluster basis to find which assets have a high degree of correlation of interest-income changes in response to moves in interest rates. That is, it must determine which assets will see their income move in lock-step with changes in the base interest rate. Since these highly correlated assets will account for a large degree of the upside and downside to the payment stream, they may be the portion of the portfolio to hedge. For example, if 60% of the portfolio is set off 90-day LIBOR with a reset the first of each quarter, then any mispricing of LIBOR on that date will highly influence the income stream. By hedging just this portion of the portfolio for the affected dates, the pension plan can reduce a major portion of its risk in cash-flow mismatch while reducing transaction costs. The hedge would be done as previously described, but would not apply to the total portfolio. The plan manager might choose to identify specific payment indices to hedge; in that case basis swaps could take care of differences between a LIBOR asset base and a T-bill liability base. The plan manager could also look at individual corporate names that are overrepresented in the portfolio.

Some of the newer products will help here as well. The pension fund might see its best investment opportunities in fixed-rate instruments. It could then purchase a cap, so that a minimum spread would be guaranteed. For example, assume that the average interest payment on the assets is 10.25% while the average liability rate is 7.50%. The current spread is 2.75%. By purchasing a cap on the cost-of-living index (often one-year Treasury bills), the pension plan will receive payments when the COLA index exceeds the pre-specified cap rate. Therefore, if the 360-day bills move to 8.00% and the cap rate is at 7.75%, the pension fund will receive from the bank the difference between the base rate (8.00%) and the cap rate (7.75%) multiplied by the notional principal (the value of the liabilities). In this way, the fund receives not only the 10.25% fixed income stream, but also receives the additional .25% to make up for the increased liability payments. However, remember that a premium was paid to purchase the cap that will eat into the additional monies received.

To optimize or find the least costly portfolio to fund the liabilities usually requires a computer program providing a data-base of acceptable issues versus market price. Setting up this type of program can be expensive, as the most sophisticated logic is also the most technically advanced. Hiring programmers to build this data-base or purchasing it outright will also be costly. In addition, the prices of the issues can be somewhat inaccurate. Therefore, the supposed optimal portfolio will be one of several lower-cost alternatives, but it may not be the cheapest. This optimal portfolio should be re-evaluated on a regular basis, at least yearly. Quite often, due to changes in the yield curve or outright interest-rate levels, a new and cheaper optimal portfolio can be constructed. However, this apparent take-out in cash is usually paid back as commissions for re-structuring the portfolio. On the other hand, since most of the coupon payments are used to meet the pension liabilities, there will be less reinvestment risk than usual.

CASE 3. MINIMIZING FUNDING COSTS

Almost every institution has a niche in which it has a borrowing advantage. For one, its client base may like to lend short-term for fixed rates. A larger institution may borrow from regional institutions for longer terms at a floating rate. One large institution might be able to borrow from other large institutions on a short-term floating-rate basis. Whatever the specialty, almost every firm has one area in which it receives advantageous rates for borrowing.

Strategy 1—Swaps

Minimizing funding costs is the problem that swaps were designed to solve. By employing swaps, two firms can exchange flows and can exploit their relative advantages to lower borrowing costs in other sectors as well.

Suppose that a small bank, Alpha, can borrow from the retail market at 8% for two years; to borrow floating, it must pay LIBOR plus 4.25%. On the other hand, a mid-sized investment bank, Beta, must pay 10.50% fixed, but can borrow floating from its commercial bank for LIBOR plus 3.00%. By exchanging cash flows, both banks can lower their funding costs. For example, assume a straight swap in which Alpha pays 8% to the retail lender, receives 9.25% from Beta, and pays LIBOR plus 3.50% to Beta. Alpha's net cost for borrowing floating is now LIBOR plus 2.25%, a full two percentage points lower. On the other hand, Beta pays LIBOR plus 3.00% to its commercial bank, pays 9.25% fixed to Alpha, and receives LIBOR plus 3.50% from Alpha. Its fixed costs have now dropped to 8.75%, one and three-quarters percentage points lower. Both companies have benefited. See Figures 4.23A, B, C, and D.

The disadvantage to this type of transaction is that costs are incurred to look for the perfect counterparty to match up the opposing needs and advantages. Since borrowing costs are seldom revealed, matching is not a simple chore. In addition, the length of the swap

Figure 4.23A. Relative Funding Costs

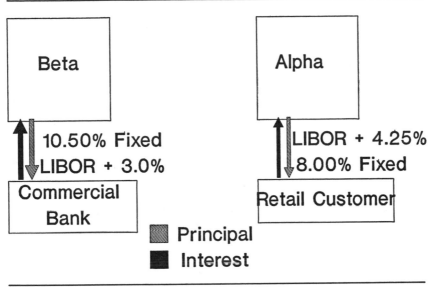

Figure 4.23B. Minimizing Funding Costs via Swaps

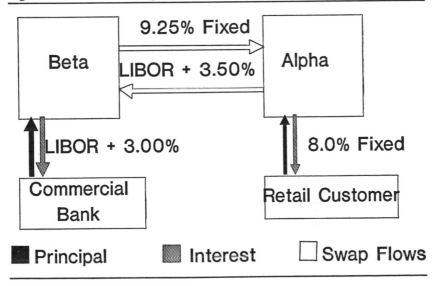

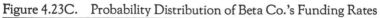

Figure 4.23C. Probability Distribution of Beta Co.'s Funding Rates

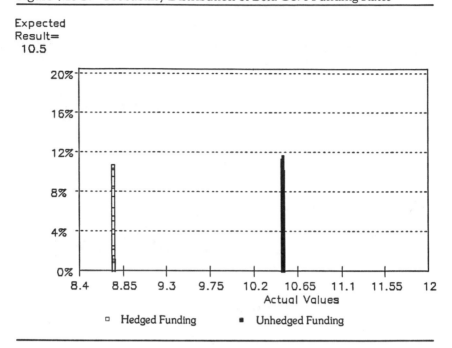

Expected
Result=
10.5

Figure 4.23D. Probability Distribution of Alpha Co.'s Funding Rates

Expected
Result=
11.99

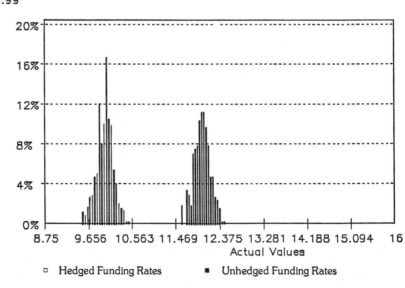

must match, which does not often occur, and each party must be acceptable to the other's credit department.

To meet these concerns, certain banks have developed as broker/dealers in swaps. Since they are likely to add the bid/ask spread to the cost of the swap, they do not generally offer the levels of savings achieved in the example of Alpha and Beta. However, the added liquidity can make up for the loss in savings.

To determine if you will have a natural advantage in borrowing, simply calculate if it will be cheaper to trade a unit of fixed borrowing for floating or vice versa. Using the example of Alpha and Beta, when LIBOR is at 6.50%, Alpha's ratio of fixed-to-floating costs is 8.00% to 10.75%, or .744. That is, each unit of fixed costs is .744 of a comparable unit of floating-rate borrowings. For Beta, the ratio is 10.50% to 9.50%, or 1.10. Each unit of fixed borrowing costs 1.10 times the cost of a unit of floating borrowings.

Note that this is not a stable calculation. For example, if rates increase, so that Alpha must now borrow fixed at 9.00% and floating at LIBOR plus 4.50%, then the ratio might move to .783 when LIBOR is at 7.00%. For Beta, the ratio might see less movement, since a change in costs is dependent on perceptions of the credit quality of the institution doing the borrowing. As a general rule of thumb, a small company is viewed as being less able to withstand adverse times. This includes higher interest rates for an inflation scenario and lower rates for a recession scenario. Thus, a smaller company will generally see an increase in borrow costs for any change in rates, while changes will be smaller for larger institutions of decent credit quality.

Strategy 2—Purchase a Cap

Another way to minimize the cost of borrowing floating is to purchase a cap. While there will be the additional upfront cost of the premium, there will also be an offsetting differential between the cap rate and the base rate for any interest rate above the prespecified "pain threshold."

If the premium for such a cap is too expensive, the company might be offered a participating cap. This is the same as selling a floor with the same strike price but with a smaller notional principal. However, in the case of the participating cap, no premium changes hands. While it may not actually minimize borrowing costs, the purchase of a participating cap does minimize funding-cost volatility, which may prove even more valuable in the long run.

For example, if a bank purchases a cap on a notional principal of $10 million with a cap rate of 9.00% and a base rate of LIBOR, it might pay an upfront premium of 2.00% of the principal and receive the difference between LIBOR and 9.00% every time LIBOR was greater than 9.00% on a reset date. Using a participating cap, the bank would neither pay nor receive a premium. It would still receive the full differential when LIBOR was greater than 9.00%. However, if LIBOR fell below 9.00%, the bank would pay only a percentage of the differential. The level of "participation" is determined by what percentage of the premium for the floor will equal the premium for the cap. Participating caps are common in the 25% to 50% range, so it is essential to price the corresponding floor before entering a participating cap. However, from a borrowing point of view, keep in mind that selling the whole floor will eliminate the chance to participate in a favorable interest-rate move. See Figure 4.24 for the formula to calculate the participation rate and Figure 4.25 for the probability distribution of returns.

Another way to lower the expense of buying a cap on borrowing costs is to purchase a corridor. The success of this strategy depends a great deal on the institution's confidence in the accuracy of its interest-rate forecast. A corridor limits the protection obtained on a floating-rate loan. Returning to the previous example, the bank would have protection if its borrowing costs rose above 9.00%, but its protection might at end LIBOR greater than 12%. The disadvantage to corridors is that the protection ends when it is most needed. It might be preferable to tolerate the smaller shifts in rates and own a cap for higher levels. The actual level would depend almost entirely on the current spread between borrowing and lendings and the pain threshold.

Strategy 3—Foreign Exchange Risk Management

If a funding officer has the responsibility to raise deposits in non-dollar currencies, he will want to minimize both his funding costs and his foreign-exchange risk. If the non-dollar currencies are needed on a specific date, he might choose to lock in a funding rate by buying forward. This protects against an increase in funding rates, but permits no participation if rates fall. However, it also locks in the exchange rate, so both components of risk are stabilized. This forward is referred to as a forward exchange agreement.

An officer with an ongoing need for currencies will also watch Euro-

Figure 4.24. Calculating the Percentage for a Participating Cap

Generally speaking, the purchase of a participating cap is an alternative to the purchase of a straight cap when the premium is considered too expensive. As a result, the percentage of participation chosen for the cap will depend on the price of the cap. The formula for calculating what percentage of participation in a favorable move must be sacrificed to eliminate the premium is as follows:

$$\%C = 1 - \left[\frac{(SR_c - SR_{om}) \times \left[\frac{1}{SR_c} - \left(\frac{1}{SR_c} \times \frac{1}{(1 + SR_c)^t} \right) \right]}{\left(CPr + \left[(SR_c - SR_{om}) \times \frac{1}{SR_c} - \left(\frac{1}{SR_c} \times \frac{1}{(1 + SR_c)} \right) \right] \right)} \right]$$

where SR_c = Current Market Swap Rate
SR_{om} = Offmarket Swap Rate
t = Time until Maturity
CPr = Price of the Cap

Let's look at an example. Perhaps the price of the 2-year 9.00% cap is 2% of the notional principal. If the current market rate to enter a swap with this strike rate is 8.65% and the offmarket rate is 8.80% for a differential of .15%, when we present value this differential according to the annuity formula in the equation, the present value of the annuity is .265%. Then the percentage amount of the cap is

$$\%C = 1 - \frac{(.265)}{(.265 + 2.00)} = 1 - .117 = 88\%$$

The price of the cap for this short period of time is excessively high. To avoid paying the premium, 88% of participation in favorable moves must be forgone. Consider pricing a plain swap instead as it may be cheaper, or set the strike rate on the cap at a higher level.

---

dollar and Diff futures contracts closely. When these contracts are priced above their break-even value, funding can be locked in at below-market rates. To lock in a funding rate, the futures price should approximate the cash price of the security plus the carrying costs, which are the costs of borrowing the monies to invest in the futures contract. The calculation can be expressed in an equation in which futures price minus cash price divided by cash price equals carrying

Figure 4.25.   Probability Distribution of Funding Costs via a Participating
Cap

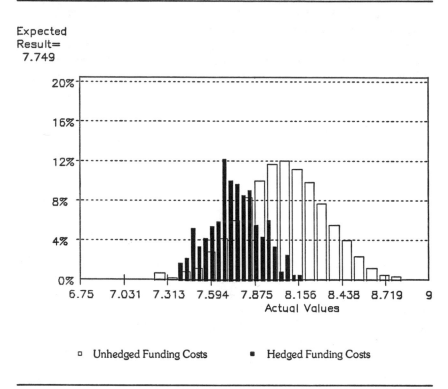

Expected
Result=
 7.749

cost minus income rate. When the income rate is zero, this becomes
the break-even relationship. By keeping an eye on Euros, the funding
officer can offset the cash position and lock in below-market funding
costs when the contract is held to maturity. For example, a transaction
could be as follows: Watch the pricing relationship; when funding
costs fall to an attractive level, buy the cash Euro and sell the futures,
thereby locking in that attractive funding level until the contract expires. This strategy has the problems of margin calls and volatility, but
is relatively cheap to place.

The exchange rate might be hedged by using currency futures. Buying yen futures, for example, is similar to using an FXA. It assures that
a certain number of yen will be delivered upon expiration of the contract. Spreads between currencies can be set as well, for example, by

buying deutschemarks and selling Swiss francs simultaneously. A combination hedge can be placed by using Diff futures contracts. The Diffs reflect the difference between 90-day Eurodollar rates and the same 90-day Euromark, Euroyen, or Euroswiss rates. Buying a Diff implies that the difference between the two rates is attractive; selling implies that the difference is too great. Using futures contracts of different types can provide for customization of differing tolerances to the different risks. Therefore, they can become complex.

When it comes to minimizing funding costs, many companies today will consider borrowing overseas in different currencies. Such a borrowing might work as follows: You need to borrow $100 million at a fixed rate to fund a certain investment for one year. Due to attractive short-term nominal rates, you decide to borrow in Japan. Your company issues a one-year note at 7.00%. At a current exchange rate of 133.20, this means that you must issue a principal amount of 750,750 yen. Your liability is to repay 750,750 yen in principal and 52,552.50 yen in interest. Your risk is primarily due to exchange-rate fluctuations, but you might also find a change in interest rates between the date of your decision and the security-issue date. At the same time, you note that the Eurodollar futures price is trading above the break-even rate. Since you will profit with lower funding costs if rates fall, you need to hedge the upside. Therefore, you buy the Euroyen Diffs at break-even and sell Eurodollars at better than break-even. This allows for attractive funding on the Euroyen side, as the two Eurodollar positions cancel each other out. At this point, your net exposure is to the Euroyen interest rate. This position gains value when the Euroyen rate increases and loses value when the Euroyen rate decreases. You sell the near-by yen futures contract to lock in an exchange rate for the borrowing; you also buy the one-year-out yen futures contract so that you own the currency for redeeming this investment at a fixed exchange rate. Once the borrowing is complete, closing out the Eurodollar and Euroyen positions and closing out the near-by yen contract leaves you with $100 million for your investment. You still have the longer-dated yen to assure a fixed rate when paying back the security holders.

As an alternative, you could sell a yen forward. As you issue the security, you are borrowing yen. To lock in the foreign exchange rate, you can sell this forward until maturity. That combination is similar to a currency repo agreement. You need to pay yen on the issue date, but you also need to receive sufficient yen to redeem the securities on the maturity date. Therefore, you can sell and buy on the forward market for different dates or use the futures market to buy and sell the different expiration dates. You might also enter a forward exchange swap in which you receive dollars and pay yen. However, a swap is generally sufficiently attractive only if the foreign borrowing is longer in term than a year.

The costs of hedging a foreign borrowing can be enough to erase a relative advantage. However, when the liabilities to be funded are also denominated in the borrowed currency, using a combination of Euro and Diff futures can help to lock in a more advantageous rate.

CASE 4. HEDGING TOTAL RETURN

When we look at total return on a security or a portfolio, we see that there are three sources of risk where the risk is to the principal invested: a capital component, a coupon-payment component, and an interest-on-interest component. Coupon risk is slightly ambiguous in that it comprises the credit risk of actually receiving the coupon owed as well as the risk that the value or purchasing power of the coupon will change over time. Interest-on-interest risk is the risk that the expected earnings on the coupons received will not be as expected due to changes in reinvestment-rate levels. Case 4 will focus on this reinvestment-rate risk. Since credit analysis is not a topic for this text, coupon risk will be mentioned only in passing.

The risk that the purchasing power of a coupon will erode over time is linked to the required rate of return or discount level. When nominal interest rates are higher than the historical average and are expected to stay high, the required return will be higher than it would be in an environment of historically low and decreasing rates. In addition, the risks that the coupon will be received as promised and that the principal will be repaid is tied to the credit risk of the security. If you feel that there is a substantial likelihood of a problem with one or more coupon payments over the life of the security, you should include this factor when pricing the security.

The value today of a future cash flow, also known as the present value, depends on the interest rate used for discounting purposes. This required rate of return is also the reinvestment rate when using the yield-to-maturity measurement. This risk is the uncertainty associated with reinvesting future cash flows at the rate assumed at the time the security was purchased. In other words, buying a bond with a yield to maturity of 9.125% means that all the coupons are assumed to be reinvested at a 9.125%. Since the interest earned on previous interest received is a large portion of total return, a drop in reinvestment-rate levels can cause the actual return on a fixed-income security to be less than anticipated. In times of interest-rate volatility, the stability of reinvestment rates is in question. This is one reason that lower coupon securities are generally more attractive than higher coupon securities with the same yield to maturity.

There are a number of ways to hedge reinvestment-rate risks.

Strategy 1—Buying a Floor

Buying a floor locks in a minimum rate, but that rate will be at a level below the current market. In that way, a floor is best suited to pension fund managers. Pension fund managers generally have actuaries that calculate a required reinvestment rate that will assure payouts to pensions. In recent years, this required rate has been substantially below market rates, although market rates are now starting to edge back toward the actuarial assumptions. Buying a floor means that the pension fund manager will pay out a premium initially, but will receive additional monies when the level of market rates falls below the strike level, thus adding to the return on the portfolio. If the pension fund manager is concerned about the premium payout, then selling a cap would be a way to recover it. This is called a reverse interest-rate collar. It will prevent the fund manager from participating in an upward move in rates beyond a pre-specified level, so purchasing the floor is the most necessary source of protection.

For example, if the current level of interest rates for the maturity of the security is 8.00%, then the purchaser of a floor with a strike rate of 6% will receive from the counterparty the difference between the 6% strike and the base rate when the base rate is below 6%. Although the purchaser will be reinvesting his coupons at a lower interest rate than expected, he will have more money to invest at this lower level. In this way, the reinvestment level can be locked in, but it will be at levels below the current market. See Figure 4.26 and Figure 4.27. Note on the probability distribution of returns, the level where the cut-off in

Figure 4.26.   Hedging Reinvestment-Rate Risk via a Floor

Purchasing a floor allows for additional monies to be received in a portfolio when market rates fall below the level required to assure a particular return. For an example of the possible cash flows, see the table.

	Market Rate	Amortized Premium	Cap Flows	Net
Q1	8.00%	−.25%	0	7.75%
Q2	7.00%	−.25%	0	6.75%
Q3	6.00%	−.25%	0	5.75%

This puts a minimum reinvestment rate per period of 5.75%. Any increase in rates, however, has full participation.

Figure 4.27.   Probability Distribution of Funding Costs Using a Floor Strategy

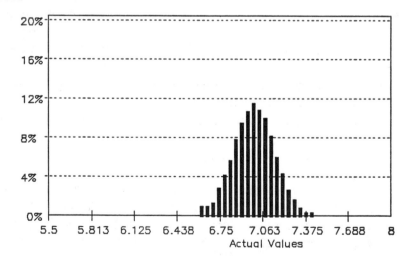

reinvestment rates occurs is so far below the mean that there is only a slight likelihood of its occurrence. In this case, even though the distribution is truncated, it looks very like the normal distribution of returns.

Strategy 2—Buying Calls

The same type of protection for reinvestment-rate levels can be achieved by purchasing a series of interest-rate call options. Remember that the goal is to receive money when interest rates fall. If you own a series of calls at 8% that expire every three months, you are replicating the pay-off structure of owning a floor. In the case of the floor, if the interest rate at quarterly settlement is 6%, you will receive the differential on the notional principal, or 2%. If you own the series of calls, the call expiring at the quarterly date will still pay the 2% differential, because you can exercise the option to buy at 8% and sell the proceeds in the market at 6%. In both cases, any gains will be reduced by the premium paid. At levels above the 8% strike, the option will expire worthless. If you could buy in the market at 10%, for instance, you would not exercise the right to buy at 8%. See Figure 4.28.

Strategy 3—Buying Options

Things are a bit reversed when buying interest-rate options. The right to buy a security at a 6% level means that the price of that asset will be higher than in an 8% environment. A profitable strategy of buying at the low price and selling at the higher price means that you will purchase at higher interest rates and sell at lower interest rates.

Since the bank from which you purchase your floor will likely hedge it with options, you should compare the options premiums with the floor premium. Sometimes the floor will be preferred because of its customization capability and the longer-term nature of the product. Options may also create a liquidity problem if they are purchased too far in the future. In addition, they may be governed by different accounting procedures and regulations. However, despite their volatility, options are generally more reversible and allow more strategic flexibility than caps, floors, or swaps.

Strategy 4—Selling Cash Flows Forward

A minimum reinvestment rate can also be replicated by selling the anticipated cash flows on the forward market or by entering a swap. For

Figure 4.28.   Purchasing a Strip of Call Options

Owning yield calls is equivalent to owning price puts, so this strategy is similar to owning protective puts on the portfolio. See Table I for an example of the time table to place this hedge. Table II shows the possible cash flows under a scenario of decreasing rates.

January 1

Purchase Floating-rate securities at an average Yield-to-Maturity of 9.125% and an average maturity of one year.

Purchase March 8% calls in an amount equal to the current principal value of the portfolio.

Purchase June 8% calls in an amount equal to the future value of the portfolio on June 1.

Purchase September 8% calls in an amount equal to the future value of the portfolio on September 1.

If you wish to provide a cushion for future re-investment opportunities, purchase December 8% calls in the amount of the future value of the portfolio. Most of the portfolio will be maturing at the time these options are available for exercise.

Table I

	Reinvestment Rate	Premium	Call Flows	Net
Q1	8.125%	−.25%	0	+7.875%
Q2	7.125%	−.25%	+.875%	+7.750%
Q3	6.125%	−.25%	+1.875%	+7.750%
Q4	5.5%	−.25%	+2.500%	+7.750%

Table II

instance, if a security will pay you a coupon of $50,000 on June 1, you can sell that amount on the forward market and lock in a known reinvestment rate. You would enter a contract on January 1 (the day you buy the security), promising the delivery of $50,000 on June 1 (the payment date). In return, on the settlement date, which might or might not be January 1, you would receive a pre-arranged amount of money. Using the present value equation [PV $=$ c/i], the reinvestment rate of that flow is assured. To hedge more than one flow, you might enter a swap, which is a series of forward rate agreements.

Strategy 5—Selling Futures

You can get the same effect by using futures. You can sell the present value of the cash flows in the futures market and gradually stack the contracts, since the present value over time changes as the cash payments are made. Note that you are selling the value of the coupons, not the principal amount of the security or portfolio. By offsetting the inflow of the cash coupons with the outflow of the short futures position, a variable relationship becomes a fixed relationship. For example, assume that you have calculated the present value of the coupons to be received on a three-year security on the day you purchase it at $202,503.57 for every million dollars invested in an 8% coupon and a 9.0% yield to maturity. Using a hedge ratio, this would approximate selling two five-year futures contracts. Over the course of the first year, this short position could be rolled from contract to contract or could be initially placed in the back-month five-year contract that expires in one year. After the first year, the present value is re-calculated. This time the discount is the current market rate for a two-year security, or 8.0%, which gives a present value after one year of $142,661.17. The five-year position would be closed out or rolled to the two-year futures contract. The second-year calculation points out a problem with this strategy. Since it requires the sale of 1.4 contracts, the position will be underhedged or overhedged. Whether you sell only one contract or two, this could be rolled every three months or could be placed in the back-month contract. In the last year, the level of interest rates for one-year securities is now 7.5%, so the present value of the payments is $74,418.60. You would now need to place the hedge in the back-month Treasury bill contract or Eurodollar contract to match the maturity. At this point you have to overhedge, as the required protection is only about three-quarters of a contract. The way the number of contracts changes over time is called **stacking**. This type of action permits an approximate hedge to be placed and then fine-tuned as the receipt of funds approaches. Note that this resembles using the forward market. We take the value of the anticipated cash flow and sell it today. This type of selling is equivalent to re-investing the flow; by investing money, you are selling one dollar today for more than one dollar tomorrow. The difference between the value of a dollar today and the value tomorrow is the rate of return on the money and, in this example, the reinvestment rate. Also note that this is a hedging strategy rather than a trading strategy, in that the interim volatility before delivering on the contracts will not affect the reinvestment rate. The match is not perfect because it adds basis risk, as well as a significant volatility component, but the reinvestment-rate risk is significantly reduced. The only real problem with this strategy is that it might require significant cash management to meet margin calls.

Strategy 6—Immunization

The market price of a security will not affect its total return if it is held to maturity. However, that is not always the case today. Volatility in the price of the security is common, as the price is based on credit evaluation, expectational components, estimates of present value for the cash flows, and similar factors. These will depend on the shape of the yield curve, the current maturity of the security, the state of the economy, and other non-stable factors. If a portfolio of securities needs a very stable total return, it can be achieved by using a form of immunization. The purpose is to decrease the sensitivity of returns to interest-rate fluctuations by setting the changes in the capital appreciation/depreciation equal to changes in interest income. For example, when the level of interest rates rise, the price of the fixed-income security will fall and the total return will decrease. However, the coupon payments could be reinvested at a higher than expected rate, which will increase the total return. Unfortunately, the calculations are extensive and difficult to do accurately without a computer program, as the capital component is affected by the convexity of the security. This increases with time to maturity and the size of the coupon payment. In addition, the capital component is non-symmetrical for interest-rate movements. Under most circumstances, price will appreciate more for a drop in rates than it will fall for an increase in rates.

However, we can approximate, which will simplify the arithmetic, by including convexity but assuming that the price moves symmetrically. For a simple example, suppose you have a note maturing in one year with an 8% coupon. Interest rates are also currently at 8%, so the price is par. However, if rates increase to 9%, then the interest component will move from $81,600 ($40,000 invested at 8% for six months adds $1,600 to the coupon income) to $81,800. At the same time, the price of the note will fall to 99.063%, so there will be a capital depreciation of $9,363.34. Therefore, with an interest-rate sensitivity concentrated on the capital end, you would want to add a security with more sensitivity in the interest end. Typically, this would be a security with a high coupon payment and currently priced at a discount. This type of interest-rate sensitivity hedge does well at minimizing fluctuations in total return, but it severely limits the available investment alternatives. However, once placed, it requires little management except as the securities mature. See Figure 4.29

Figure 4.29. An Example of Immunization

As interest rates increase, the price of fixed-income securities decreases, but the coupon payments can garner more additional income. When the capital loss approximates the increase in income, we achieve *immunization*.

	Current Market Rate	Current Security Price	Capital Gain/Loss	Interest Gain/Loss	Net
t = 0	8.00%	100.000	0	0	0
t = 1	9.00%	99.063	−0.937%	+.04%	−0.897%
t = 2	10.00%	91.906	−8.095%	+.16%	−7.935%

Owning this security alone opens the investor to a risk of capital loss. To immunize, add another security to the portfolio with more interest sensitivity. An example would be a security with a high coupon currently priced at a discount. Note that this type of security may open you to a credit risk, though. See the next table for an example of how owning two securities can reduce the interest-rate sensitivity.

	Current Market Rate	Current Security Price	Capital Gain/Loss	Interest Gain/Loss
t = 0	8.00%	A = 100.00	0	0
		B = 96.54	0	0
Net Gain/Loss = 0				
t = 1	9.00%	A = 99.063	−0.937%	+.04%
		B = 96.430	−0.110%	+1.01%
Net Gain/Loss = +.003%				
t = 2	10.00%	A = 91.906	−8.095%	+0.16%
		B = 96.380	−0.160%	+6.80%
Net Gain/Loss = −1.30%				

CASE 5. HEDGING FOREIGN-PAY
SECURITIES

Cash flows will sometimes be denominated in a non-dollar currency, which will add a dimension of currency or exchange-rate risk. The appreciation or depreciation of the non-dollar currency can add to or detract from the security return. Typically, you will be invested in a foreign-pay security for any of three reasons: (1) you will have cash flows denominated in that currency that you want to invest until they are needed for internal corporate use, (2) you will have liabilities in that currency that you are trying to match, or (3) you see an opportunity for superior real returns by investing overseas. The translated or domestic returns are more volatile than those on domestic securities because the interest-rate differential and the currency exposure are added to all the factors that generally influence returns on the domestic securities.

Strategy 1—Using Diffs

One strategy for managing currency risk is similar to minimizing funding costs using foreign borrowings, which was discussed in Case 3, but the focus will be different. In borrowing overseas, you will be the issuer and will wish to minimize the spread between interest payments and your domestic investment. As the investor, your emphasis is on the dollar translation of your investment and your goal is to minimize any reinvestment risk. Depending on the currencies, Diff futures can be used to hedge the interest-rate differentials for dollars versus yen, marks, and sterling. If you are comfortable with the exchange-rate risk—and accounting procedures allow using the average rate of exchange to figure returns—then hedging this interest-rate differential will reduce the foreign-pay security to the same level as domestic-pay securities. Since ownership of the security equates to ownership of the differential at the current market rates, you hedge by selling the appropriate futures contracts. For the hedge ratio, the "conversion ratio" is the rate of exchange, since there is no actual deliverable security at expiration. This is a cash-settled contract traded on the Chicago Mercantile Exchange.

Strategy 2—Using Swaps

If you are concerned about exchange-rate risk, several tools are available.

You should be aware that exchange-rate risk will provide the most short-term volatility, but that the difference between interest rates tends to be fairly stable over time. It will take a very large position to be significantly affected by change of one-tenth of a percentage point in the interest-rate differential, but it is not that rare to see the deutschemark move a pfennig in one day's time, which translates to around $6,000.00 per million invested.

A plain-vanilla currency swap eliminates this exchange risk by essentially swapping the foreign-pay security for a domestic-pay security. The principal is exchanged when the swap is initiated and is re-exchanged at expiration. This is the primary difference between the currency swap and the domestic swap. For example, a United States firm with assets invested in Great Britain might like to transform the floating-rate sterling payments into a fixed-rate dollar payment. The U.S. firm would find a counterparty and exchange the principals at the current spot rate. Thus, the U.S. firm would pay out dollar principal and receive sterling principal. This offsets the firm's initial investment which paid out a sterling principal and receives the interest payments in sterling. As these floating-rate sterling payments are received, they are sent to the swap counterparty. In return, the counterparty pays dollars to the U.S. firm at a fixed rate. At maturity, the principal amounts are re-exchanged at the same exchange rate as before. See Figure 4.30.

The disadvantage of this strategy is the loss of any upside possibilities, as the price of the swap will eat into a favorable interest-rate differential. However, reducing the currency risk can be worth a relatively high premium.

If the exchange-rate risk is usually acceptable but is increasingly uncertain, forward exchange-rate agreements can be used to periodically hedge the risk. In this way, the present value of the expected cash flow in the foreign currency can be sold to lock in the exchange rate, but it does not solve the problem of interest-rate risk.

Strategy 3—Swap Variations

Swap combinations can be used to handle both the interest-rate risk and the currency risk. This type of swap is generally called a "circus swap," but other terms are also used. A circus swap is specific to using LIBOR for the floating-rate side. A circus swap is specifically a combination of a fixed-for-floating rate interest-rate swap and a fixed-for-

Figure 4.30.   Currency Swap

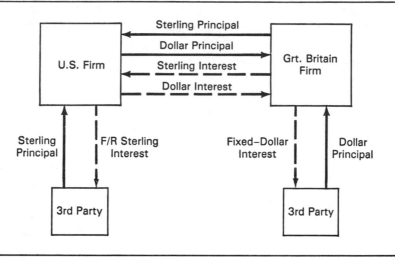

floating rate currency swap when both floating rates are based off LIBOR.

A convertible currency-indexed swap can also be used. This involves the sale of an out-of-the-money call option for the currency. In other words, the investment rate is hedged in return for giving up any potential favorable currency moves. Since the hedger already owns the currency in the form of its expected cash flows and invested principal, selling the right to buy if the exchange-rate moves significantly involves no additional risk. Moreover, the premium received helps enhance returns.

In this type of swap the investor is the intermediary between the asset cash flows that he receives and the payments made to the counterparty. In this way, it is no different from any other swap. The counterparty will then pay the investor another type of cash flow that is fixed to a preferred index or at a fixed rate. This tying of the cash flows to an index rather than LIBOR is the primary difference between an induced swap and a regular swap. In addition, the cash flows paid to the counterparty are somewhat reduced because the investor also sells a currency call to the same counterparty. See Figure 4.31 for the structure. In this way, the cash flows are favorably hedged, but they cost the opportunity of taking advantage of any currency appreciation.

Figure 4.31. Convertible Currency Indexed Swap

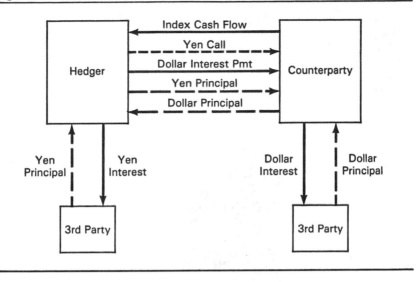

This investor might choose to buy an out-of-the-money currency put to limit his downside currency risk, since he has already sold his potential upside reward. However, this additional put decreases the enhanced return even when the premium required to buy the put is less that the premium received for selling the call. Moreover, the put premium may not always be less than the call premium, since currency options have a large expectational component in their pricing.

Strategy 4—Protective Put

In general, unless there is a reason to want the cash flows in another form, it will be simpler to buy a protective put for the currency. By owning the foreign investment, you are naturally long that currency. By purchasing the right to sell that currency at a below-market rate, you can lock in a "worst-case" scenario while allowing yourself the right to participate in the upside potential. However, remember that currencies are volatile. If the strike price for the put is too close to the current market exchange rate, it might reach levels where you would exercise the option only to find that the increase was a temporary aberration in the market. See Figure 4.32 for the probability distribution of returns.

Figure 4.32.   Hedging Risk Through the Purchase of Protective Currency
Puts

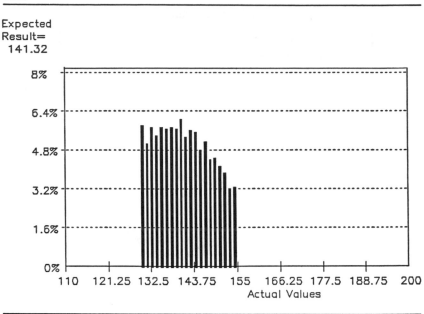

Expected
Result=
141.32

Strategy 5—Currency Futures

The currency risk can also be hedged with currency futures. The process is similar to using forward exchange agreements, but there is more
volatility and generally lower transaction fees. The coupon flows can
be hedged with Diffs or by selling and buying the respective flows forward.

Strategy 6—Hedging Cross-Rates

Sometimes the situation overseas does not involve buying a standard
security. For example, a U.S. firm might lease equipment abroad in a
foreign currency or an importer might work a "triangle trade route"
that involves purchases of goods in currency A for resale in currency
B, then purchases of other goods in currency B for resale in currency
C. In this case, currency C must then be exchanged for currency A to
start the cycle again.

        This type of cross-rate risk can be most easily hedged using one of three methods. Either the hedger can choose to (1) sell cross-rate futures contracts, which trade on a branch of the Philadelphia Stock Exchange, or (2) purchase a combination of spot rate currency C calls and spot rate currency A puts. This last can be very expensive, since as many as four separate options contracts might be needed to hedge the risk. As the last possibility, the hedger can request bids on the OTC market for the specific cross-rate option. Note that rather than design the hedge yourself, you may choose to tell your broker how much you are willing to spend for protection, and see what he can provide.

There also may be a contingent liability, a case in which the currency liability is uncertain. This may be faced by a contractor who submits a bid for a job overseas. Once the bid is submitted, any appreciation or depreciation in the currency could wipe out the potential profits. Using currency options is the classic solution to this problem. However, it also could be managed with forward exchange agreements. In case the bid is not accepted, the agreement to purchase the currency at a pre-arranged price at a certain date in the future could contain a clause to terminate early. While this raises the cost of the currency slightly, the goal here is to lock in rates and reduce risk. To account for the added cost, the anticipated fee for early termination could be estimated and added into the bid.

There also may be contingent assets in foreign currencies when an importer is in negotiations to purchase goods. These possible outflows in a foreign currency must be hedged so that the cost of the goods does not increase suddenly due to currency fluctuations. Again, a forward exchange agreement with an early termination clause can be used or currency futures can be purchased in the contract month that has an expiration date most closely matching the date on which the currency would be paid out. The position can be closed out if the negotiations fall through. If the negotiations work out, the importer can simply take delivery of the currency at expiration. This method leaves an exposure to short-term mispricings, but it is easy and liquid. If the importer found the cost of an early termination clause too expensive, it could buy a put for the currency as an alternative.

To illustrate, consider the example of a manufacturer who is delivering two shipments of wickets to West Germany in January and September and who is receiving two shipments of wockets from Switzerland in February and October. The wockets are used to make the wickets. In December of the previous year he had set a price of

$125,000 per shipment for the wickets and agreed to pay a price of 125,000 Swiss francs for the wockets. The spot rate at that time had been used to determine the prices. Therefore, he is vulnerable to changes in the value of deutschemarks and Swiss francs during the year.

There are a number of suitable strategies for hedging this exposure. The manufacturer could sell deutschemarks forward and buy Swiss francs forward (an FXA). He could also sell D-mark futures and buy Swiss futures on the IMM, or he could buy at-the-money D-mark puts and at-the-money Swiss calls. He could even sell marks on the spot market, use the funds received to purchase Swiss francs on the spot market, and invest those francs in Switzerland until needed. The difficulty with these strategies is that the manufacturer is not necessarily reducing his risk. Instead, he is exchanging it for a risk that respective funding rates between Germany and Switzerland will change. To sell the D-marks spot he needs to borrow at West German rates. The Swiss francs are invested there, so the interest-rate spread between Germany and Switzerland is the new risk exposure. This strategy is viable, though, because the historic volatility of the interest-rate spread between the two countries is less than the volatility of currency moves. In addition, the dollar/mark part of this strategy can be hedged using Diff futures, although there are no Swiss franc Diffs at this time.

In any event, marks and Swiss francs are highly correlated, so the currency moves are potentially offsetting. As such, the manufacturer should determine if protection is desired at all. If there is no real desire to hedge the currency move itself, then a strategy that matches dollar flows to reduce the gap would be helpful, and this could be done with a plain-vanilla currency swap. Still, given that input prices should be more highly managed than final output prices, because of the profit margin, it might be enough to hedge the Swiss francs and just purchase out-of-the-money puts for the deutschemarks.

CASE 6. ASSET-ALLOCATION STRATEGIES USING DERIVATIVES

Although derivative products were not designed with a view to asset management, they have become an important tool. When a portfolio includes various asset classes, such as fixed-income, equity, mortgage securities, and so on, there is an ongoing need to adjust the percentage of the portfolio represented by each asset. For example, suppose the portfolio manager has decided to make up the portfolio by purchasing 75% equities, 15% fixed-income securities, 5% physical commodities, and 5% precious metals. As the value of the purchases changes over time, the dollar value that equates to 5% of the total portfolio will change. So there is a need to sell portions of one asset category and buy portions of another asset category.

Different asset mixes are usually compared by looking at their risk in terms of the standard deviation of return versus the mean or average return for the portfolio. Given certain requirements for each portfolio, a portfolio manager tries to construct an optimal portfolio to achieve the highest return for a specified level of risk. Quantitative methods that employ put/call parity can copy the stances and exposures of options strategies for portfolios that are restricted from using options. For example, instead of owning a put option, the portfolio might choose to sell short a part of the asset and invest another part in a "riskless" investment. In addition, there are methods of comparing strategies to achieve high portfolio returns by shifting the asset mix. Depending on the price behavior of an asset, a portfolio manager can devise payoff functions to compare strategies. Most strategies are compared to the basic buy-and-hold, which is the simplistic strategy of purchasing an asset and holding it until maturity or, in the case of an equity, until the price objective is reached. In this strategy, an asset is never re-evaluated in terms of changing market conditions after it is purchased. By contrast, strategies that continue to monitor asset returns in the light of changing market conditions are known as dynamic strategies. These will be discussed in more detail at the end of Case 6.

There are a number of standard asset allocation techniques that will be addressed. Fundamental Asset Allocation uses derivatives as a substitute for the cash security. Other standard asset allocation techniques that will be discussed are Strategic Asset Allocation, Tactical Asset Allocation, Portfolio Insurance, and Directional Asset Allocation.

One of the most important uses of the derivatives market is as a substitute for an actual cash position in an asset. This is called *Fundamental Asset Allocation*. For example, by purchasing bond futures you can participate in the growth of that market without expending time or money to establish a position in the cash market or to choose specific securities. In the same way, by selling S&P 500 futures you can decrease an exposure to equities without having to sell a cash portfolio in a thin market or at a loss. You can achieve international portfolio diversification by purchasing bund or gilt futures. Equally, you can obtain the same type of directional exposure with options without needing to choose specific securities within the asset category. Owning calls is the simplest way to add a contingent right to an asset category. Buying puts also earns a contingent right, but in the opposite direction. Therefore, buying either puts or calls is less risky than selling either of these options.

There will not be an exact match between a specific security and the futures contract for the general asset, in that the futures will not have one-to-one correspondence in price moves to a specific instrument. Certainly, futures and options will not take advantage of credit-spread appreciation or depreciation in securities, but they provide a way to establish an exposure or to diversify into an asset. This can also help for yield enhancement for portfolio-management purposes, but there will be the corresponding cost of some added risk.

Strategy 1—Fundamental Asset Allocation

A newly appointed pension fund portfolio manager might use fundamental asset allocation in the following way. On his appointment on January 1, he is given $100 million with a commitment for $50 million more on March 1 and again on June 1. This will give the manager a total of $200 million to invest in a fixed-income portfolio. On January 1 the manager buys enough fixed-income futures to replicate the exposure of $100 million today, $50 million on March 1, and $50 million on June 1. Suppose the $50 million due March 1 is purchased on January 1 using the bond futures contract expiring approximately March 15 as a substitute. Regardless of the interim price movements in the contract, upon expiration the manager will own $50 million worth of bonds at that price. He receives the cash from the portfolio sponsors and pays it to the exchange to take delivery of the bonds. The manager would be aggressive about this strategy if he anticipated a bull market in the asset so that he could lock in a lower price for the securities. Using the hedge ratio to calculate this exposure can be a little tricky though. Since no securities are currently owned, using the conversion factor method is inappropriate unless the portfolio manager has already determined the duration desired for the portfolio. In that case, he could use the deliverable instrument with a duration closest to this desired level as the proxy to calculate the conversion ratio. Equally, he might choose to use a weighted-average conversion ratio of all the deliverable securities. This is similar to building an index. I tend to feel that since the purpose of this derivatives position is to act as a substitute for the cash portfolio until a security selection is made, the hedge will be inexact at best. Thus, it seems counter-productive to spend too much time calculating a hedge ratio.

The portfolio manager's major reason for wanting a substitute position is that the basic level of rates may move lower while he is looking for attractive cash securities. Obviously, if the manager feels that there is a significant bear market for price in the asset category, he may choose to not place a substitute position and simply wait for prices to move lower. However, there is a substantial risk attached to this. Instead, by placing the derivatives position, the portfolio manager can wait for more attractive levels in cash while not losing the right to own the asset at the current levels. In addition, there is the time value of money to consider. For fixed-income assets, the interest-on-interest earned is a sufficiently large portion of total return that waiting for slightly lower prices to enhance capital return might sacrifice an offsetting return in the interest portion. Although there is the added cost of commissions, owning a substitute reduces that risk. In this example the portfolio manager will earn interest for an additional quarter-year on the first $50 million and an additional half-year on the last $50 million.

The portfolio manager can buy the face value of the future monies outright, rather than buy the present value of the additional monies because only margin is required to place the investment.

As an alternative, on January 1 the portfolio manager might choose to buy the present value of the March and June monies on the forward market. The forward market strategy locks in a given rate of return, as opposed to the futures strategy, which locks in a price. The difference is in time frame. Using the forwards market locks in the return for a prespecified time, so that the difference between the beginning and ending prices is the lock-in. In the futures market, the lock-in is the initial price less any commissions.

Another way to obtain the exposure is to buy a combination of at-the-money and out-of-the-money calls with exercise dates at March 1 and June 1. Buying at-the-money calls with an expiration of March 1 duplicates the exposure of purchasing futures. However, this is a contingent right; if prices are lower when the funds become available, there is no obligation to exercise the call and own the securities at the higher price. Instead, the securities themselves can be bought at the lower price. However, the premium paid can be higher than the margin for three months. That will depend on the consensus market view for rates in the short term. The options due June 1 can really be either out-of-the-money calls or at-the-money calls, although at-the-money calls will cost more.

If the portfolio manager is particularly cautious, he can lock in a specific return for a portion of the portfolio by buying futures and selling forward to either March 1 or June 1. This provides a bit of "padding" for future market moves. This also can be done on a yield-enhancement basis. For example, the portfolio manager might purchase 500 bond contracts on January 1 at 98-00 to approximate $50 million. The margin call will be around $1,000,000. He would then sell $50 million forward three months in a non-standard agreement to receive the difference between the reference rate, LIBOR and the agreed-upon contractual rate of 6.75%. If LIBOR is 6.64% on the settlement date, then the .11% annual rate difference multiplied by the $50 million notional principal for the time period and discounted by the reference rate gives the portfolio manager receipts of $13,746.22. On March 1 the portfolio manager accepts delivery of his bonds. The amount to be paid is calculated as 500 contracts × 100,000 × .9800 × a conversion factor of 1.018, or $49,882,000.00, of which $1,000,000 has already been paid on the margin account. Because of the $13,746.22 received on the sale forward, the actual price per bond is calculated at 97.97%, slightly lower than 98-00. Although this may seem to be a minor difference, it may pay the commission and management costs of hedging.

In general, the options strategies will be slightly preferred, as the portfolio manager is a "natural" long. If the portfolio manager owns futures and plans to invest in corporates and mortgage-backed instruments as well as in government securities, then either he will expend a great deal of effort to design a substitute portfolio or there will be a fairly inexact price correlation. Again, the government bond futures do not hedge any credit spread for nongovernment securities. In addition, by using futures he would need to close out the position gradually as he accumulated the cash securities or took delivery of government securities he might not necessarily want. Because of these factors, the portfolio manager might opt to replicate with futures only the portion of his portfolio that he already planned to devote to government securities.

Moreover, owning cash and derivative securities lowers the portfolio manager's cost of changing his mind. Therefore, not only will he be able to replicate entirely different asset classes, but he will also be able to manipulate the duration and maturity of specific sectors within the chosen asset classes. For example, if he owns both three-month and six-month cash securities, the three-month portion can be changed into a six-month equivalent by adding the next futures contract to the portfolio. The cash flows are demonstrated by purchasing a 90-day security on March 1 and then in April buying a 90-day T-bill future expiring June 1. In this way, the portfolio manager might pay out $96,000 on March 1, pay out $2,000 in margin on April 1 for one contract at 93.24, receive $1,000,000 on June 1 when the three-month security matures, and pay out $930,400 ($932,400 minus $2,000) for a three-month security maturing September 1. By purchasing the futures contract, the portfolio manager has achieved an exposure to a six-month security.

On the other hand, the horizon of a nine-month security can be shortened by selling bill futures or by selling bill forwards with a settlement in six months. However, this will be more expensive. By purchasing a bill on March 1 to mature December 1, the maturity date can be shortened by selling the contract that expires on June 1 or September 1. The cash flows are demonstrated by paying out the cost of the bill on March 1, paying the futures margin at the time the maturity is shortened, and receiving the payment on the security on June 1 when the futures expire and the security that matures December 1 is delivered.

Yield-curve trades, in which the relative exposure to different maturity sectors is changed, can be entered into quickly and without moving the market by re-positioning large amounts of cash. This differs from changing the duration of the portfolio. As is described in Case 2, the desired duration for a portfolio can be managed with derivatives. The trade-off is between frequent rebalancing for accuracy and the commissions paid on the trades. There are exchange-traded futures and options contracts available on almost every sector of the U.S. yield curve. As well, there is a decent OTC market in some bonds.

Another way of changing the relative weighting of the portfolio is by using options. For example, by purchasing ten-year note calls, more exposure to moves in that sector can be added. By buying bond puts, a decline in the long end can be minimized and the relative weight in the short end increased. The only disadvantage to options is that the commission costs on some trades can outweigh the possible return. Some of the newer products also provide protection alternatives for the portfolio manager. For example, a floor can lock in reinvestment rates.

Strategy 2—Rebalancing a Portfolio

Another primary user of the derivative market is the manager of a balanced fund. The relative weight in the fund between fixed income and equity can be managed with futures. For example, if the portfolio is currently 60% equity and 40% fixed income, simply purchasing bond futures will decrease the relative weighting of equities. Equally, the manager might choose to own gold or silver futures or options to achieve a small asset allocation when he anticipates severe economic times.

This sort of rebalancing also works within asset classes. Selling the Dow Jones utility index can decrease exposure without actually requiring the sale of stocks at a loss. The manager can diversify internationally by buying currency futures and foreign equity and fixed-income futures. An equity manager might hedge a downturn by owning S&P 500 futures or options.

There are even a number of mixed asset-class indices with derivatives attached. If the manager has the authority, he might buy into the CRB index or Maxi Major Market index for either futures or options as an inflation hedge. A domestic manager might buy International Market Index futures to take advantage of faster overseas growth. In this way, some exposure is gained, but the manager does not need to spend time choosing specific securities in an area in which he has little information or expertise. These indices are also a good diversification tool, since non-correlated asset classes can be matched in a portfolio without paying the full upfront cost. It detracts from the potential maximum return, but generally the goal of risk management is to avert the worst-case scenario. When yield-enhancement strategies are placed, it is therefore quite imperative to make sure that too much risk is not added to the portfolio.

Strategy 3—Asset Allocation Techniques

Strategic Asset Allocation (SAA) is the next strategy to discuss. It assumes a longer horizon and resembles asset/liability management for the most part. The investment policies and decisions are made more in conjunction with liabilities incurred than any particular view on the markets.

Since the horizon for most liabilities is longer term, this asset strategy will need only infrequent rebalancing. For example, a company with a younger work force would have a larger percentage of its pension fund in equities. As the work force aged and liabilities increased, a higher percentage would be moved to fixed-income investments. The purpose of this strategy is more to manage risks than to achieve superior returns. The rebalancing is usually in response to changing investment goals due to shifted liabilities. To rebalance, if the original goal is 60% equity and 40% fixed-income, the percentage of the total portfolio represented by equities would decrease as the price of equities fell. Equally, when fixed-income levels rally, the percentage represented would increase. The pension fund would sell the more expensive fixed-income asset and use the funds obtained to buy more of the less expensive equity asset. This decreases the percentage represented by the more expensive class, increases the percentage represented by the cheaper class, and brings the portfolio back to a 60/40 mix.

Tactical Asset Allocation (TAA) is a more actively managed strategy and requires more rebalancing than SAA. This strategy assumes that there is a long-term expected return for each asset class and that short-term asset returns will regress or retrace to this expected level. This translates for practical purposes into buying more of the asset class that sees price levels drop and selling the asset class that experiences rises in price. In theory, this strategy ensures buying the lower priced category and selling the higher priced category, but it is essential to have a long-term horizon for measuring returns. While the short-term returns may well move around the long-term expectations for an asset class, the return can be lower than desired when total returns are measured over shorter horizons. This is because TAA is a contrarian view, so it will trade opposite any trend in price for an asset. Purchasing stocks in a bear market may offer nice returns when measured over three years, but the returns would be disappointing on a quarterly basis. Another rationale for this strategy is that there is a segregated market for various asset classes. This means that there is relatively little flow of principal between classes. Most portfolio restructuring is done within a single class, and purchases of a different class are rare. Although there has been a gradual increase in inter-asset flows, there is still a lot of market friction to prevent it. To the extent that such friction exists, purchasing the lower priced asset is the same as purchasing an undervalued asset.

Portfolio insurance is an asset-allocation strategy specific to equity assets, although it is also used in the fixed-income market. This strategy is the opposite of TAA, in that portfolio insurance tries to join a trend rather than go against it. Unfortunately, from a theoretical basis this means buying the highs and selling the lows. While this strategy can offer superior returns if the trend is sustained, in a ranging market the returns can be well below expectations. These low returns have been justified by explaining that portfolio insurance is intended to protect against unfavorable market moves, not to earn superior returns. However, the failure of portfolio insurance during the 1987 market crash was a good example of how some protection does not work in extreme conditions.

Directional Asset Allocation (DAA) is another way to buy breakouts, but generally it is restricted to using out-of-the-money call options to buy and out-of-the-money puts to sell. This gives the strategy a higher upfront cost, but it generally offers better protection in the extreme case as long as the credit quality of the option counterparty is good.

These dynamic strategies can be implemented with futures or options or can incorporate mixed strategies. Futures are attractive because of their smaller transaction costs, good liquidity, price lock-in, and simultaneity, which is the capability to do several trades at once. However, futures are mark-to-market and carry possible tax implications. Also, the mark-to-market may need additional funding due to margin calls, and there are sometimes short-term pricing errors caused by expectational factors, and there is not a perfect correlation between the futures and the generic asset class.

Options generally protect against locking-in a higher-than-necessary price for an asset, but they require a larger upfront payment in the form of the premium. Options can also see short-term mispricing due to expectational factors and short-term aberrations caused by market volatility. Options need more rebalancing to maintain a neutral delta, particularly as expiration approaches. Exchange-traded options also have a shorter life-span, so they require more rolling; using an option with a longer expiration date, that is, a back-month options contract, adds the risk of poor liquidity.

CASE 7. HEDGING FLOATING-RATE SECURITIES WITH DIFFERENT BASES—THE QUESTION OF BASIS RISK

When asset payments due are based on one floating-rate index, but the liability payments are based on another floating-rate index, the portfolio becomes subject to *basis risk*. That is, there is a risk that the current price relationship between the two indices will change. As an example, suppose payments are due based on 90-day LIBOR, and payments are paid based on 90-day Treasury bills. Any unexpected additions to Treasury-bill supply at the weekly auction, or changes in demand for overseas funds can affect the relationship between the two.

Basis risk is pervasive as price paths move irregularly, leaving the spread between two correlated securities unstable.

While basis usually is defined as the price difference between a spot security and its future contract, it can be more informally defined as the price difference between any two highly correlated securities. For example, there is a basis difference between 30-year cash bonds and bond futures, and there is a basis difference between two different AAA-rated 10-year notes.

Basis seems simple, but the implications of its measurement are more subtle. For example, generic basis is spot price less futures price, but the quoted futures price is not the price that will be listed on an invoice, as it must be multiplied by the conversion factor for the security. In addition, part of the futures price is determined by the cost of funding an equivalent cash position, and the cost of funding will depend a great deal on the nature of the borrower. There will also be the nebulous factor of time decay as the fixed-income securities approach maturity.

Therefore, it is often more convenient to speak of **rate basis,** which is the difference between the spot rate and the futures rate. It is significantly more useful to use rate basis when hedges are not being held until expiration or maturity. After all, as a security approaches maturity, the price will change even if the rate basis does not. Therefore, at times the relationship between price basis and rate basis will be unclear. Both types of basis have hedging instruments and sometimes one rather than the other will be the source of risk. However, for a portfolio-based hedge, the rate basis is usually the greater source of risk. This is because rate basis is the risk you are exposed to when moving from a fixed-rate cash stream to a floating-rate cash stream. If the obligation you own is based on floating rates, but the obligation owed to you is based on fixed rates, then rising rates hurt you and falling rates help. Equally, if you owe fixed and are receiving floating, then a fall in interest rates should be protected against and a rise in rates should be participated in. In an even more arcane example, if you are paid on a prime-plus rate, but pay out on a LIBOR-plus rate, you are still exposed to rate basis.

Strategy 1—Swaps

The basic tool for managing rate-basis risk is the interest-rate swap. You can match assets or liabilities to their opposites by entering a fixed-to-floating swap. Swaps can be sufficiently customized that almost any desired index can be used, although LIBOR is most common. By purchasing a fixed-to-floating swap, the buyer commits himself to paying the fixed rate and receiving a floating-rate interest payment instead. The actual cash exchanged is the difference between the two rates, so the intermittent cash flows are relatively small. However, these flows reduce the variability of the difference between the rates. The cost is the loss of the ability to profit from a favorable move between the rates. For example, if your portfolio is designed to receive fixed and pay floating on the liability side, you might purchase a fixed-to-floating swap for the assets when you anticipate that rates will increase. If you are wrong and rates fall, you will have committed all of the favorable increase in the spread to your counterparty. However, the volatility of the spread between the two rates will have been reduced.

Strategy 2—Using the Forward Market

If less protection is desired, selling or buying either the asset or liability cash flows forward can permit hedging of only the near-term flows. Quite often, hedging just a portion of the position is all that will be needed when some of the risk on future cash flows can be tolerated, although leaving the entire position at risk might be uncomfortable for extreme moves. For example, buying the floating-rate liabilities in the forward market locks in the rate for those specific cash flows. Suppose you need to pay out LIBOR plus 2.75 on a principal amount of $5,000,000 on June 1. If it is now January 15 and you forecast an increase in LIBOR, buying those flows will lock in the base-rate level. You might buy a 1 × 4 forward with a reference rate of LIBOR plus 2.75 and a contractual rate of 9.40%. In one month you calculate the difference between the LIBOR plus 2.75 and the contractual rate. If LIBOR has moved from 6.64% at the time you set the contractual rate to 6.70%, then the difference between the two rates is .05 (9.45 − 9.40). The resulting $25,000 is present valued for the three months, and you are paid $24,423. Then on June 1 you pay the semi-annual liabilities of $236,250. If rates had not increased, you would have paid out $234,750, but by purchasing the cash flow forward you were able to add $24,423. Therefore, the net pay-out was $236,250 minus $24,423, or $211,827. The hedge lowered your liability base to 8.47% plus commission.

This example appears to have generated a significant saving, but it has not yet accounted for commission costs. If the commission was 1% of the notional principal, or $50,000, then the sum of the payout of the liability and the commission cost raises the funding cost to 10.47%. For the hedge to be worthwhile, you would have had to think that LIBOR would rally above 7.72%, an increase of 16% over the current level. This graphically shows why you need to include commission costs in deciding whether or not to place a hedge. Running a long-term history of LIBOR to find an expected mean and standard deviation for this rate can help you decide if this 16% increase is likely or not. First, determine if the 7.72 break-even for the hedge is within the expected level for LIBOR plus 1 standard deviation. If the mean or expected level of LIBOR is 5.0% with a standard deviation of 3.0%, then levels of LIBOR between 2.0% and 8.0% are reasonable over the long term. Therefore, if 7.72% is unacceptable for paying the liability, it should be hedged, since this is a reasonable expectation for this interest rate.

Strategy 3—More Swaps

Suppose you want to invest in a floating-rate asset and have issued fixed-rate securities at market rates. This translates as a borrowing. By the time your securities have seasoned for a year or two, the coupon rate you have to pay out may be substantially above the market. In other words, you will be paying out more than your floating-rate asset is paying in. If you wait until rates have already moved, the protection will be too expensive, as no one will want to take the other side of the trade. However, if at inception you enter a swap to receive fixed and pay floating, the costs of the security will be fixed and your payments will be linked to whatever index is preferred. Generally, this will be the index that matches the assets whose cash flows are earmarked to the liability. For an example, see Figure 4.23B.

Strategy 4—Combination Strategies

The same effect can be achieved with additional upside potential by entering a series of forward purchases. For instance, the coupon payments for the first few payments owed can be bought via a forward rate agreement, which will lock in the real rate of the borrowed funds. This is the same example illustrated in Strategy 2. As perceptions and market conditions change, more coupon payments can be hedged or not, depending on the direction of rates. This strategy requires more maintenance and more ongoing costs, but it allows a better opportunity to profit if interest rates increase. In such a case, your payments out will be unchanged but the payments in via the asset will increase.

For the best profit opportunity, you want to be able to participate as interest rates move higher but retain protection as interest rates move lower. Therefore, an alternative to hedging with a forward rate agreement might be the purchase of a floor for the investment, thereby ascertaining a minimum return for the invested borrowings. Buying a floor is discussed in Case 4, Strategy 3. You could also purchase an at-the-money put for the investment and be able to sell your investment at near market rates at a minimum loss. This carries a high premium though. On the other hand, since you own the investment, selling a slightly out-of-the-money call would add cash upfront and lock in a profit on the asset if the call is exercised. The funds received should the call be exercised can be invested at a higher rate of return, thus making profits on the spread between the asset and the fixed-rate liability. Although this strategy limits the returns on the asset, but it accomplishes the purpose of minimizing risk without giving up too much return.

Strategy 5—Hedging Mismatches

If the asset and the liability are both floating, but float off different indices and at different reset dates there are a number of ways to manage the risk. This situation is actually a combination of two different basis risks: the mismatch between indices and the mismatch between reset dates.

The index mismatch might be handled by floating-to-floating swaps or fixed-to-floating swaps. In the former, you would pay the asset index and receive the liability index to achieve a match. In the alternative, you could hedge just the liability side by receiving fixed and paying the floating index of the liability. For example, if you own a security that pays based on prime, but you pay borrowing based on LIBOR, you can receive fixed and pay floating based on LIBOR for the liability hedge or simply match up the two sides by entering a swap in which you receive based on LIBOR and pay based on prime.

You also could buy the liabilities forward as was discussed in Strategy 2. Using forward rate agreements, you would buy the liability index forward and sell the asset index forward to minimize costs. Of course, buying only the liabilities forward would offer protection, as well. Since the liabilities are obligations you owe, generally speaking hedging them is the preferred strategy. However, if the assets are subject to greater volatility, or if their credit quality has declined, hedging that side may be preferred.

A somewhat different type of protection results from using futures. Some markets exist for spread mismatches of this type, primarily the TED (Treasury bills over Eurodollars) spread. Buying a TED spread is a combination of owning T-bills and selling Euros, so it protects T-bill/LIBOR disparities. You can also use futures to hedge dollar/LIBOR and deutschemark/LIBOR with a diff contract. There is also a small Federal Funds contract for 30-day interest-rate levels, but it is very illiquid and not recommended for large positions. In the Federal Funds contract, the liquidity premium is such that entering almost any position will move the market and subject you to additional price risk. The one-month LIBOR contract is more useful. Although the one-month LIBOR contract is not very liquid, when you feel that it is underpriced in the short term, buying a position can be a cheap alternative to owning a floor. There is no futures contract for indexes set off the prime lending rate, but the basis risk is fairly small for substituting T-bills. There is an extremely high correlation between the T-bill rate and the prime rate and there is almost no time lag, as prime can be reset any day. For investing overseas, in addition to the LIBOR differential contracts, one can hedge using the Paris Interbank Offer Rate (PIBOR) contract traded on the French Futures Market, the Matif.

The mismatch between reset dates for floating-to-floating instruments is handled by duration hedging. The idea is to equate the duration of the assets to the duration of the liabilities. In addition, there is often a subdividing done so that the duration of the floating assets matches the duration of the floating liabilities. The duration can be lengthened by buying longer term futures and shortened by either purchasing shorter termed futures or by selling bond futures. There are several PC programs that quickly calculate the effects of futures purchases and sales. However, duration matching must be remeasured frequently, as it is affected by both the interest payments made and the time to maturity. Thus, the futures portion must be changed, which implies ongoing commission costs. This is really the only way to deal with date mismatches on a portfolio basis.

There is also a dispersion factor in matching reset dates. Dispersion measures the lifetime variability of cash flows around a security's measured duration. Since duration changes over time, dispersion will not be a stable measure. However, if we use the square-root-dispersion (SRD) instead, we arrive at a type of standard deviation of payments around the duration. Securities with a smaller SRD have more of their flows nearer the duration date, while larger SRD implies more variation in large payments at times other than the duration time. Therefore, when trying to manage different reset dates, there is less risk of needing to borrow unexpectedly to make a payment if the SRD of the assets is greater than the SRD of the liabilities. This is a secondary condition to establish a more conservative stance.

If you follow a dedication strategy, with assets matched to liabilities, a floating-to-floating swap can be customized to cover the difference in reset dates. In this way, a dedication strategy can be more cheaply implemented in some cases. However, it also means that each asset-liability pair needs to be separately evaluated. If your portfolio does not change much, this evaluation will be only a small problem. However, as a certain critical size is approached, dedication becomes less feasible, mostly because it severely limits your alternative investment choices.

CASE 8. MANAGING THE YIELD CURVE—TWISTS AND SHIFTS

Most quantitative management tools work best for parallel moves in the yield curve, or shifts. For example, this is when the entire curve moves in lock-step up or down a few basis points. Many quantitative methodologies add the further assumption that the curve is flat. However, a flat curve is a rare occurrence, and parallel moves are rare for either the short term or the long term. Most often, what we see are yield curve twists. This happens when money flows out of one time horizon into another, thereby making funds relatively cheaper in one sector and more expensive in another. An example of this would be an increase in yield in the intermediate period of 3 to 5 years and a decrease in the short term of 3 to 6 months. This is a special case of basis risk. See Figure 4.33. Hedging this type of risk can be complex, so you must be sure to state your goals rather precisely. You must know in advance whether you want a fixed relationship, or spread, between two specific maturities or whether you want a minimum yield to be locked in in a specific sector.

Strategy 1—Using Futures

Some futures markets allow a hedge for either spread or minimum yield. For instance, the NOB (Notes over Bonds) spread is the purchase of 10-year note futures and the sale of bond futures. Buying this spread implies a desire to move into a more intermediate-term sector of

Figure 4.33.   Yield-Curve Shifts

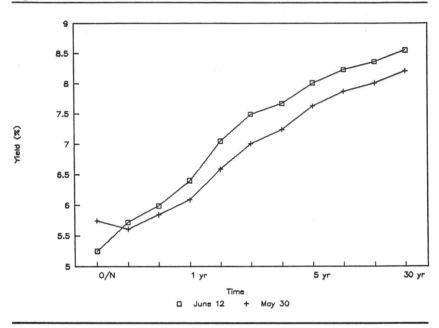

the yield curve. The note futures contract has a duration of around seven years, while the bond futures contract has a duration of around twelve years. Therefore, the time periods of the hedges are shorter than it initially appears. This also can be done in other maturity sectors. The futures exchanges offer fixed-income futures for almost every maturity of the yield curve. There is the 90-day T-bill, the two-year note, two different five-year notes, the 10-year note, and the 30-year bond. By paying a relatively small commission and margin, your portfolio can be weighted to any particular horizon you feel is attractive. Also, as your portfolio matures, the same maturity profile can be maintained.

The maturity profile of an investment portfolio can take on a number of different shapes. It can be evenly distributed across the curve so that 20% of the principal is expected to mature every five years for the next twenty-five. On the other hand it might show a more biased distribution with 30% or more placed in one time sector. This type of weighting can subject the portfolio to disproportionate capital gains or losses if the shape of the yield curve changes suddenly. By owning futures contracts in underweighted areas of the curve, this risk can be minimized. For example, if the portfolio is structured for 65% to mature four years from now, then by purchasing bill futures and bond futures the structure can be reconfigured to a flatter shape.

Equally, a mildly speculative flavor can be given to an evenly distributed portfolio by owning some futures contracts for sectors expected to appreciate near term. A common example would be the purchase of bill futures when easing by the Federal Reserve Bank is anticipated. This would weight the portfolio to the shorter maturities where the bulk of price reaction would take place if the easing occurs.

To widen the maturity exposure of a portfolio, using the futures market allows an immediate impact on decision making. You would buy the futures contract where additional weight is needed and, to conserve cash, you would also sell the futures that have maturities where the portfolio is overweighted. The margins will net out to some extent, reducing the cash outlay needed for this strategy. The futures would be redeemed as the cash transactions took place. An advantage is that you will never be caught with the portfolio only partially restructured when the yield curve moves.

Strategy 2—Using Options

Since the futures markets replicate the cash security, futures offer the same type of price exposure—both positive and negative. To change this probability distribution, you might decide to use alternative derivative instruments. Options products allow you to participate in price appreciations but avoid price depreciations. Therefore, buying protective puts or owning calls offer different ways to lock in price.

For example, if your portfolio is heavily weighted toward the five-year maturity sector, you could simply sell five-year futures. However, any capital gains in the portfolio resulting from price rallies will be decreased by the futures losses. Instead, you might choose to buy out-of-the-money puts, that is, purchase the right to sell at a price that is currently below the market price. If the five-year futures are priced at 101–20, you might buy a put with a strike at 101–00. If prices fall below 101–00, you can exercise the put and sell the value of the portfolio at 101–00. The funds can then be re-invested. Since the price of this sector of the portfolio cannot fall below 101–00, you have locked in a maximum capital loss for this sector. However, if prices rally, you will allow the put to expire worthless. You are still losing some of the participation in the upside move, but it is limited to the amount of the premium paid for the put.

The call strategy is less advantageous, but it can work. Owning a position in your portfolio can be seen as owning an exercised call option. Selling a covered call is a way to hedge this. Essentially, you are selling to someone else the right to purchase that portion of the portfolio from you at a higher price. For selling this right, you receive a premium. Receiving the premium means that the price of the portfolio must fall farther to reach the same decline in value as another, unhedged portfolio. However, the price distribution is such that, while it reduces the downside effect in a relative manner, it does not reduce it in an absolute manner. Also, it places a limit on the upside advantage that results from price increases. Since you have positioned your portfolio to take advantage of the greatest risk-adjusted opportunity, limiting yourself on the upside is not very sensible. On the other hand, if you plan to re-structuring soon anyway, or if you are not very committed to owning your portfolio if prices change, this can be a cheaper way to hedge.

Strategy 3—Using a Cap

Owning a cap is similar to the protective put strategy, but it can be structured for a longer term and involves a lower upfront cost. Buying a cap means purchasing a maximum yield for the value of the hedged portion of the portfolio. As yield increases above the value of the cap and prices decrease, you will receive the difference between the cap rate and the base rate, which is usually some version of LIBOR. The amount of the difference serves to offset the capital losses. If you think that the cost of the cap is unattractive, some upside price advantage can be given up by selling a floor for this portion of the portfolio. In this way, the product becomes a collar. If you want to stabilize the price of the portfolio, a collar can be constructed with the same strike rate for both the cap and the floor. In this way, you would receive the difference for downward price moves but would pay out the difference for upward price moves. If your view is for sideways prices and the portfolio sponsors want to stabilize a certain portion of the portfolio, this strategy can work very well.

Strategy 4—Using Multiple Options

Some options strategies are so common that they have their own names. Some of these work well in hedging yield-curve twists. For example, you could purchase a straddle on an underweighted maturity sector of the portfolio. A straddle means owning both a put and a call. This is almost a "disaster" hedge, in that it will be unprofitable for the currently expected range of prices but will offer good earnings if there is a price break-out in either direction. By owning a slightly out-of-the-money call, you become long as the price appreciates. By owning a slightly out-of-the-money put, you become a seller as price moves lower. You might even choose to have the same strike price for both the put and the call.

If the hedged portion of the portfolio is underweighted, placing a straddle allows the weighting to be changed if there is a twist and relative prices move significantly in either direction. For example, suppose 15% of the portfolio is short term. If short-term prices rally, you will be able to take only slight advantage of the move. By purchasing a call option on this sector, you can re-weight it for an upward price move. However, there is still the chance of downward appreciation. The straddle earns no additional monies when price remains stable, but it permits a re-weighting of the portfolio to take advantage of any substantial price change—up or down. If you consider this type of hedge desirable from the point of view of probability distribution, you can regain some money by selling a similar type of straddle on the overweighted sector of the portfolio. For example, you would sell a 10-year straddle and buy a six-month straddle. In this way, as long as the ten-year sector remains stable, money is earned on the options portion of the hedge. If there is a large break-out, the note straddle will lose money, but with luck the six-month straddle will be earning money at that time. See the detailed example in the Figure 4.34.

Options strategies are also ideal for locking in relative spreads between sectors. By simply owning calls on the underweighted sectors and puts on the fairly represented or overweighted sectors, the principal value of the entire portfolio can become more stable. The disadvantage is the inexact correlation of price between cash and options. Exchange-traded options are options on futures, and they are designed to correlate most closely with the near-term futures contract.

Figure 4.34.   An Example of an Options Straddle

The straddle strategy involves owning both a put and a call option for the same market. Generally, the strike price for both options is the same, but can be somewhat different with both options purchased slightly out-of-the-money. See the table for a scenario where the straddle is used for asset allocation purposes.

	Market Price	Option Premium	Put Gain/Loss	Call Gain/Loss	Net
t = 0	92–05	−.34	0	0	0
t = 1	94–23	−.34	0	+2–18	+2.225
t = 2	95–22	−.34	0	+0–31	+0.629
t = 3	94–27	−.34	0	−0–27	−1.184
Total earned on the straddle: 1.67%					

The table demonstrates the two primary risks to this strategy. First, the total premium is so high for even the short-term that the price move needs to be large to compensate for it. Second, if the price move is not sustained, one can end up owing a portion of the asset class at a higher than desired price.

To see the mechanics for using this strategy for asset allocation, see the next table.

t = 0   Purchase a $100 million balanced portfolio with 60% equity and 40% bonds. Also purchase a straddle on the $40 million bond portion of the portfolio, with a strike price of 92–00 for a total premium of 1.36% and an expiration in three months.

t = 1   The bond market rallies and the call portion of the straddle appreciates. Half the call option is exercised, so the portfolio manager now owns an additional $20 million of bonds. Since the total size of the portfolio has increased to $120 million, the portion represented by fixed-income is $60 million or 50%.

t = 2   The bond market continues to rally and half of the remaining call portion is exercised. The manager now owns $70 million bonds and has a relative weight of 46% equity and 54% fixed-income.

t = 3   It is now expiration time. The put portion of the straddle is out-of-the-money and expires worthless. The call portion has decreased in value from its last mark-to-market, but is still in-the-money. However, since the portfolio manager does not wish any additional fixed-income exposure, he sells his bond futures in the market to realize a gain of 2–27 (91 ticks) on the $10 million or $284,375. This works to enhance yield by .4% on the $70 million fixed-income portion of the portfolio.

However, if the cash security differs in credit quality or maturity, there can be an inexact match in price movements. This is why you must be concerned with the premium paid for the option. Since the protection will likely be inexact, you should not give away too much upside potential. See Figure 4.35.

CASE 9. ASSORTED YIELD-ENHANCEMENT STRATEGIES

Yield is enhanced when the proportion of cash flow to principal increases. We can add to yield by reducing funding costs, by maximizing the average reinvestment rate to increase the interest-on-interest component of return, or by improving the cash flow. Some yield-enhancement strategies improve funding costs by using swaps or minimize reinvestment-rate risk by using floors. These strategies have been discussed in other Cases. Other strategies introduce the idea of giving up less likely future gains to improve the income stream today. Most of these strategies are variations of options strategies designed to receive premium.

Strategy 1—Selling Covered Calls

In some investment portfolios there will have been a large move in prices since a portion of the portfolio was purchased. In that case, ac-

Figure 4.35. When is the Price of Protection Too High?

The process of evaluating how much you are willing to spend for protection is actually quite simple. When you have decided what type of strategy is most attractive in theory, ask a broker/dealer for a *bid indication*. Amortize this premium over the life or total maturity of the derivative product and the underlying security or portfolio needing the protection. The protection offers an economic good for the entire life of the security, even though it may not exist for the entire life. Subtract this amortized percentage from the probability distribution of price. Paying commissions skews the probability distribution to the left. If the resulting worst case still provides an acceptable return, then the strategy is acceptably priced. Otherwise, look for a strategy or strike price closer to at-the-money. However, as the strategy strike price approaches at-the-money, the increase in commission price will increase faster.

counting provides for booking the securities at "lower of cost or market," which means that there may be large, untaken capital-gains profits for these securities. However, quite often the cash stream for these securities is lower than if the funds were invested today. Derivatives can provide the chance to improve yield without totally repositioning the portfolio.

For example, by selling covered calls you will receive the premium, which adds to the cash flow. Even if the call is exercised, you will book a profit and can re-invest the monies at higher interest rates. On a risk profile, writing a covered call sets a maximum to any upside, while only offsetting any downside by the amount of premium received. This is basically a no-lose proposition when the security has already made a capital gain. See Figure 4.36. As long as you do not mind losing the security from your portfolio, the concept is sound, but if the security cannot be replaced easily, you should not write the call. For example, suppose you own the Anheuser Busch 8.75% due XX/XX/99. These were issued in 19XX and you bought them at issue. Currently, the market price on this seasoned issue is 101–16, so there is a point-and-a-half of capital gains in the trade. However, the 8.75% coupon is below the current market, so this is a prime candidate for writing a call. If a slightly out-of-the-money call is written on this issue, then 18 points of premium can be received. This increases the yield by increasing the cash flows. If this call goes unexercised due to a sideways price action, then another call can be written to gain more premium. If the call is exercised, a profit will be booked, and the money can be reinvested at market rates, thereby keeping the reinvestment risk relatively low but increasing the coupon. Since the current profits are unrealized, no new loss is incurred if the price of the security falls. Even a dramatic fall in price will be reduced by the premium earned.

Strategy 2—Selling Puts

In general, selling calls works best when there has been a movement upward in price that has either topped out or stabilized. If you think that the upward move is mostly finished but has not topped, selling puts on the security can also increase the yield. This is a riskier position and is directionally somewhat equivalent to owning calls. However, the position will be profitable as long as there is not a large price

Figure 4.36. Profit Probability Distribution for a Covered Call Strategy When the Underlying Security Has Unrealized Gains

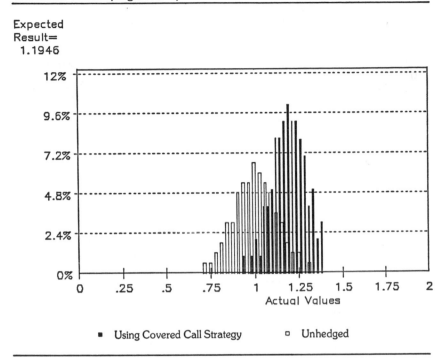

Expected
Result=
1.1946

• Using Covered Call Strategy □ Unhedged

decline. Selling a put on the Anheuser Busch bond in the previous example can gain a larger premium and will be net profitable as long as the price of the bond at expiration is not less than the strike price minus the premium. For instance, with a strike of 101–00 and a premium of 18/64ths, price must fall to 100–23 for the put to cost additional money. For an example, see Figure 4.37.

Strategy 3—Selling a Straddle

If you think prices will be moderately stable, the yield can be increased by selling a straddle. This is a type of wing strategy in which you sell both a put and a call. Wings are the part of the probability price distribution that are possible, but currently have a low probability weighting assigned. Strategies using the wings generally try to take advantage

Figure 4.37.   Short Put Strategy: Profit/Loss Diagram

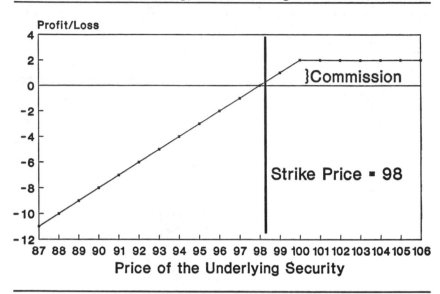

of the anticipation of large price moves. For puts and calls individually, you must be correct about the direction of prices for maximum profitability. Selling a straddle brings in less premium but is profitable for a wider band of price activity. The gains from the short call position offset the losses from the short put position as price moves. As long as price moves moderately, the premium offsets any losses. Only for extreme price moves will the loss from one of the short options positions overweigh the premium.

Strategy 4—Doing Bond Swaps

Bond swaps were a traditional method of enhancing yield. Arbitrage has caused this strategy to virtually disappear. The strategy involved trading one security for a similar one at a yield differential. Sometimes this meant that you were taking advantage of a broker's need for an illiquid security that you owned by trading for a similar but more liquid issue. At other times there was a question of "strong AA" or "weak AA" credit ratings. Years ago, it might have meant taking the risk of an unfamiliar issuer of securities in trade for an older and more established name. There were times when one could sell a two-year 8% coupon for a similar 8%-coupon two-year security to both increase yield to maturity and take in a cash payment. Today, these mispricings are avidly searched for. Now, with greater computer and analytical capabilities, such mispricings seldom exist for long. If you find a mispriced security, be careful, since it may be mispriced for a reason.

Strategy 5—Sector Weighting

As an alternative to strategy 4, you might choose to invest a portion of your cash flow in the futures market with either a combined stop-loss order to close out the position at a predetermined level below the market, or a put. This limits the possible losses but effectively overweights the portfolio in your chosen sector. This is a more speculative posture. This strategy introduces the trading concept known as "pyramiding," that is, adding to longs as the price increases or adding to shorts as the price falls. The underlying purpose is to keep the average price of the position moving in the same direction as the market. For example, straight pyramiding would entail selling futures at 98–22, again at 98–07, again at 97–16, and again at 97–10. This gives an average price of not quite 98–00. As price moves higher, the position can be unwound. While the gains per unit are not as large as the original position, there are more units involved in the trade. In addition, it will be rare that all the units will be traded at a loss, even in the worst possible case. As opposed to actually purchasing more of the chosen security or maturity sector, owning futures requires less upfront monies because of the use of margin. As the price increases, the long futures positions add to the gains.

The same type of additional exposure can be had by owning a series of out-of-the-money calls with varying strike prices. For example, you might own a series of March Eurodollar calls with strikes at 9325, 9350, and 9375, or you might own a March Eurodollar call at 9325, a June call at 9350, and a July call at 9375. Your choice will depend on the price and on the time expected for the bullish move to run. This is also a more speculative strategy because there will be no income added to the position unless you are right about the direction of price moves.

Strategy 6—Managing Fund Costs

Minimizing funding costs by various means is discussed in broad terms in Case 3. This can also be used as a specific yield-enhancement strategy.

Occasionally, a company will decide that lowering funding costs is a priority, generally because current rates are well above historical costs or because there is an actuarial mandate that requires the investment of additional funds at current levels. By assuming a small credit risk, the company can lock in below-market funding rates. In addition to the added credit risk, the company may also face a problem if rates suddenly fall. However, a company usually makes funding costs a priority only when it believes that market rates are sustainable.

Interest-rate swaps are tailor-made for this situation. By taking on the small amount of added credit risk, a company with a comparative advantage in borrowing in a niche market can achieve lower funding rates in other markets as well. For example, if Toys Inc. is AAA-rated and Boys Inc. is A-rated, a swap might take place as follows: Toys can borrow directly in the market at 13% fixed or 3.0% over LIBOR. Boys can borrow at 15% fixed of 4.25% over LIBOR. When LIBOR is at 8.125%, then for Toys the ratio of floating-to-fixed rates is .856, while for Boys it is .825. Boys has a comparative advantage in floating rates because it can substitute one unit of fixed-rate funding for .825 units of floating funding. Therefore, the least expensive borrowing cost is for Boys in floating. Both parties can benefit if they set up a swap with each other. Boys will use its comparative advantage to borrow floating in the direct market at LIBOR plus 4.25%. Toys will borrow fixed at 13%. The swap between the two pays fixed to Toys and floating to Boys. Essentially, Toys pays Boys at LIBOR plus 4.25, and Boys pays Toys at 14.50%. By entering the swap, Boys has actually borrowed fixed at 14.50%, one-half percentage point cheaper than it could on the direct market. Toys has borrowed floating at LIBOR plus 2.75%, the difference between 4.25 and 1.50, one-quarter point cheaper than on the direct market.

In this strategy, there will be added commissions and documentation costs, but they may be outweighed by the decreased costs of borrowing.

Reducing the costs of borrowing can be the easiest way to add value to a portfolio or a securities position. The gross profits are the returns on the investment, but the net returns are what keep you in business. Every financial institution has a method of charging off the cost of funds between departments. If you direct a portfolio, it is important to keep an eye on what you are being charged by your own company, because those charges can turn a marginal trade into a losing trade.

That is one reason that funding costs and transaction fees should be included when you calculate return. There are a number of theoretical investment manipulations that look like "free money." However, after adding in all the costs, these profits disappear.

Strategy 7—Managing Interest-on-Interest

Maximizing the interest-on-interest component of return can also enhance yield. This component is maximized by investing idle funds and by setting minimum reinvestment rates. See Figure 4.38. This may be done by purchasing a floor, as is described in Case 2. In addition, you may sell the cash flows forward, which locks in the rate for that specific flow for a period of time, or you may enter swaps. Swaps accomplish the same purpose as forwards but generally run for longer periods.

CASE 10. HEDGING ISSUANCE COSTS FOR SECURITIES

There is generally a delay of a day or so between setting a range of prices for issuing a security and setting the actual price. Should a move in credit spreads or general interest rates ensue, then either the broker or the issuer could lose a great deal of money. Hedging against a move of this type can keep a broker in business and guarantee that a company will not have to pay more for its funding than expected.

When a company needs to borrow a great deal of money for a longer term, it will write a contract known as a bond to specify the interest rate it will pay, when it will pay, and what legal recourse the investor has if the company defaults. An investment bank will assist in ex-

---

Figure 4.38.   The Cost of Idle Funds

If you have a fixed-income portfolio of $100 million and it earns an average coupon of 9.875%, you receive $9,875,000 in coupon payments annually. This works out to an average $27,054.79 daily. This daily cash flow itself can earn at least $4 when invested overnight at minimum-risk rates. While this does not sound impressive, the cost of leaving one week's cash flows idle one week is $200. If this cash is not reinvested on a regular basis, the cost could be $10,387.55 annually, or .1%.

---

change for a fee for legal and advisory services and commissions for selling the contracts. As the issuance date approaches, the brokers call their customers and determine the rate at which the bonds will be attractive enough to be purchased. They also take orders for the bonds and may guarantee a rate or a range of rates to the company. Therefore, a large move upward in interest rates will either add significantly to the company's borrowing costs or cost the broker the difference between the market rate and his guaranteed rate. If the issue does not sell as well as expected, the broker may also have to own a larger percentage of the paper than he desires simply to avoid booking large losses. This might occur when credit spreads widen rather than when general interest-rate levels increase. For its part, the issuing company wants to protect against both last minute upside interest-rate increases and credit-spread increases. However, some or all of a downward move should remain available.

Strategy 1—Selling Futures

General interest-rate levels can be hedged by the issuing company by selling the appropriate futures contracts. This replicates the cash position, although somewhat early. The futures will be closed out after the issuance is complete. This offers only general interest-rate protection, however, and the company is still subject to credit risk.

The broker may buy out-of-the-money puts, which establishes a lower limit of price for the security. However, since the security is not yet issued, the puts are likely to be government-security puts traded on one of the exchanges, and there will not be an exact correlation in price movements. These puts also do not offer protection against credit-spread moves. Another alternative is buying an interest rate cap, although the transaction fee can add significantly to borrowing rates and credit risk again will not be managed.

Strategy 2—Hedging Credit Risk

Protection against credit risk might be achieved by using regression analysis techniques to calculate a hedge ratio that includes the credit risk. However, this will be inaccurate because the security is a new issue with no history of price behavior. An alternative would be to use a portfolio of similar securities to do the regression analysis, but there would again be an inexact correlation. An additional, theoretical difficulty with using regression analysis is that it requires a straight-line relationship. However, since the relationship between price path and expectations follows a curved path, regression analysis will infrequently be an accurate forecaster of future events.

The best way to hedge credit-spread risk is to offset the cash position with another highly correlated instrument. For corporates and mortgage-backed securities, this can be difficult. In extreme cases, where credit spreads jump unexpectedly and unfavorably during the issue period, the issuing company may be better off choosing to delay the borrowing rather than pay the increased costs.

There also are some unorthodox theories for hedging credit-spread risk, such as hedging the interest-rate portion using futures and hedging the credit-spread risk using the company's equity. However, when the company is issuing its own securities, shorting its own stock may create regulatory problems and send a possibly disastrous message to the market. Moreover, there is no strong short-term correlation between equity prices and credit-spread changes.

Although it is scarcely orthodox, you may believe that credit spreads widen when the general level of default risk increases and that, when such credit-spread changes occur, the level of volatility in the market increases. In that event, you may hedge a change in credit spread by using options strategies to go long volatility. If price volatility increases, the issuing company will lose money due to increased funding costs. However, by going long volatility, it can offset this increase in costs. Since there will be an inexact price correlation to this hedge, it is best to pursue the cheapest possible strategy. Depending on market conditions, the cheapest strategy might be buying a straddle. A straddle consists of owning both a put and a call and loses money when price is unchanged. However, it earns progressively more as price moves one way or the other, that is, as volatility increases. Straddles will also be discussed as a strategy for hedging event risk in Case 13.

An example will explain the mechanics of placing a straddle hedge. Suppose you intend to issue $100 million out three years at 8.75%. One week before issue, the issuing syndicate determines that 8.75% is attractive to the market, and it takes preliminary orders. Your actual cost will be around 8.92% to fund the position after paying the syndicate 2% of principal. If the syndicate guarantees a rate to you, the syndicate will hedge for the next week. If there is no guaranteed rate, then you must place the hedge. After the rate is estimated, you or the syndicate will purchase approximately 1,000 futures contracts, depending on the method used to calculate the hedge ratio. To create the straddle, the hedger will buy puts with an at-the-money strike price. The other part of the straddle, owning the calls, is already copied by owning the futures contracts. In this way, there will be participation to the upside if rates decline. There will also be protection against a move downward in price via the put. In addition, the derivatives will earn money when market volatility increases, which is a substitute for an increase in credit spreads. After the issue is placed, the futures position will be sold. Depending on the market, the puts will either be sold or allowed to expire worthless.

CASE 11. MANAGING COSTS FOR FOREIGN EXCHANGE TRANSACTIONS

Any firm that has ongoing foreign exchange transactions or a foreign exchange trading desk has gains and losses due to funding costs and the speculative issue of currency appreciation/depreciation. In principle, it is cheaper to own currencies with high interest rates than currencies with lower interest rates. For example, buying Canadian dollars implies selling another currency in exchange, that is, paying U.S. dollars to receive Canadian dollars. To pay the U.S. dollars, you must borrow them at 6.20% for 90 days but, by receiving Canadian dollars, you can invest them at 12%. Therefore, you can earn interest at a 5.80% relative rate if the exchange rate does not change. In other words, the Canadian currency can depreciate 5.80% before any real loss occurs. Managing this type of cost is a big part of whether or not the trading desk or foreign exchange operation will be profitable.

Relative interest rates can be hedged in a number of ways.

Strategy 1—Using Interest-Rate Futures

There are futures exchanges around the world offering contracts for Euromark, Euroyen, Euroswiss, short sterling, and the like. Therefore, you can hedge the relative interest-rate differential Diff contracts or you can hedge just one side or "leg" of the relationship by fixing the rate in one of the futures markets. Since you already own the security, the offset is to sell the futures. If you know the approximate time frame for the holding period, you can pick the contract that has an expiration most closely matching the unwinding of your foreign-exchange holding. If you use Diffs, by borrowing in the U.S. market you can sell Diffs and have a net long position on the Eurocurrency. Since you will be receiving payments in Eurocurrency, this effectively hedges you against downward moves in that interest rate.

When discussing the management of foreign exchange costs, it is very important to note time frame. For example, if your exposure to a currency exists because you have future liabilities in that currency, then that exposure requires less management. However, if the exposure exists because of speculative interest or some other type of short-term commitment, then it requires more management. As currencies are very volatile, a small position can quickly become a large loss.

Strategy 2—Buying a Straddle

For a short-term commitment, buying a straddle might be attractive. Since this is a "break-out" strategy, the most money is made when the market moves extremely in either direction. However, if the volatility is tolerable for a particular range, then this is an easy hedge for levels outside that range.

A straddle consists of owning both a call and a put on a currency, each with at-the-money strike prices. Therefore, when the currency exchange rate is sideways, the two options cancel each other out and you incur the commission costs. However, as the exchange rate appreciates, the effect of owning a call dominates and you make money. Equally, as the exchange rate depreciates, the effect of the put starts to prevail.

A variation on the straddle is the strangle, in which the premiums are less because the options strike prices are out-of-the-money. That is, with a current exchange rate of 132.37 dollar/yen, a strangle involves owning a call at 133.00 and a put at 131.00. In addition, the premiums are less because the protection is less. However, if you feel again that the current exchange rate is close enough to longer term expected levels, then the lower cost might be a consideration. A strangle will also allow you to adjust the hedge to reflect your view on prices. For example, the call can be less out-of-the-money than the put if you are somewhat bullish. A strangle will expire worthless most of the time. Deciding if it is worthwhile to spend the premium for a strangle depends on how badly you will be hurt if the market does move.

As an alternative to buying a straddle or a strangle, although it is risky, the opposite trade can be done and you can sell either a straddle or strangle to generate premium. As long as the exchange rate stays within the range, the cash flow will increase. However, if volatility increases and the market moves, the loss will be mitigated only by the premium received.

Strategy 3—Using Currency Futures

Another way to manage the exchange-rate exposure is to offset the currency positions with futures or forwards. However, buying currency futures to offset a long dollar/yen position reduces gains as well as losses, and all gains in the currency position will be offset almost equally by the futures. As an alternative, you could adopt a somewhat riskier stance by hedging only a portion of the currency position in futures, but that allows less downside protection.

If the horizon for the currency exposure is known, you can sell the position forward to lock in the exchange rate. This is advantageous in that the cash flows are minimal. However, it again permits no chance to take advantage of a favorable move.

Strategy 4—Buying a Put

A strategy similar to a straddle is buying a put. The difference is there is no need to add to a long posture by owning a call, since you already own the currency. Choosing the strike will be a trade-off between the cost of the premium and your pain threshold. The closer the strike price is to being at-the-money, the higher is the chance that the put will be exercised and the higher will be the premium. As a general rule, look to place the strike one standard deviation below the longer term expected value for the exchange rate, if you can tolerate that much pain. For the yen this is currently around the 127.00 level, or 7800 on yen options.

A more attractive way to manage the exposure is to use futures and options to manage the length of the currency exposure. Just as the maturity of domestic securities can be lengthened or shortened using futures, the foreign pay investments can also be lengthened or shortened. To maximize the interest-rate differentials, you could move to a longer term maturity overseas and to short-end maturities domestically.

Strategy 5—Using a Collar

You can also use collars as a way to manage foreign-exchange exposure. This is a combination of buying puts, as in Strategy 4, and selling a call to add the position. This recoups some of the premium paid to own the put. However, you are again sacrificing some part of an advantageous move to obtain lower costs. For example, owing the 79 strike yen put and selling the 84 strike yen call translates as owning the right to sell yen and buy dollars at 126.50 and selling the right to buy yen and sell dollars at 119.00.

In the preceding example this is the correct risk posture if the yen is your primary concern. However, if you intend to hedge dollars, then the appropriate combination is to buy puts on the dollar (buy calls on the yen) and sell calls on the dollar (sell puts on the yen). The first combination sets a maximum loss on yen, the second sets a maximum loss on the dollar. Remember that every currency transaction is really a dual-currency transaction. Be sure that you hedge the appropriate currency.

Also remember that the collar does not need to be symmetric in terms of protection. By simply varying the strike prices, a collar can take on a more bullish or bearish tone. Setting the call strike higher means that you need to give up less of the move. Equally, moving the put farther out-of-the-money gives less protection but costs less. If you are bullish, this lesser downside protection may be adequate, since you will not really feel that you need it anyway. However, it is wise to buy at least some form of cheap protection in case you were mistaken in how you foresee the future.

Strategy 6—Buying a Corridor

When you anticipate that you will need only limited protection, you can also purchase a corridor. This has the effect of buying a cap at one strike price and selling another cap at a higher strike price. In this way, the payments you receive when the market exceeds the second strike price will be canceled out by the payments you owe when the market exceeds the higher strike rate. In other words, you receive the difference between the market rate and the base rate for increases in the exchange rate, but only for a limited move. For instance, assume that you purchase a corridor when the dollar/mark is at 1.4950, that the strike price of the first cap is 1.5100, and that the strike of the second cap is 1.5250. When market rates increase to 1.5200, you will receive the difference between that rate and the cap rate of 1.5100 on the notational principal. However, when the market rate exceeds 1.5250, you no longer have any protection against additional increases. This strategy has the advantages of being inexpensive and of not requiring a high credit rating. Generally, selling a cap along or in combination to form a reverse collar requires a high credit rating, as the counterparty wants to be sure that it will receive its money in the event of an extreme move in rates. See Figure 4.39.

Strategy 7—Using OTC Options

The preceding Strategies have used the exchange-traded currency options for illustration. There is also a large OTC market in currency options. These can be used for odd-lot amounts or for longer time frames than the CME options currently allow. The OTC market also will permit you to customize the strike price to your exact tolerance. While they are slightly more expensive, there is a decent amount of volume to the market, and the market-makers are usually large com-

Figure 4.39.   An Example of a Currency Corridor

See the accompanying table for an example of the cash flows involved when a foreign-exchange corridor is purchased. Note that a portion of the cash flows nets out for extreme moves. The purchased cap has a strike rate of 1.5100, and the strike rate of the sold cap has a rate of 1.5250. In general practice, the costs of a corridor this tight will be excessive. Usually the strike rates are farther apart.

Exchange Rate	Cash Flows for Purchased Cap	Cash Flows for Sold Cap	Net
1.4950	0	0	0
1.5100	0	0	0
1.5200	+.0100	0	+.0100
1.5250	+.0150	0	+.0150
1.5300	+.0200	−.005	+.0150
1.5350	+.0250	−.010	+.0150

mercial banks that can offset the OTC options through the exchange-traded options or through their extensive client base.

CASE 12. HEDGING FORWARD FOREIGN-EXCHANGE EXPOSURE

The forward dealer for a foreign exchange department is generally viewed as separate from the spot dealer. In effect, the forward foreign exchange dealer treats the spot dealer as a separate entity, as if he were another customer. As a result, when a client wants to buy a currency forward, the forward dealer sets a price and covers his exposure in the spot market when the transaction is completed. In effect, the forward dealer is buying spot and selling forward, as if he were conducting a currency swap. However, there is an underlying exposure to funding this position, since the dollars needed to buy the currency in the spot market must be borrowed. Admittedly, this cost of borrowing is offset by the interest earned in the foreign market, but it is still an added risk. Managing this risk can be done in several ways.

Strategy 1—Buying Diffs

As the spot position is usually rolled daily, the exposure is the difference between currency and dollar nominal interest rates. Therefore, buying Diffs will lock in rates. Because the foreign currency is earning interest, increases in rates are favorable. However, increases in U.S. rates are less favorable, because that is the rate the forward dealer is paying, so the relative difference can be locked in using Diffs. However, Diffs require management because the hedge ratio will change frequently, and Diffs do not offer good protection for non-parallel moves in the yield curve. The hedge ratio is generally calculated by dividing the effect of a move of one basis point in relative rates on the cost of carry by $25 (the value of one basis point on the Diff contract). Then, the cash position divided by the size of the futures contact multiplied by the hedge ration is the number of contracts needed to offset the cash position.

Strategy 2—Dealer Offsets

Since the forward dealer makes a market for both buyers and sellers of the currency, an alternative is to simply offset the portion of the trade he does not wish to assume. Although this can mean lowering the price of the forward exposure he wants to move off his books (called "having an axe" between the dealer and the sales force), it is still the alternative that requires the least management. However, it can be impossible to find a counterparty willing to assume that exposure, since there seems to be a consensus on which currency is attractive at any one time. This strategy also provides no upside opportunity in case your forecast is wrong. In addition, it may involve booking a loss, which is often unattractive to management. Usually, a combination of methods is most appropriate or try to use the sales force to offset an unattractive position and hedge the rest in diffs.

Strategy 3—Interest-Rate Futures

Another choice is to hedge the currency interest-rate differential by using cash T-bills and Euromarks when the Diff is inappropriate. The futures contracts for these instruments can also be used. After all, a Diff is only one contract, but it equates to owning one interest rate and selling the other. The same can be done with T-bills and Euroswiss or short sterling. These foreign cash securities will have higher commission costs, but they will require less management. They will also work better for twists in the yield curve, since their maturity spreads can also be hedged. However, you need to have access to the Frankfurt or London exchanges. This strategy works for yen, French francs, deutschemarks, pound sterling, and Swiss francs.

Strategy 4—Using FX Options

A final choice is buying and selling foreign exchange options. This will require high levels of management. In addition, commission costs will be high because the dealer will need to adjust his hedge often—probably daily. However, the upfront costs are low, so the commission as a percentage is not high in absolute dollar terms. For a longer-term position, this can be attractive.

CASE 13. HEDGING CALLS AND PUTS—THE OPTION-ADJUSTED SPREAD

The fixed-income asset class got its name because the securities originally issued offered fixed payment streams for a fixed amount of time.

It was considered a low-risk investment because the owner of the income stream had access to legal recourse even if the concern went bankrupt. There have been a number of innovations in this asset over the years and today almost every fixed-income security in the market with a maturity over two years has some sort of attached option.

Fixed-income securities with attached rights for early call or put are also known as option-adjusted paper. The option on the security can be on the interest rate, or the maturity. When the option concerns shortening the maturity of the security, we can look at it as either a right for the issuer to buy the security from the investor on a specific date for a specific price, or a right for the investor to sell the security to the issuer on a specific date for a specific price. The right for the issuer to buy is a call while the right for the investor to sell is a put. Although these securities are now the norm, they are a relatively recent phenomenon.

One methodology for pricing these securities involves looking at similar but non-callable paper and then adding or subtracting the additional fee for the option. Therefore, one way of hedging these callable or puttable bonds is by effectively stripping out the call option to divide the hedge into two parts: the bond itself and the option. That way, if the risks of owning the straight security are within your tolerance levels, you might choose to hedge only the option portion. For example, if you are interested in owning a security with a ten-year life, but the most attractive one is callable in five years, you might choose to hedge the option to neutralize it. Equally, if the price of the option when incorporated into the bond makes it too expensive, you could create your own option-adjusted security. An example of this would be when the non-puttable version of the security is offering a yield of 10.75%, but the puttable version is offering 9.375%. You may find it more attractive to own the higher yielding security and purchase your own put.

Floating-rate securities can also be thought of as base-rate plain-vanilla instruments with an attached series of puts or calls. As with the floating-rate CD discussed in Case 1, when a floating-rate security with a minimum coupon level is issued, the cash flows are equivalent to issuing a plain-vanilla security with a minimum coupon and a series of calls. That is, the investor purchases a non-floating security plus a series of calls that offer a choice of exercise on the coupon-reset dates to own the difference between the minimum coupon and the index rate based on the notional principal of the bond. The issuer must hedge a short call position. If you prefer to own the non-floating issue, you might choose to buy a series of calls on the open market to create the equivalent exposure.

Other securities are more complicated. Some issues are floating rate, callable and puttable. In this case, the issuer sells a plain-vanilla security, sells calls for the floating-rate portion, sells puts, and buys another series of calls with different expiration dates to replicate the call option. This is similar to selling a straddle, whereby the issuer will make additional money as long as rates stay within a given broad range while owning the effect of a protective put on the borrowing. For an issuer to own the call right to a security is the same as owning a put on the borrowed money, since buying the security equates to giving back the money originally borrowed if the cost of the borrowing becomes prohibitive. Admittedly, the put on the borrowed money is probably set at a level where the investment spread has become negative, that is, the amount earned on investment is less than the amount spent to borrow, but it sets a maximum loss to the spread. As well, the spread need not be negative. The strike price for the call on the security can be set for a minimum positive spread. There is a greater chance of a call in this case, however and a company with a poorer credit rating may find it too expensive to borrow under these conditions. On the other hand, for a company rated AA or better, such a minimum spread may not make much difference in borrowing costs.

An investor is more likely to find the put option attractive for credit considerations than for interest-rate considerations. After all, the security has a minimum rate guaranteed for the downside but will allow for appreciation to the upside. However, if the credit rating of the company is declining or is anticipated to decline, or if credit spreads widen, there may be other more attractive opportunities for investment. For those who wish to limit the volatility of the value of an investment, floating-rate securities tends to be priced near par and, the more frequent the resets, the nearer par it will trade. Thus, for those trying to squeeze every basis point from an investment, keeping tabs on relative prices of callable securities versus their non-callable counterparts can offer opportunities. As a caveat, however, it appears that this sector of the market is quite efficient. This implies that a lot of looking is required to spot a mispricing and to take advantage of it. There also seems to be a recent structural change to this sector of the market. As more securities are issued with attached call or put options, the spread between non-option-adjusted and option-adjusted paper becomes less reliable. Therefore, be sure that the price difference you see is due to option differences, rather than to credit differences or differences in company debt ratios.

Option-adjusted securities are a perfect case for using synthetic strategies, both to hedge or to create your own type of option adjustment. These strategies are based on the following fundamental relationships. Being long a call on a security is equivalent to owning a long cash or futures position and being long a put. Being short a call is the same as selling a put and selling either cash or futures. Being long a put is the same cash-flow equivalent of being long a call and selling the cash or futures. Being short a put is the same as selling a call while owning the cash or futures.

Strategy 1—Entering a Swap

For the investor, adding the call-option portion of the security to create a floater from a fixed-rate security is as simple as entering a swap. Trading fixed-rate cash flows for a floating-rate cash flow can be attractive to an asset/liability manager acting as the counterparty. Doing this might expose the manager to a slight time lag, since the payment dates follow rather than anticipate actual market moves. However, owning the floating security would have the same drawback. The real difficulty is that a swap does not guarantee a minimum coupon for a security, so the investor might be safer entering a swap with an attached call option for that swap, which equates to an early-termination option.

Strategy 2—Anticipatory Hedging

If you like the advantage of owning a fixed-rate security when you think interest rates are declining, you might hedge only when you think rates are about to increase. To do this, you might purchase a forward rate agreement to buy forward those cash flows that you feel will be affected by the increased rate.

For example, suppose that you own a fixed-rate 9.00% note maturing in two years. For the first year, this level of interest is acceptable. However, as the second year approaches, you note certain inflationary pressures, so you approach a commercial bank for quotes on the 1×7 and 6×12 forward rate agreements. The purchase of these FRAs would settle in one month and six months respectively to cover the two semi-annual payments to be received on the note in the second year. The reference rate will usually be LIBOR plus a spread, but it can also be customized to prime, T-bills, or some other index. The contractual rate will usually be as close as possible to the fixed rate you are receiving. As time goes on and interest rates do increase, assume that LIBOR moves from 6.15% to 7.00% and the spread is +275 basis points. On the first settlement date you will receive the difference between the LIBOR-based reference rate, now at 9.75%, and the contractual rate of 9.00%. This .75% is multiplied by the notional principal of the bonds and by the term of the contract, in this case 6 months, and you will receive an additional $3,575.69 for every million in notional principal. This calculated additional payment is discounted by the reference rate for the six-month period, because settlement is at the beginning of the contract period, not at the end. This additional payment increases the interest rate for that payment to 9.71% annualized (minus commissions) versus 9.00% annualized. For the last payment, if LIBOR falls back to its previous 6.15% level, the reference rate will be 8.90%. You will pay out $478.69 plus commissions, so for that payment you have transformed the fixed-rate security to an 8.89% security. Note that, by hedging the individual payments one at a time, you transform the security into a floater, but you can more easily change it back to a fixed rate by simply ceasing to buy forward. The drawback to this arrangement is that, as rates move higher in a steady manner, each successive FRA either will be more expensive or will not permit a contractual rate close to the fixed rate of the security. Therefore, if rates move higher, hedging each interest payment individually enables you to efficiently hedge against additional increases but may require you to take the opportunity loss of the change in interest rates. Although the price of the fixed-rate security will fall as the level of general interest rates rises, this is not really a consideration if you hold the security to maturity.

Strategy 3—Cross-Hedging

The preceding strategies have used swaps and FRAs to create call options in series or individually. You also can own a fixed-rate instrument and purchase futures contracts to create a floater, although again there will be no minimum coupon created by this method. Of course, you always may choose to simply purchasing calls on the OTC market or use bond options to take advantage of the conveniences of exchange trading. Using an alternative instrument to hedge a position, rather than using the perfect substitute, is known as placing a cross-hedge. Since generally there will be no exact price correlation anyway, placing a cross-hedge takes advantage of liquidity preferences or some other factor.

Strategy 4—Using Synthetics

There is a difference between placing calls on yield and placing calls on price. The right to own higher interest rates is the same as the right to own lower prices. You can make up for less-than-optimal cash flows by adding to those cash flows or by owning more of the security at a lower price to add capital gains. When you use swaps or FRAs to create a floater from a fixed rate, you are hedging only the cash flows, and the principal remains unchanged. If you choose to purchase calls at a lower price, it will be very expensive and the greatly in-the-money calls will act like the futures contract underlying the calls. Since you already own the security, this is simply adding leverage rather than protection. To solve this, you can create a synthetic by purchasing a protective out-of-the-money put on the security. This allows for a maximum capital loss on the security, which generally translates as the maximum permitted opportunity loss between actual cash flows received and potential cash flows that could have been received. The monies received from exercising the put are then invested at higher interest rates.

On the other side, if you are an issuer, you will have sold calls. To replicate the long call position that neutralizes this position, owning a put and futures is the classic solution. While being long around 1,000 contracts will hedge an issuance of $100 million, it subjects the issuer to margin calls, management time, the costs of rolling the hedge, and the ever-important question of where to book the mark-to-market. It also may subject the cost of borrowing to unacceptable volatility. The sale of the calls is usually offset by investing in some instrument with a floating rate. In this way, you simply will have bought calls to offset the series that you sold. However, if you plan to invest in capital equipment, rather than a commercial property, you might prefer to pay the possibly higher fixed rate to borrow so that the projected cash flows are not disrupted halfway through the project.

Caps, floors, and collars are other ways to handle this, but the approach will be different. These instruments acknowledge that there may be a difference between the invested rates and current market rates, but they allow you to set a maximum difference between the two. On a psychological level, this can be attractive; it means that small mistakes are generally acceptable and will be permitted, but large mistakes that sometimes occur will be protected against. This division of the market is generally quoted in yield. Therefore, if you are receiving a 9.0% coupon, you might place a maximum on the difference between your receipts and market rates by purchasing a cap with a strike of 12%. In this way, you have transformed your fixed security into a lagged floater. For interest moves above 12%, you will receive the difference between the base rate, usually LIBOR, and the 12% strike. This means that the coupon flow becomes the base rate minus the difference between the coupon rate and the strike rate, in this case base minus 3%. Thus, when the base rate moves to 14%, you will receive 9% on the coupon of the fixed security and 2% from owning the cap to net a security worth 11%.

CASE 14. EVENT RISK—WHAT WORKS UNDER EXTREME CONDITIONS?

Events around the world can have a significant influence on asset prices. Election results, the assassination of a national leader, natural disasters, the threat of war, or any other imaginable event could damage the value of your portfolio. This effect is called event risk.

For example, late on Friday afternoon in New York you learn that the Japanese Minister of Finance will make an important speech early Monday morning in Tokyo. This news will break in New York on Sunday evening and may influence world markets before the local markets open for business on Monday. You fear that the speech will cause a move in interest rates, but you are unsure of whether this will be a yield-curve twist or a parallel move. You must decide whether the speech will have an effect on your asset prices and what you should do about the risk.

Strategy 1—Selling a Straddle

The easiest strategy is to sell a straddle. This is an options strategy that consists of owning both a call and a put at-the-money. While this strategy will lose income if prices remain stable, it will protect you if volatility sharply increases. This is a balanced strategy, in that both the upside and downside moves are protected. For moves lower in price, the effect of owning a put comes to dominate; for price increases, the effect of owning a call predominates. Although a straddle can be expensive, it also can be customized to own out-of-the money puts and calls. Since your intention is to protect against large moves, this lower level of protection will often be adequate. By using exchange-traded options, there will be little credit risk to this strategy, which is always an advantage when dealing with extreme circumstances.

Strategy 2—Buying Puts

Quite often, a move in only one direction will cause you pain. If you are the issuer of a floating security and the minimum coupon rate is already hedged, then only increases in interest rates will concern you. If you own a portfolio of securities with generally market-rate coupons, then only a decrease in rates will affect your reinvestment income. If you own a trading portfolio, reinvestment income will be only a secondary concern. Instead, you will want to protect the market value of the portfolio and will hedge only increases in rates that will lower the value of your portfolio.

Owning puts is the solutions to these varied situations. The technique is to own puts on the item you want to hedge. If you want to protect the value of your portfolio, own puts on the securities or construct a cross-hedge using government securities futures or options to take advantage of the low credit risk and the high volume of trading. If you are concerned about the reinvestment-rate risk, owns puts on the reinvestment rate, which translates as buying a floor. If you are making payments, owning a cap is a viable way to hedge extreme moves.

For event risk, it is best to use exchange-traded instruments so that you can minimize a credit risk that might result if your counterparty is unable to make the payment. If your counterparty defaults, you will be in a worse position than if you had not hedged at all, since you will have already paid out the premium without getting the protection you wanted. A second reason to prefer exchange-traded instruments for specific event risk is that quite often such protection is not desired for the longer term. Both institutions and individuals are seeking short-term protection against extreme moves. That is why the straddle—simply the put or call half of a straddle—is the most effective protection. After the period of risk is past, these hedges are easily unwound. While they do not offer complete and perfect protection, they often overshoot expected price in extreme moves due to volatility expectations and so give adequate coverage.

Strategy 3—Wing Strategies

Other types of wing strategies will work, as well. A type of corridor strategy can be constructed using options. This would be used when you think that volatility will increase but that any change in prices will not be sustained. You would look for an opportunity to lower the average cost of assets if prices moved lower and also take advantage of an opportunity to sell at higher levels if prices move upward. For example, for bonds with a current pre-event market price of 96–00, buying a put with a strike price of 95–00 ensures a maximum loss for the portfolio currently owned of one point. Owning a call with a strike of 94–00 reinvests those monies at the new, lower price level. In addition, selling a call with a strike of 98–00 recoups a small amount of premium. The amount will be small because it is well out-of-the-money. This type of combination is one of many known as a butterfly.

Butterfly options strategies are generic when the expiration dates are the same but strike prices are different. The example in the preceding paragraph is non-standard in that it consists of calls and puts. A more standard example might be owning one call at a higher strike price and one call at a below-market price and going short two calls near the current market. For an example of this, suppose that you think that the Japanese Finance Minister's speech might temporarily depress price. Overall, however, you are bullish regardless of short-term price gyrations. By going long the call at the higher strike price, you will own the right to purchase the security at the higher price, which allows you to do the trade at a worse price if you miss a better opportunity. However, even though the price is relatively less attractive, you will still have the right to place the position. Equally, by going long the call at the lower strike price, you are retaining the right to take advantage of a short-term attractive price move. The near at-the-money calls that you sell are both to recover some of the premium and to work as a yield-enhancement strategy in case they are executed. This is the same strategy as writing an at-the-money covered call. The ratio of 1-to-1 keeps a delta-neutral posture, which ensures that one wing of the trade does not overpower another wing as the market-level price moves.

A delta-neutral condition exists when the delta of a portfolio is equal to 0. The delta of a position will only equal zero when it is perfectly hedged, and a perfect hedge means that the portfolio or position is protected against a price move in either direction. Delta can be used as the number of units of the underlying needed to construct a riskless hedge. That is, a call option strategy with a delta of five needs a sale of five futures contracts to be "riskless," that is, for price moves to net out in dollar terms.

Wing strategies have a disadvantage in that the gamma for the combined options position can be larger than for a less complex strategy. A position with a high gamma will have a delta with a greater sensitivity to price moves. Thus it will require more frequent rebalancing to maintain a delta-neutral posture. Gamma tends to increase as a position move into-the-money, and wing strategies normally have at least one option at- or in-the-money.

In general, both a generic wing strategy and the best event risk protection will be options that limit loss on the current portfolio to a pre-specified level and that also permit you to take advantage of potential short-term price aberrations to execute longer-term strategy decisions at attractive price levels. Thus, owning an out-of-the-money put or selling an at-the-money covered call is often a part of this strategy. The call strategy will be exercised if the market sees large volatility swings, but it is less protective because of the issue of control. That is, when you own the put, you are the one who chooses to exercise it. However, when you sell a call, you must trust to market levels and arbitrage opportunities to convince the new call owner that it is attractive to exercise it. The two are not the same. For example, suppose that the upward price movement is so swift and so quickly reversed that the call is not exercised. If there was no practical arbitrage opportunity on the other side due to chaotic conditions, such a call might not be exercised. This is not a usual case, but it has been known to happen especially in the OTC market. In that event, you would not have the protection that you had counted on.

You must be aware that unusual things happen in unusual markets. True event risk is hedged by having the protection exist even during chaotic markets. The most secure way of limiting loss is to own an exchange-traded put. Since the other part of a wing strategy usually has to do with re-purchasing the assets at attractive levels, there is less need for a secure execution, as there will always be another opportunity to attain the desired exposure.

CASE 15. MANAGING THE DERIVATIVES PORTFOLIO

Due to changes in the market environment, suppose that you have derivatives in your portfolio that are not specifically linked to particular assets or liabilities. These positions might have been taken on in a speculative outlook and add risk. To individually offset or even partially hedge each futures position, swap, or FRA can be timeconsuming and expensive. The usual solution is to consolidate the assorted non-matched derivatives into a portfolio and measure the net risk of the resulting derivatives portfolio.

Remember that most derivative products can be looked at in a number of different ways. For example, forward rate agreement is the same as a futures contract when measured in cash flows, and a series of forwards can be thought of as a swap. Equally, a swap can be looked at as owning two separate bonds with different cash flows—one fixed and one floating. This disaggregates the asset-liability offset. When an interest-rate swap is owned to receive fixed and pay floating, it is the same as owning the cash flows for a fixed-rate bond and being short the cash flows for a floating-rate bond. When we add a zero-coupon security with the same maturity as the swap, the fixed-rate cash flows become a fixed-rate bond. The hedge to this fixed-rate part of the swap is an offsetting cash flow equal to the notional principal of the swap, so that the floating-rate cash flows become a floating-rate note. Thus, the value of the swap is the net of the value of this fixed-rate bond minus the value of the floating-rate bond. To hedge the swap we need only hedge the equivalent floating-rate note, and a floating-rate note can be looked at as a series of short-term securities with monthly or quarterly "maturities" and reissuance. As an example, then, a note that floats semi-annually will have a sensitivity that falls between the sensitivity of a note that matures today and one that matures in six months, so a possible strategy is to add these series of short-term securities to the regular cash portfolio for calculation purposes and hedge them along with the other near-term paper.

With the disaggregation approach, you can see how important it is to determine the cash flows. Since a swap is just a series of FRAs and since FRAs can be replicated by futures, the entire derivative portfolio can be translated into a series of cash flows. These flows then can be netted out and a composite bond formed. This composite bond represents the risk of the entire derivative position that is not offset by specific assets or liabilities. However, remember to distinguish between speculative derivatives and those placed as hedges, since the derivatives placed as hedges certainly do not need to be re-hedged. Note that disaggregating the derivatives also allows more simple hedging of any non-vanilla deals that were placed. Since the portfolio is now represented as the net cash-flows, there will also be fewer transaction costs for hedging.

Once the assorted net cash flows are determined, they must be discounted to arrive at the current value. There are a number of methods for this. Creating a zero-coupon yield curve is one way to discount cash flows. A zero-coupon yield curve is a graph of yield against time, but it uses securities that have no income stream. This removes the reinvestment-rate risk component of return from the curve. A zero-coupon curve can be created by observing the market prices and yields of government issued zero-coupon securities of assorted maturities. Using the zero-coupon curve is more theoretically appropriate but can expose you to liquidity-premium mispricings. For more accuracy, you can construct a fitted, smooth curve to the more ragged actual curve. Spline regression methodology is the newest and hottest technique at the moment. However, curve smoothing can be done more simply as well. Using a ruler and doing the smoothing by hand can help minimize any aberrations due to specific liquidity problems.

This strategy becomes routine once the present value is obtained. You simply calculate the duration of the portfolio and offset it with an equally interest-rate-sensitive instrument. The problems are the same as hedging any interest-rate instrument. There will be cash-flow mismatches and volatility mismatches, and the hedge will be vulnerable to shifts in the yield curve. Here again it will be useful to gauge the relative dispersion of the hedge to the derivatives, as was demonstrated in Case 7.

CASE 16. CHANGING THE PROBABLE
PRICE DISTRIBUTION

There will be times when you simply do not like the payoff probabilities of a position, perhaps because of a price change over time. When the ratio of probable price to possible price spreads becomes too small, using derivatives can help improve the ratio. This is almost a classic example of the use of options. For example, owning puts and calls for the same issue at the same strike price gives the investor rights but not obligations. However, usually the cost of owning both options is prohibitive unless an increase in volatility or a large swing in price is expected. Sometimes, however, there are occasions where the ambiguity of the federal government's macroeconomic figures leads to several viable interpretations of the state of the economy and several opinions of attractive trade positions. In such a case, an increase in market volatility is a reasonable assumption.

Strategy 1—Buying Puts

Buying puts changes the probability distribution for a price taker by truncating the downside. There is also the case of selling a collar, that is, buying a put to establish a floor and selling a call to establish a cap. This creates a most favorable probable-to-possible ratio by limiting the possible decreases in price. By owning a floor, you receive payments when rates fall below the preset strike rate. However, this sacrifices some potential upside, since you must make payments when rates move higher than the preset strike rate. It does not become a loss, because the asset is owned at lower rates, but it truncates both the upside as well as the downside price moves.

Strategy 2—Buying Calls

Buying naked, out-of-the-money calls also provides a good probable-to-possible ratio at the cost of an upfront payment. Since the position is naked, this method obtains the asset at a low-probability price, which translates as a price below the long-term expectations for price. This does not actually truncate the probability distribution, but it makes a loss of more than one standard deviation extremely improbable. However, this strategy reduces the actual realized yield by the premium and requires a long-run horizon to be effective. After all, getting the call executed may require you to sit with the position somewhat underwater for a while. Seeing the price move low enough to be attractive will usually happen only when the short-term to intermediate-term expectations are such that even lower prices are due. This may happen because of excess supply or decreased demand or because the market expects either of the two to happen.

Strategy 3—Selling Puts

Selling a put also truncates the probability distribution, but it limits the advantage to an increase in prices. Unless you are already short the item, selling a put is best done as part of a combination strategy to recoup other commissions or premiums. Remember, selling a put is selling to someone else the right to sell to you. That is, you have a contingent obligation to purchase the asset at a price currently above the market. If you are already short, it provides a contingent offset to that short. However, if you are not short, then it has the possibility of doubling your exposure to the security. Owning one bond and selling a put on the same bond provides the same exposure to owning two bonds if the market moves.

Strategy 4—Wing Strategies

Another group of strategies that change the ratio of potential-to-probable price is the wing strategies discussed in Cases 14 and 9 on the subject of event risk. In this case, the risk involved for movements around the expected price are deemed acceptable, but "break-outs" need hedging. Wing strategies include buying calls at the upper or lower end of the price range and selling an offsetting call at or near the current market price. Be careful about pricing wing strategies, as they have a strong speculative audience. Generally speaking, when wing strategies are placed for reasons other than event risk, there is an assumption that sharp moves from the mean price will be sustained and it will be best to follow that move. Portfolio insurance is an example of that type of thought. The cash flows of such strategies are referred to as convex payoff strategies which are often short-term. Strategies that are based on reversion to the mean—assuming that price will fluctuate around the expected price and only gradually move away—are called concave payoff strategies. These are usually longer term. The payoff functions are used most often in asset allocation analysis. The incre-

Figure 4.40A.   Convex Payoff Strategy vs. Buy-and-Hold

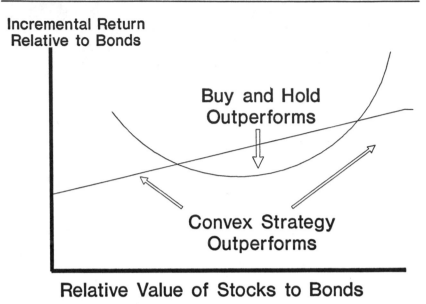

Incremental Return
Relative to Bonds

Buy and Hold
Outperforms

Convex Strategy
Outperforms

Relative Value of Stocks to Bonds

Figure 4.40B.   Concave Payoff Strategy vs. Buy-and-Hold

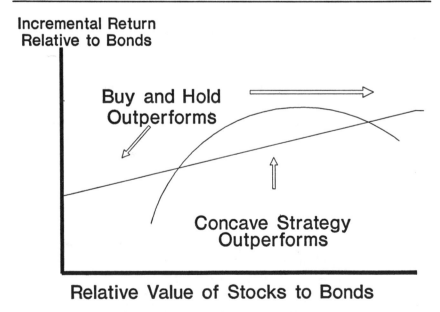

Incremental Return
Relative to Bonds

Buy and Hold
Outperforms

Concave Strategy
Outperforms

Relative Value of Stocks to Bonds

mental relative return of asset A is graphed on the y-axis and the relative value of asset B to asset A is on the x-axis. So a 100% holding of asset A is a horizontal line along zero while a 100% holding of asset B is a 45% line running from the origin. If you have a portfolio with a buy-and-hold strategy and compare it to one of these dynamic positions, we see that the wing strategies outperform buy and hold for large moves in bond prices. That is, when the relative value of this security versus another security is either high or low, then this convex function will outperform. On the other hand, a concave function outperforms if prices converge around the mean. See Figures 4.40 A and B for details.

Finally, it is important to remember that all of these strategies to "improve the odds" are options strategies, and options can become mis-priced, as they are particularly sensitive to unexpected changes in the price of the underlying.

CHAPTER 5

The Hidden Costs of Regulation, Accounting, Taxation, and Manpower

When we evaluate alternative solutions to problems of interest-rate risk, we often base a decision on relative cost. The costs we discussed in previous chapters are direct costs, which have a specific dollar worth attached. However, the choice of a hedging instrument can also be affected by other factors, such as regulatory issues, accounting methods, tax treatment, and servicing requirements or manpower hours. This chapter will be an overview to the subject of hidden costs. You should consult the appropriate experts before you begin any major programs.

REGULATORY ISSUES

Generally speaking, the regulatory environment is considered to be part of the industry, rather than a source of additional costs. However, the financial industry is more highly regulated than most, and is also seeing more ongoing regulatory legislation. Due to the uncertainty of future new legislation and how it will affect hybrid securities and derivatives, in this case there is indeed a regulatory cost, since choosing one hedge strategy over another could cost the corporation additional taxes in future. This section will examine the current regulatory environment.

The agencies with regulatory authority are the Federal Reserve Board (FRB), the Comptroller of the Currency (OCC), the Office of Thrift Supervision (OTS), the Commodity Futures Trading Commission (CFTC), and the International Swap Dealers Association (ISDA). These agencies sometimes overlap in their duties as they were established with different primary duties.

The Federal Reserve Board has as a primary duty to act as the agent of the U.S. Treasury in the global arena. It issues government securities of various maturities through auction at the Federal Bank of New York. It also puts into action the monetary policy decided upon by the U.S. government. The function we are mostly concerned with here is its duty to set reserve requirements for depositary institutions and also to regulate the makeup of the asset base for those depositary institutions. Both of these regulatory duties are designed to manage the risk exposure of commercial and non-commercial banks, and so protect the public. As well, margin trading falls within the jurisdiction of the FRB. The objective is to restrain excessive use of credit in the securities markets. Note that while the FRB sets the credit limits, the enforcement of these limits is the responsibility of the Security Exchange Commission (SEC) which regulates specific securities with an eye to protecting the public from fraud. The Comptroller of the Currency (OCC) is an agent of Congress and acts as the auditor for national banks. It examines the asset makeup and risk exposure of specific institions. The Office of Thrift Supervision acts in the same capacity for thrifts and savings institutions. It was created only recently as a result of the passage of the Financial Institutions Reform, Recovery and Enforcement Act (FIRREA) in 1989. The Commodity Futures Trading Commission was established as part of a 1974 amendment to the Commodity Trading Act. It also reports to Congress. All commodity exchange rules must be approved by the CFTC, and it has broad-based authority over anything that can be the subject of a futures contract. The International Swap Dealers Association is the only non-governmental agency to be discussed here. Although they have no official power, any institution desiring to participate in the swaps market is unofficially required to become a member. It has attempted to provide standardization for swaps and common solutions to problems.

With regard to the total derivatives product market, the OCC issues the essential guidelines for bank participation in all derivatives markets and usually leads the way to standardized practices. The OTS is primarily concerned with capital adequacy and encourages the practice of risk management via asset/liability gap management. As a result, the OTS seems to encourage the use of forwards and swaps, but it seems to have a bias against the use or misuse of futures and options. The FRB has also recently been involved with capital adequacy issues. In 1989 the FRB issued risk-based guidelines for U.S. banks capital requirement. This was in conjunction with the *Basle Accord*, which will require standardized levels of global bank capital by 1992.

Trading in futures is regulated by two federal agencies: the Commodity Futures Trading Commission and the Securities Exchange Commission (SEC). The CFTC regulates the trading of futures and options on futures contracts. The SEC regulates the trading of securities and options on securities. Thus, the difference between these agencies relates to the difference between the exchange-traded markets and the over-the-counter markets.

The CFTC enforces two major principles of futures trading; customer protection and market integrity. So it does regular daily analysis of the futures markets to assure no price manipulation or exchange disruptions occur.

Companies that broker futures contracts, known as *futures commission merchants* (FCMs), are regulated instead by the FRB and the OCC. Specifically, the FRB assures that for banks desiring to enter the business, benefits to the public will outweigh any disadvantages such as unsound market practices. The OCC assures that internal standards are developed, ethics standards and supervision are devised and maintained, and CFTC registration of personnel is obtained.

The trust department of a bank is constrained to operate within the context of the "prudent man" rule. This requires bank fiduciaries to perform their duties in the way that a prudent man would handle his own property or as the rule has been revised, to act as a prudent man who is familiar with such matters and is acting in accordance with the same goals.

Employee benefit plans are within the scope of the Employee Retirement Income Security Act of 1974 (ERISA), which includes a general guideline to diversify assets "unless . . . clearly prudent not to do so." As this applies to derivatives, the requirement is for prudence. ERISA guidelines still contain a good deal of ambiguity. Thus, while risk management is deemed prudent, questions remain as to which instruments are considered safe hedging instruments and whether futures and options are acceptable. The use of FRAs and swaps has been accepted, but there is on-going work to make these off-balance-sheet instruments more standardized and more regulated.

National banks are empowered to use financial futures in three different ways. The first is asset/liability management to hedge general interest-rate exposure for mismatched assets and liabilities. The second is that non-dealer operations may use futures to reduce their risk in overall investment activities. The third is more general, in that dealer activity should be in accordance with safe and sound banking practices and reasonably related to the bank's trading activities.

Swaps

For the swaps market, there has been long been domestic and international concern over the advent and popularity of currency and interest-rate swaps. The concern has focused on the capital adequacy of institutions as they performed off-balance-sheet transactions with little regulation, which opened them to unacceptably high levels of contingent credit risk. That is, by entering a long-term swap with a partner of lesser credit, a bank might find itself with uncollectable receivables at sometime in the future.

Domestically, although credit and capital are a concern, encouraging the process of interest-rate risk management has been a counterbalancing concern. For thrifts, the Federal Home Loan Bank Board, superceded by the OTS in 1989, was one of the first agencies to encourage interest-rate risk management. The FHLBB used a risk-adjusted capital requirement by issuing a maturity matching credit. This reduced capital requirements for thrifts that reduced interest-rate risk by minimizing their asset-liability gap. For example, if a thrift could keep its one-year and three-year cumulative gap under 15%, it could reduce its capital reserve requirement by 2%. As a new and more stringent encouragement to risk management, the recently published Thrift Bulletin 13 requires insured thrifts to set a limit on changes in interest income and changes in the net market value of the institution due to changes in interest rates. The new risk-based capital requirements set reserve requirements based on the sensitivity to interest-rate changes. Since thrifts now must hold one-half of the change in market value resulting from a change of 200 basis points in interest rates, a thrift will need to hedge its risk to reduce the capital reserves.

Internationally, the central banks have focused on the effect of swaps on bank credit risk and capital adequacy, rather than on interest-rate risk. There is a current plan for international capital regulation on a risk-adjusted basis, which is referred to as the Basle Accord. Under the agreement, institutions with high levels of interest-rate risk will be required to hold more capital. This will be fully in effect at the end of 1992 for the nations of the Group of Ten, including the United States, as well as for Switzerland and Luxembourg. This risk-adjusted posture of commercial banks will include off-balance-sheet financing methods and will weight the banks' activities according to their credit risk. As a result, capital held has been divided into two types: Tier 1 and Tier 2. The final result will be that the ratio of tier 1 capital to risk-adjusted assets must equal 4.00% by December 31, 1992. The ratio of total capital to risk-adjusted on- and off-balance-sheet items must equal 8%. Tier 1 capital consists of shareholders's equity, noncumulative perpetual preferred stock that is non-callable by the institution, and minority interests in consolidated subsidiaries. Tier 2 capital consists of general reserves, such as loan-loss provisions, other types of preferred stock, subordinated debt and the like. Total capital is the sum of Tier 1 and Tier 2 capital. The Basle Agreement also specifies that swaps must be marked-to-market for the capital requirements, but that the mark-to-market may be done by each institution according to its own methods. In addition, the Agreement will allow swaps to be netted only by an offsetting method called netting by novation, which allows for a mutual offset between two swaps only if there is a specific contract between two institutions for the same currency, the same value date, and the same delivery date.

One limitation to the Basle Agreement of interest to U.S. markets is that the Agreement does not apply to investment banks or insurance companies, although they are important swaps participants. This limitation exists because these companies are not regulated by the Federal Reserve Board. In addition, swaps dealers are not regulated by the SEC as registered broker-dealers because a swap is not defined as a security. However, the CFTC is currently reviewing whether swaps will be included in its jurisdiction in the future. In 1987, the CFTC published an Advance Notice of Proposed Rulemaking to consider the potential regulation of hybrid instruments. In 1988 it announced certain qualifications that will give swaps a "safe harbor" from regulatory interference. These unregulated swaps must (1) not be marketed to the general public, (2) be reasonably related to the counterparties' lines of business, (3) not be subject to any mark-to-market variation of a margin settlement program that works to eliminate the individualized credit risk of the swap, (4) have individualized terms, even if the documentation is standard, and (5) be structured so that the obligations created by the swap can be terminated only with the consent of the counterparty. The combined effect is that an unregulated swap must be non-standard and that one of the counterparties cannot act with the usual freedom of an intermediary.

For insurance companies, there has been recent and relatively untested legislation based on the Model Act adopted in 1987 by the National Association of Insurance Commissioners. This act provides for regulation of financial guaranty insurance, which is a type of insurance contract covering the obligations of issuers of public debt, including bank deposits and limited obligations. An issuer with a poorer credit rating sometimes buys this insurance contract to improve the rating on the security and lower its funding costs. In the market, these are generically referred to as GICs (Guaranteed Investment Contracts). Since some contracts provide insurance against changes in interest rates and foreign-exchange levels, rather than absolute principal protection, this legislation may regulate all types of GICs. However, it is intended to regulate the insurance contract, not the swaps dealers themselves.

Forward Rate Agreements

Like swaps, forward rate agreements are not "real" securities. As off-balance-sheet transactions, FRAs have only recently seen any attempts at regulation. Since the revised capital guidelines requirements were instituted in 1989 by the Federal Reserve Board under the Basle Agreement, there have been credit-based limitations to the execution and trading of FRAs, but such regulation is still in an early stage and additional developments can be expected.

ACCOUNTING COSTS

Accounting Methods

The primary underlying principles of accounting methodologies are accurate representation and timely recognition of earnings. Since recognition of earnings is open to interpretation for the most part, certain accounting standards and practices have been developed. The Financial Accounting Standards Board (FASB) issues bulletins on a periodic basis regarding new financial standards. These apply to all types of business income and earnings. For the financial derivatives sector, the current primary guideline is mark-to-market, which recognizes variances between value in the last reporting period and value in the current reporting period. Since any positive or negative changes go into earnings, it is important to understand which derivative under what circumstance must meet this mark-to-market criterion.

The mark-to-market procedure is one of three traditional accounting methods. The mark-to-market method treats the value of an investment as being at market level in each reporting period. That is, in every period an investment is treated as though it had been sold and a new, identical security had been purchased. Therefore, the difference in market value from the last period to the current period is recognized as either a gain or a loss to income. In a highly liquid market, the value is less liable to be manipulated. However, the mark-to-market treats realized and unrealized earnings in the same manner, so it can subject the income sheet to greater volatility. On the other hand, periodic repricing means that changes in credit, interest rates, exchange rates, and the like always will be fully incorporated. The changes from a mark-to-market method are usually fed into the income sheet, but sometimes an alternative shareholder's equity account is used, instead.

The accrual accounting method treats earnings as a constant, regular cash flow over the life of the investment. For example, when a zero-coupon security is purchased, its price is less than the face value, and the face value is received at maturity. Instead of recognizing the difference between the discount price and the face price as income at maturity, which after all is the day the owner will receive the check, the accrual method recognizes a little bit of income in each reporting period. Therefore, a 10-year zero will see income reported every year, not just a bullet payment at maturity. This method smooths the company's earnings flow, since it is much easier to forecast average expected earnings on the accrual system. However, a drawback occurs when an investment is terminated early or when the final value of the earning decreases dramatically due to credit changes. In that case, income recognized but not earned might not really exist. For income that is particularly subject to volatility, there can be problems with recognizing earnings ahead of time.

The lower-of-cost-or-market method immediately recognizes unrealized losses but defers any unrealized gains. This has an asymmetric effect by skewing the income sheet to the downside. This skew is also susceptible to timing effects. Since losing trades are recognized but winning ones are not until they are offset, then at any given reporting period two otherwise identical companies can look very different just due to the accounting methodology.

There is no regulation requiring consistent reporting methods, so a company may change methods as it desires. Quite often in fact, the method stating the largest income will be used for the annual report and the method stating the least amount of income will be used for tax reporting. As the Financial Accounting Standards Board (FASB) increases their efforts to standardize the reporting of off-balance-sheet items and derivative products in general, there may be less choice available in the future. This may result in additional taxes paid in the future.

When dealing with international assets and liabilities, there has been more regulation done on translating foreign currency amounts into domestic terms. Let's look at putting all the transactions into the same currency first. Translation of foreign exchange into the home currency is covered by Financial Accounting Standards Board Bulletin (FAS) #8 and FAS #52. FAS #8 was issued in 1976 and was superceded in 1981. It required that all the gains and losses resulting from foreign-exchange translation be entered on the income statement. Prior to FAS #8, losses were recorded on the balance sheet, but gains could be held indefinitely or used to reverse previously recorded losses. The method of exchange translation under FAS #8 was usually temporal, meaning that all current accounts were translated at current levels but noncurrent accounts were translated at the historical level in effect when the asset was acquired or the liability was incurred. In addition, any inventory valued on a historical cost also used the historical exchange rate from the time that the inventory was acquired. As a practical method, this ensured that temporary exchange levels could not be manipulated to give unrealistically high or low materials costs.

In 1981 FAS #52 became effective. This introduced the concept of functional currency. The functional currency is the currency in use in the main economy in which a company operates. This differs from the reporting currency, which is the currency in which the company's financial reporting is done. The distinction is made because a multinational company may have subsidiaries for which the functional currency is different from the reporting currency. However, the functional currency concept can subject an individual transaction to a double translation. For example, suppose a German subsidiary of a U.S. company makes a purchase in Swiss francs. The Swiss francs must be translated into deutschemarks, which then must be translated into U.S. dollars. While these currencies will offer little discrepancy in the double translation, using a more restricted currency can add to the apparent costs of a transaction by including a liquidity premium and two bid-ask spreads in the FX quotes. Any company operating in the Far East (with the exception of Japan and the yen) or in Eastern Europe will encounter this problem.

FAS #52 also allows translation gains and losses to bypass the income sheet and hit equity directly. It also requires that the translation be done on a current method, that is, that all assets and liabilities be translated at the current-market exchange rates. The equity account is used to show any variation or residual translation, so the equity account will reflect the volatility of participating in foreign-exchange derivatives. This alone may change whether or not a hedge is considered attractive.

When a swap is a dual-currency interest-rate swap, accounting procedures generally separate out the exchange rate. This is one case in which swaps are easier to use than other foreign derivatives. Since the exchange rate for the notional principal is specified in the contract, then that is the rate used in the accounting process. The difficulty comes in accounting for the cash flows. There is no specific standard of whether to account for them on an average exchange rate or a historical one.

Note that the mark-to-market rule varies depending on the type of business and the derivative security used. There will be more regulatory scrutiny for financial companies, for instance, while a basic commercial business will have no accounting restrictions on hedging its interest-rate risk and will be allowed to book the derivatives at the lower-of-cost-or-market value. Banks and insurance companies tread a middle road, with longer term financial investments carried at cost and amortized or depreciated over time. These gains and losses are recognized in income only when they are realized and the security transaction is closed out. However, any financial instruments carried as short-term investments are required to be marked-to-market. The broker/ dealer community has the most restrictive practices, and all financial-instrument assets must be marked-to-market. When securities are marked, the resulting gain or loss is immediately recognized as an income effect whether or not the position is closed out. The effect of volatility on unrealized gains and losses may be sufficiently unattractive that a broker/dealer will refrain from entering certain markets.

Futures

The most comprehensive guideline on the mark-to-market process for derivatives is FAS #80, Accounting for Futures Contracts. Most of FAS #80 discusses how to determine if a specific futures transaction is a hedge or not. All non-hedge, that is, speculative transactions are required to be marked-to-market and variations recognized as income immediately. Hedges may or may not be marked-to-market. A hedge that is marked-to-market can affect either the income account or a shareholder's equity account. Otherwise, if it is allowed to be carried at historical cost the variations can be deferred until the underlying instrument matures or is otherwise closed out.

FAS #80 defines a hedge in the following way. The price movements in the hedge vehicle must correlate closely with the underlying risky asset or liability. FAS #80 also addresses the question of a hedge vehicle that used to have a price correlation. When the correlation stops, so must the hedge accounting and any gains or losses must be immediately recognized. A hedge can be placed in anticipation, such as for event risk or purchasing an asset. However, the expected date of the event transaction, the type of underlying involved, the principal amount of the underlying, and the expected maturity must all be identified for an investment to count as a hedge.

One difficulty with using futures contracts as a hedge is that there is no definition of a macro-hedge. A futures position can be defined as a hedge only on a specific security or group of securities. Any hedge based on macro-economic risk is treated as speculative and so must be marked-to-market.

Forwards

One of the reasons that the FRA market is still so popular is the accounting differences between FRAs and futures. As opposed to futures, FRAs are not required to be marked-to-market, as they are exclusively off-balance-sheet items. Although there is a current trend to require all derivatives to be accounted for on a mark-to-market basis, this is likely to take many years to put into effect if it does occur at all. The mark-to-market treatment with the accompanying volatility of gains/losses is called accounting-profit volatility and is seen as an undesirable occurrence.

Swaps

Swaps are an unusual case because the standards are new and rudimentary. Therefore swaps are the hedge instrument most subject to "interpretative" accounting procedures. Swaps are officially an off-balance-sheet instrument, as are forwards. Thus, these derivatives can affect the payables and receivables, and now can affect the capital requirements under the Basle Agreement, but need not affect the calculation of certain key financial ratios. However, this non-standard treatment is changing. Moreover, since interest-rate swaps are a way of modifying or exchanging the original cash flows for a more preferred structure of cash flows, they can be treated as a part of the original transaction or as a completely separate entity.

In addition to indirect costs, swaps have indirect benefits, which also usually go unmeasured. For example, an interest-rate swap can lower a firm's average cost of borrowing. It provides an alternative to usual methods of borrowing and can delay the need to renegotiate a loan. As a result, the firm can take advantage of short-term market inefficiencies and exploit any comparative credit advantage. Second, swaps also have the advantage of separating out two decisions, since the choice of how to fund is different from the choice of a rate at which to fund. Third, swaps are more advantageous than issuing debt or equity, in that regulations are simpler and require no lead-time for registration. Finally, swaps let companies acquire funding from non-standard portions of the market. This allows the firm to "spread around" its name and preserve its credit supply from becoming devalued through too much use in any one sector. However, this advantage may disappear due to the capital requirements of the Basle Agreement that are soon to become effective. Since these capital requirements are risk-adjusted, swap counterparties with poorer quality names will need more capital behind them. This last indirect benefit is a bit subtle. The swaps market allows firms to mildly speculate on the direction of interest rates without exposing themselves to more risk than is acceptable. Most of the costs of this speculation are opportunity costs implied by a higher-than-necessary funding cost if they are wrong. There are few absolute and large cash "hits" to being wrong about the direction of rates.

Because many of the accounting procedures for swaps are still being formulated, the periodic payment from a swap may be recognized in various ways depending on the company. The essential underlying principle is to accurately reflect the economic substance of a transaction. To do this, there are a number of issues to be addressed by the accountants. First is the question of whether interest-rate swaps should be on the balance sheet and, if they are, whether they should be fully or partially entered. This question arises when the swap has been done to provide asset/liability gap management. A second question concerns whether the revenues and expenses associated with the swap should be treated in the income statement differently than other expenses and revenues. Related to this is how the Internal Revenue Service treats the associated cash flows. The periodic payments of a swap have been variously treated as interest income, exchange gains or losses, or even "other income and expense."

As a general rule of thumb, the purpose and final effect of the swap is the important issue for determining how swaps payments will be recognized. Any swap executed to hedge either an asset or a liability should be treated in the same fashion as that asset or liability to minimize accounting volatility. However, if the swap is a speculative event, then it should absolutely be marked-to-market to reduce risk.

The one difficulty in the mark-to-market concept is that some non-vanilla swaps are difficult to accurately price. However, for the more standard currency swaps or fixed-to-floating swaps, this will not be a problem even in a thin market since the base rates are very liquid. Like all other investments, it is not until maturity that a final profit or loss can be determined for a swap, particularly a puttable swap, but questions remain as to how a swap should be treated while ongoing. Regardless of whether the accounting method is mark-to-market or accrual, should there be a running Profit/Loss for the internal books, thereby again subjecting those books to volatility, or should any anticipated flows be recognized early? Should swap flows be accounted for as variations in a company's funding costs? These questions have added to the confusion about accounting procedures by raising arguments about the essential nature of the cash flows and whether they are interest or whether they are separate transactions to be treated as ordinary gains and losses. Regardless of the accounting procedure chosen for tax reports or for internal departmental treatment, the swaps cash streams on the annual report are usually tied to the underlying debt issue. Thus, these are "adjustments" to interest expense, which is appropriate because it adds to or decreases the interest amount associated with the debt for the period.

Swaps accounting can also use the cost method, which means that any interim profits or losses need not be recognized as such but can be deferred. Some authorities feel that all swaps should see mandatory marking-to-market regardless of their purpose or effect. This is particularly so when treating the swap cash stream as an adjustment to funding costs.

A choice must also be made for accounting at termination. A termination can be at maturity or it can end before the actual maturity date if the counterparty wishing to end early pays his counterparty a fee. The fee is usually tied to the interest-rate differential to approximate cash flows lost by ending early. For accounting purposes a question remains as to whether the fee is part of the other gains and losses or whether it is a premium to costs and should be amortized for the rest of the hypothetical lifetime of the swap. Currently, the Financial Accounting Standards Board believes that early terminations of swaps should be treated like the termination of futures positions since both terminations minimize interest-rate risk. This interpretation means that the gain or loss of the position is deferred and is recognized only as the interest is actually accrued. This is a logical interpretation if the counterparty receiving the fee turns around and uses it to enter another swap in order to remain hedged.*

The following example of common treatment of a swap will illustrate some of the complexity. Company CDE assumes a credit risk to reduce basis risk and move from floating-to-floating funding via a plain-vanilla swap. CDE's counterparty is Company DEF, which has a lesser credit rating and therefore must pay more for funding in conventional markets. Because CDE has the better credit rating, its cost of funding is less for both fixed and various floating rates. However, it has a comparative advantage over DEF in the LIBOR-based market. That is, while the difference between costs for the two companies in the market based on T-bills is .75%, it is 1.25% in the LIBOR-based market. See Figure 5.1.

The base of the swap is for both companies to borrow $100,000 for the same period of time, two years for this example. This match is what makes the additional swap most simple. CDE borrows based on LIBOR plus .75% and DEF borrows on T-bill plus 1.25%. To employ its advantage, CDE pays DEF T-bill + 1.25% and DEF pays CDE LIBOR + 1.75%. In this way, CDE is paying out .75% more than it has to on a T-bill basis, but is receiving 1.25% more than it could otherwise get on a LIBOR basis. Equally, DEF is receiving the same amount on a T-bill basis, but paying .25% less than it could otherwise fund on a LIBOR basis. Both companies are experiencing benefits of trade. The net effect is that CDE is transforming its LIBOR debt to a T-bill debt and getting an improvement of .25% on funding costs. DEF is also improving its funding costs by .25%. As for the mechanics, the $100,000 notional principal is not exchanged. The credit risk assumed by CDE is minimized, in that the actual cash transfers are the differential between the two payments. For example, if LIBOR is at 7.00% at the beginning and T-bills are at 7.22%, then the cash flow is a payment from CDE to DEF of 8.47%, or $705.83 for the first month, and DEF

---

*Accounting issues for swaps become more complex when one of the swap counterparties is a bank acting as an intermediary. The accounting position of a money center bank that holds a book of swaps is very complicated and even less standardized. The bank may be a principal counterparty in some swaps, act as intermediary to others, or use an unhedged swap (one with no underlying debt) as a vehicle for speculation. All of these require different treatments in order to reflect the economic value of the transaction. See Benjamin Neuhausen's "Accounting Guidelines for Swaps in the United States" for a more complete picture.

Figure 5.1.   Basis Swap

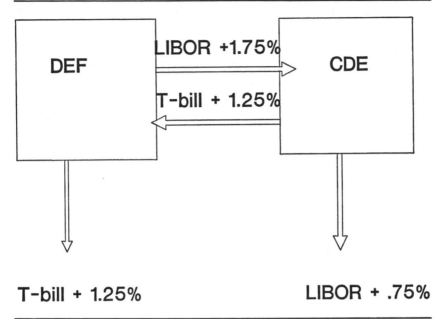

T-bill + 1.25%   LIBOR + .75%

pays an effective 8.75%, or $729.17. The actual payment of the differential is a check for $23.34 from DEF to CDE. Future movements between T-bills and LIBOR will account for the size of the payment exchanged and for who pays whom.

Next, the basic arrangements must be translated to the accounts side. First, since the principal amount is not actually exchanged, the current practice is to value the attached borrowing (the $100,000 debt) at its transaction price, so that the bond or loan issuance will be equal and offsetting items on the balance sheet. Second, the associated swap must be valued. One way is to treat the present value of the swap as a payable/receivable offset. The present value is calculated as the present value of the cash flows. The discount rate to calculate the present value is generally the cost of funds. Since we are dealing with floating rate funding, this will change over time. One of the reasons this practice is not standard is that it subjects the earnings of the company to quite a bit of variability as the present value changes. Remember that the present value will change both as time passes and as discount rates change, that is as the yield curve shifts. In addition, if the swap is a currency swap, it must be handled as two transactions: a currency borrowing and a swap transaction. Also, the swap is not consistent with the accounting treatment of FRAs, even though the cash flows of a swap are the equivalent to a series of FRAs. Therefore, the more common practice is to treat the swap as an off-balance-sheet item. This makes it a swap more appealing to the company at any rate, since there is no effect on key financial ratios when the financing decisions are off the balance sheet. These ratios are followed closely by industry analysts and could have an impact on the company's stock price, so keeping them stable is important.

Options

Options are subject to an underlying accounting decision established by The American Institute of Certified Public Accountants. In their seminal paper *Accounting for Options*, the Institute determined that options must meet the criteria for hedges to be treated as such. However, once a purchased option meets those requirements, its price is divided into time value and intrinsic value. The time value is then amortized over the life of the option and only the intrinsic value is subject to the mark-to-market requirement. The intrinsic value is defined as the difference between the strike price and the market price. However, when an option is sold, there is no split in value and no amortization of time value. As a result, the premium gained from the sale is often judged less attractive than the additional volatility from the mark-to-market of the total premium. When an option does not meet the criteria for a hedge, it is marked-to-market for the entire premium whether it is bought or sold.

Compound Options

The accounting method for captions, floortions, and swaptions is not clear-cut. However, the basic practice at the moment is to use the mark-to-market method when these compound options are part of a trading portfolio. The accrual method can be used when these instruments are used to reduce funding costs by a corporate issuer. When a compound option is purchased as an interest-rate risk management tool, the cost of the premium can be amortized over the life of the contract, because the option has no value if it is not exercised. If it is used specifically as an asset/liability management tool, it should be treated the same as the underlying swap, irrespective of whether the compound option is exercised or not. Thus, the premium should be amortized over the period that the gap is being managed. The rationale for amortizing the premium whether or not the compound option is exercised is that its purchase is a hedge. If it is not exercised, it is because a more attractive cap, floor, or swap was purchased. Thus, the premium is a part of the cost of the underlying hedge, since its purchase was to protect against less attractive terms.

TAX COSTS

The treatment of derivatives in the current tax law lags behind practice, since all derivatives are relatively new. As the accounting practices become more standardized, we can expect more clear-cut tax regulations.

Futures

The treatment of futures contracts was addressed in the Tax Reform Act of 1984, and again in 1986 and 1987. The hedges are not always subject to year-end mark-to-market, although they may be marked for accounting purposes. Accounting for annual reports need not be the same as accounting for the IRS. In general, more income is desired for the annual report but less is desired for taxation purposes. Thus, sometimes income is recognized earlier for external reporting by using the accrual method and the more conservative lower-of-cost-or-market method is used for tax filing.

For taxation purposes, hedges are assumed to produce ordinary income or losses and such income or loss from a hedge is recognized when the position is closed out. However the non-hedge futures are marked-to-market at the end of the year and the income is treated as capital gains. Although there is currently no incremental difference between long-term and short-term capital gains, all speculative futures income is treated as 60% long-term gains and 40% short-term gains.

Swaps

Swaps have more complex tax regulations because of both the timing of the flows and the net exchanges of payments. For example, some swaps and interest-rate caps see the notional principal exchanged and some do not. Moreover, interest payments are generally treated as deductions from income. For the recipient of a lump sum payment, this lump sum must be included as income and amortized over the life of the contract. For instance, notional principal payment for a nine-year swap can be spread out as income over those nine years.

Although currency swaps are accounted as two separate transactions, a currency swap identified as a hedge may be treated as one transaction for tax purposes. For the transfer of a swap or its termination, the principle seems to be that they are deductible in accordance with the method of accounting of the payor of the monies if the recipient of the lump sum at termination receives no future benefit from that payment, that is, if he reinvests it in another swap to continue the hedge. In that case, the periodic payments are also deductible in accordance with the company's normal accounting practices.

There also are tax implications to a company's normal accounting practices. If the gains or losses are ordinary income, then marking-to-market could increase tax payments for a company, while the accrual method more closely matches income with expenses. However, the accrual method is more subject to manipulation than the mark-to-market method. The accrual and mark-to-market methods are the usual choices for the income stream of derivatives because of the skew that results to earnings from using the lower-of-cost-or-market method. To be safe, if the underlying debt is treated mark-to-market, so should the swap. If the debt is on the accrual method, the swap should be as well.

These payment deductions are usually ordinary income, not a capital gain or loss. A capital loss occurs from the sale or exchange of a capital asset. Since swaps are off-balance-sheet items for the most part, they accrue to ordinary income. If they are on the balance sheet, then the sale or other transfer of the contract might be treated as a capital loss. If the payments are received, they are treated as income depending on the company's accounting practices. These, as described above, will influence when the income is recognized.

Compound Options

For compound options, the same principles apply. Any payment made as part of a Notional Principal Contract Transaction is generally amortized over the life of that contract for taxation purposes. A Notional Principal Contract Transaction include swaps, swaptions, forward rate agreements, and any other contract involving a notional principal amount.

MANPOWER COST

Recalculating the Hedge

Servicing requirements, or the manpower hours needed to manage derivatives positions, are an indirect cost that is usually associated with how often a hedge must be recalculated.

For example, an FRA or FXA requires no interim servicing because the contract locks-in an interest rate for the period of concern. Futures positions require irregular servicing, which is based on price moves. For futures, the hedge ratio should be recalculated for every point or so of price movement in either the future or the underlying cash market. In addition, the correlation between the two markets should be run every two or three weeks so that any divergences can be seen early. Moreover, since a futures contract can be accounted for as a hedge only if there is a high degree of price correlation, the price correlation must be closely monitored, particularly when a cross-hedge is placed. This will also avoid losing money on both the cash market and the hedge.

Futures strips, swaps, or a series of forward contracts should be reevaluated when there is a significant movement in rates or when the cost of funding moves significantly due to a yield-curve shift or twist. It may pay to terminate a swap early or enter into another swap in that circumstance.

Options, on the other hand, have such a susceptibility to time decay that the wise investor will reevaluate the hedge every day. Therefore, while the upfront costs of an option can be less, the manpower required to service an option can be large. This is especially so if evaluating and re-calculating the hedge every day can require considerable time, such as when the position is complex.

A certain degree of expertise is needed for the person monitoring the position. The manpower hours needed to manage a derivatives position will exponentially increase in reverse proportion to the expertise of the worker, and there is also the question of accuracy. Therefore, the cost of managing the position will increase as the level of expertise needed increases. This cost also directly related to the size of your participation in the derivatives market.

Cash Management

A second indirect cost is the present value at any given time of the interim cash flows outward. Indeed, these flows are costly to manage regardless of their direction.

There are several computer systems that will provide help for a fee. Among them is SPAN, offered by the Chicago Mercantile Exchange. SPAN is a margin management system for companies hedging in futures. It lets them know about upcoming margin requirements and helps to minimize the flows. This margin requirement is an expense when dealing with futures and options on exchanges. The continual mark-to-market reduces the exposure to credit risk but equally ties up short-term cash. In addition, there is a lack of predictability to those cash flows, which means that any inward flows might soon become outward flows. As a result, margin flows must be set aside and invested overnight each night. This exposes the company to an opportunity cost, since it might be more advantageous to invest for another time period. It also means that a successful hedge might act as a cash drain for the company. After all, if the underlying cash position increases in value but is not marked-to-market, the offsetting derivative hedge is probably losing money on a mark-to-market basis and the successful hedge is a cash drain for the company.

As an alternative, a company might choose to do the cash management in-house. However, this involves a certain level of involvement to be cost-efficient. Setting up an in-house system involves the purchase of the system itself, the cost of developing, adapting, or purchasing the computer programs to run the cash management, and the cost of the expert to develop or maintain the system after it is implemented. Expert help should also be obtained in setting up a fund for cash variations. The size of the hedge reserve will depend on the market as well as on the net size of the position. Some markets are simply subject to a greater degree of short-term price moves than others, and the hedge reserve will need to be larger than for the same size position in another market.

When using futures for a hedge against interest-rate risk, some of the indirect costs can be addressed and minimized if the company prepares a statement of objectives before placing the position. See Figure 5.2 for an example. This should specify the goal to be achieved, the means of doing so, how and who shall monitor the hedge position, what the specific concerns are for the position, why this hedge vehicle has been chosen, and under what circumstances the position shall be terminated early. After the hedge is unwound, a companion report should evaluate the success of the hedge and any unanticipated problems that arose, and it should note how close actual costs were to estimated costs. This method guarantees excellent recordkeeping and achieving internal discipline. It can also offer an addition to tickets for audit purposes and serve as an educational tool for new employees. However, it also takes additional man-hours to prepare and means higher administrative costs, but it should pay for itself by narrowing the focus of the hedge and helping in performance measurement.

Figure 5.2.   Hedging Fixed-Income Securities with Futures Contracts: Statement of Objectives

---

Objective—To provide reduced volatility in the net cost of a fixed-income portfolio consisting of 60% corporate bonds and 40% government securities.

Means—This will be done by selling bond futures contracts on the Chicago Board of Trade. The hedge ratio used to determine the number of contracts sold will be calculated using the conversion factor model.

Monitoring—Both the price correlation of the portfolio to the futures contract will be followed and the duration of the two instruments will be measured on a weekly basis. The hedge ratio will be re-calculated weekly, or when market volatility exceeds 12%.

Rationale—For periods of credit stability, the price correlation between the corporate and government bonds sectors of the market have seen a close price correlation. Offsetting the cash portfolio with futures will limit capital losses while requiring little additional funds for margin. Also the futures market offers good liquidity for adjusting the hedge.

Risks and Concerns—Price correlation is poor between futures and cash instruments for changing credit conditions, and so should be closely monitored. Should credit spreads change dramatically, there is a chance of seeing a loss on both cash and hedge instruments. Also, the futures market is subject to excess volatility at times. This could cause periodic undervaluation to the hedge vehicle and a resultant mispricing in the mark-to-market.

A related cost to operating in the derivatives markets is the need for a compliance officer or department. The role is to assure compliance with the federal laws and regulations governing derivatives. There are a variety of agencies that coordinate in the regulatory arenas. For example, when dealing in futures contracts the firm is potentially subject to the SEC, the CFTC, and possibly the FRB or OCC.

Commissions

A third indirect cost is relative commission costs. As a rule of thumb, the more standardized the product and the more liquid the market, the lower the commission costs will be. This is because a standard product requires a lesser degree of expertise and because liquidity attracts entrants to the market so that competition drives down the commissions. However, a standard product is also less likely to offer the desired degree of protection, so there will be a tradeoff. Each investor must decide how much of a tradeoff he can tolerate. This decision will influence how specialized a product he will buy.

Another rule of thumb for commissions is that 2.5 times the bid-ask spread is a "normal" commission. Anything wider indicates a specialized, that is, illiquid market or few market-makers.

Reversing a Position

A frequently unacknowledged cost is the cost of changing your mind. There will always be a fee associated with unwinding a position early. Therefore, if you are not certain about the time frame in which protection will be needed, or if you want to hedge but are uncertain of specifics, then this cost must be kept in mind.

Although terminating a futures position will involve no additional costs, it will subject the holder to short-term price risk, since price paths are uncertain even if the final convergence of price is relatively sure. Terminating a swap early will add a fee based on the interest-rate differential at the time of termination. Terminating an FRA or FXA can often require adding the opposite position to the portfolio, which can double the costs and expose the position to risk.

Reversing an options position can also be expensive on a percentage basis because of the time decay of the position. However, since upfront costs are less, the absolute dollar cost is usually not that great. Options can be reversed by entering a similar position in the opposite direction or by canceling out the first position. For example, if you are originally long bond calls with a strike of 94-00, that is if you own the right to buy bonds at 94-00, you can either sell these calls or buy puts with a strike of something around the same strike price. For instance, if you buy puts with a strike of 93-00, there will be the cost of an additional premium, but there will also be more upside potential. If the market moves to 94-16, then you can exercise the call for 16/32 profit minus the premium paid and the put will expire worthless. If price moves to 92-16, then you can exercise the put with a profit of 16/32 minus the premium paid and the call will expire worthless. If you sell the calls, you will pay out less premium but you will no longer have any profit opportunities. In that case, the loss will be less, but it will be locked in. After all, a commission must be paid to the broker whether you sell the calls or buy puts. If time is close to expiration, the premium will be less because of a smaller theta.

Systems Cost

A final indirect cost that may apply to some companies is systems cost—the cost of establishing and operating a computer system to evaluate hedge decisions or the cost of paying someone else to do it.

Today, it is nearly impossible to evaluate all the costs and relative hedge ratios on an ongoing basis without a systems capability. This can be as simple as a PC or as complex as an internationally linked network for mainframes and PCs. It can involve having an analytics department or making the evaluation part of the risk-takers job. However, if your company currently has little or no computer capability, establishing a system will be a major expenditure.

Many banks and brokerages will offer their services if they feel that more trades will be generated, but the equipment and the advice will be piecemeal and not necessarily what your company needs. There are also software packages for PCs that will look for mispricings in all the derivatives markets. However, because the software is designed outside your company, it may have biases. This is particularly true for the options pricing systems.*

In general, it takes a minimum of one accounts person and one operations person for every one or two risk-takers, so farming out the job

---

*I refer you to chapter 6 for a discussion of options pricing problems.

of managing the derivatives may be very attractive. However, you must decide whether you can trust the outsider to manage these positions. The purpose of this text is to guide you to better decision-making, not to suggest that you drop the problem in someone else's lap.

Hiring an expert to set up a system is probably the best choice. However, before you hire an expert, you should draw up a set of objectives. Since a goal can be achieved in a number of ways, deciding ahead of time what priorities you have and what capabilities you need will make the expert's job easier. You should consider whether your business will be primarily domestic or whether you will need foreign-exchange capabilities, what your accounting procedures will be, how you will handle commission costs, whether you want the capability to evaluate futures only, whether other derivative products will be managed by brokers, whether you will simply want a spreadsheet to keep track of the derivatives positions with their management to be handled outside, and similar factors.

Even if a bank or brokerage offers a "free advisory service," you should remember that the costs of the service will be built into the commission. Transferring consultants fees to commissions costs is acceptable if that is what you want to do. Otherwise, look for an unbiased opinion by paying the fee upfront. Also remember that the risk ultimately will be borne by you. Although the broker who manages your account may be very sorry for his mistakes, you are the one who will pay the costs of the broker's mismanagement. Thus, decisions about the relative attractiveness of a particular hedge strategy are very individual. This is actually an economic "good" since it means that there usually will be market participants to take both sides of a given position. As a result, hedging costs will most likely be within the range considered attractive. This sort of individuality also makes it possible to use short-term price variations to lock in attractive hedge programs.

CHAPTER 6

Forecasting Outlooks and Pricing Securities

FORECASTING

Hedging strategies are very dependent on your "view," or opinion, on price action. You have **view on the market** when you accept the current market price as a given, but choose to buy or sell based on whether you believe that price will increase or decrease for a particular time period.

There are two basic ways to evaluate a market and form an opinion on price: **top-down evaluation** and **bottom-up evaluation.** In turn, this evaluation is conducted by using one of two basic methods of analysis: **fundamental analysis,** which examines the supply/demand factors for the market, or **technical analysis,** which examines repetitive patterns of price behavior. Top-down analysis is more usually fundamental. Bottom-up analysis sees more diversity in the methodology used.

Top-Down Market Evaluation

The top-down method starts with the general state of the economy and tries to determine which sectors of the economy will see the best growth. The economy has seen recurrent fluctuation in expansion and contraction since the 1930s, which is called the business cycle. If we start the cycle from a period of moderate growth, we see that positive growth and unfulfilled consumer demand lead businesses to borrow for capital investment and use any free capacity for expansion. This is the boom phase. Next, as free capacity diminishes and the cycle reaches a period of high growth, the excess demand for credit causes interest rates to rise and the unemployment rate falls as businesses add staff. Next, as consumers acquire greater debt loads at higher interest rates, demand begins to slacken. Businesses cut back due to below-expected returns on investments and excess inventory. Unemployment rates start to edge upward, consumer confidence in spending decreases, businesses continue to cut back on capacity, and interest rates fall due to poorer investment conditions. The bottom of this contraction is known as a recession, which is defined as a period of negative GNP growth. Finally, as interest rates reach sufficiently low levels, investment interest is stirred and the growth cycle starts again.

Most of the top-down evaluation involves figuring out where we are in the business cycle and how long it will be until we reach the next phase. This has important implications for allocating assets. To diversify, you would place a small percentage of assets in a more slowly growing area and place the bulk of your investment in the sector expected to see better growth. For example, cyclical stocks precede or match the business cycle, while defensive stocks are expected to outperform in slow growth or negative growth situations. Therefore, if you think that the cycle is approaching a boom or growth stage, you would want to own cyclical stocks. If you anticipate a growth stage, you would choose to own defensive stocks. For a second example, fixed-income securities are expected to preserve wealth in a recession, while in boom environments investments in equity offer more attractive returns. Therefore, in a boom phase you will want a higher proportion of equities, but you will shift into high-quality, fixed-income investments as the growth cycle ends. For a third example, you will want to own fixed-rate, fixed-income securities when you are investing at the top of the cycle, you will want floating-rate investments when you are investing during the recessionary phase.

Keep in mind, however, that each cycle is different. The demographics of every country change over time so that no expansion is quite like any other expansion and no recession is quite like any other recession. Certainly, we can note that the U.S. business cycle has been growing shorter in the past 40 years and that the absolute growth differential between boom and bust has been decreasing. Perhaps we will see in the years ahead the complete disappearance of the business cycle under the pressures of countercyclical monetary policy and the presence of a universe of investors seeking to take advantage of cyclical variations.

Fundamental analysis examines supply/demand factors to estimate where we are in the cycle and exactly how long each section will be. The first factor examined is the federal economic statistics that are announced monthly and quarterly. By keeping an eye on changes in GNP, the federal discount rate, the unemployment rate, Producer and Consumer Price Indices, and a number of more minor statistics, you can look at the trend in the numbers over time to see if the economy is expanding or contracting. In addition, since the Federal Reserve Bank works in a countercyclical manner, you might be able to infer that a tightening of credit by the Fed means good economic health while an easing of credit means a slowdown.

In addition to the statistics that reflect the longer term business cycle, which can last for several years, there are annual trends in employment, spending, and credit. The statistics announced by the government are "de-trended," or seasonally adjusted, to smooth out minor cyclical variations. For example, construction spending and building permits traditionally increase in Spring. A great deal of effort is spent to put the trend effects back into these seasonally adjusted numbers so that the actual figures can be compared with the adjusted ones. The actual numbers can show developing structural changes in the business cycle before they become overt. Since the best time to make an investment is before a trend becomes obvious, this type of analysis can be very profitable.

In addition to examining the business cycle, the fundamental analysis methods also examines three main markets in which supply/demand studies can be done to find opportunities for above-average future growth. These markets are in household spending, resource spending, and borrowing or funds spending. To illustrate, let's look at a quick overview of the economy. Households spend money on consumption and on savings. As total household income increases, both segments of spending increase. However, as disposable income increases, a larger percentage of disposable income will be spent and consumption will increase over savings. If the economy is in an expansion as well, there will be a great deal of growth in consumer spending. This might be the time to invest in retail goods or to buy a restaurant. The money from this spending then flows back to the businesses, which use the money to run the company and invest the money to expand. This is the resource market. This market provides the national income via wages to workers, rents, profits, and the like. The resource market is the place to look for investment opportunities as the economy emerges from the contraction phase. The funds market reflects the supply and demand between savings supplied by consumers and borrowings by businesses. The savings from consumers tends to be relatively steady, but the demand from businesses will be greater as interest rates are perceived to be lower and more attractive. The funds market is the place to look for fixed-rate borrowings just at the height of the expansion phase and for floating-rate borrowings as the economy emerges from the contraction phase. During the contraction phase the most reliable investment over time has been U.S. government borrowings.

An example will demonstrate the analysis of the supply/demand factors for the three major markets. Basically, as price increases for a product, more companies are enticed into the market to supply that product. If we chart price versus quantity, we see an upward sloping curve. The slope of the curve will depend on how much the price has to increase to elicit more quantity into the market. Although the curve appears to be a regular and steady increase, in actuality the additional supply moves in jerks and starts, demonstrating sticky price action. For example, at $3 each there may be 10,000 cans of applesauce on the market. If the price increases to $4, there might be 15,000 cans available. However, at $3.10 we may see no increase over 10,000 cans. Nonetheless, we can accept that, as the general price level of a product increases, more producers see the opportunity for profits and more product will be offered to the market. However, prices do not rise indiscriminately. As the price increases, consumers purchase less of the product, substituting another, lower-priced product or going without. Therefore, the market will look for an equilibrium where the supply of each product equals the demand. This equilibrium level will define the market price. However, the market price is not stable, as the equilibrium shifts in response to changing factors of supply and demand. By looking at longer term influences on supply and demand, an analyst can make inferences on whether demand or supply will be changing in a significant manner over the foreseeable future. This allows opportunities to spot short-term mispricings from the longer term price trend.

The difficulty with fundamental analysis is that it depends heavily on how much importance is given to each of a number of different inputs to the process. To continue example, the supply of applesauce will depend on the various factors that influence the apple crop, the supply of apples in inventory from the last harvest, labor costs for running the manufacturing process, the cost of fuel for cooking and canning, the price of gasoline as it influences delivery, the cost of substitutable canned fruits, and more. Demand will also be influenced by many factors. Each of the many inputs are difficult to calculate and, since the concept is to take advantage of a short-term aberration to make long-term profits, you might end up with an unprofitable position for quite a while before deciding that you made a mistake. On the other hand, the underlying supply/demand factors will ultimately determine the price, regardless of any short-term speculative mispricings.

In using fundamental analysis for asset allocation or picking investment opportunities, we look for the critical variables that influence price. Certain elements are more important at some times than at others. As a general rule, the scarcest necessary factor has the greatest influence. As each factor becomes more common, it lessens in influence. To continue the example, if a suddenly bad harvest occurs, the number of apples available will be the primary influence. However, if the price of fuel for the cooking process triples in price, that will be the primary variable. On the demand side, a product is generally less sensitive to price changes if it is a necessity or if there are few or no substitutes. For example, when Xerox produced the first copy machine, there was no real substitute for several years and Xerox had a almost a free hand with the price of copy machines. As price increased dramatically, interest in the machines waned. However, as the technology was duplicated by other manufacturers, the price of the machines came down.

Bottom-Up Market Evaluation

Bottom-up market evaluation involves looking at each security or asset class individually. Using either fundamental or technical analysis, you calculate a theoretical value for the security by discounting expected future cash flows. If this theoretical price is greater than the current market price, the security is undervalued by the market; if the theoretical value is less than the market price, the security is overvalued. The goal is to buy undervalued securities and to sell overvalued securities.

The calculate the theoretical value in a fundamental way, we must look at each class of derivatives separately. However, there is an underlying process of discounting cash flows that applies to all asset pricing. The underlying idea is that a dollar paid to you at some time in the future is worth less than a dollar today. After all, if you were paid the dollar today, you could invest it and have an amount greater than one dollar at the future time. The rate of interest at which you could invest is the discount rate. This is usually the return you could earn on an alternative investment with the same characteristics. Since the practice is to pay compound interest, or interest on prior interest, as we move forward in time those payments to be received more than one period in the future need the discount rate compounded to calculate their worth today. The value today of monies received in future periods is known as the present value. Equally, the value in next period for today's investments is the future value. The most accurate way to evaluate these cash flows is to look at each one as if it were a separate investment. For example, if the investment you are trying to evaluate offers cash flows annually, the most accurate evaluation will be to discount each cash flow at the appropriate rate for that specific maturity. See Figure 6.1 for the general equation and an example of how to use it.

While I have discussed the most common type of fundamental analysis, it comes in other forms as well. For example, after trading or investing in a market for several years, one's intuition can become highly honed in regard to price movements. Some analysts still use a Production/Consumption balance sheet that tracks the production of a security via treasury auction or corporate issuance, and also tracks rough consumption of the security by tracking portfolio and retail purchases separate from those purchases by financial institutions.

Technical analysis comes in a variety of forms as well. It is based on the concept that market participants are subject to repetitive behavior. For example, there is a relatively common occurrence of selling before treasury auctions and buying back after the results are announced. As another example, there is often a general squaring-up of positions just prior to month end. Technical analysis examines the pattern of past

Figure 6.1.   Calculation of Theoretical Value of a Security

The theoretical value for a security is determined by calculating the sum of the present values of the cash flows. In other words, the value today of an amount of money to be received in the future is determined. The equation for such a value is:

$$PV = \Sigma \ \frac{CF_t}{(1 + r)^t}$$

where PV = Present Value = Price
    CF_t = Cash flow received at time t
      r = discount rate
      t = time period the cash flow occurs

For example, suppose you want to see what a two-year security that pays 9.25% annually is worth today. Assume that an equivalent investment opportunity pays 11.50%. This will be the discount rate. The equation looks as follows:

$$PV = \frac{(92.50)}{(1+.1150)^1} + \frac{(92.50)}{(1+.1150)^2} + \frac{(1,000)}{(1+.1150)^2}$$
$$= (89.96) + (74.40) + (804.36)$$
$$= 968.72$$

This 968.72 represents the current value of those future cash flows. The $1,000 at the end of the sum is the principal amount repaid at maturity in two years. The price can be expressed either as total dollars, as above, or as percentage of par. This would make the price 96.872.

prices to look for trends or ranges or some other signal indicating the market is ripe to rally or sell-off. Although less common, it can be used with the U.S. government statistics series to evaluate where we are in the business cycle. Or it can be used on an asset class basis to determine whether to look for a greater return in equities, fixed-income, or some other class. It is also popularly used to examine price history of specific securities, both equity and fixed-income. Among the types of technical analysis there is the chart pattern method, volume/open interest analysis, price momentum analysis, Moving-Average-Convergence-Divergence, and cyclical analysis.

PRICING

Forward Rate Agreements

Forward rate agreements are contracts that obligate a buyer and a seller to transact an agreement at a future date at a set rate. The forward rate itself can be derived in two ways. One method assumes that the interest rate for a period starting in the future and ending farther in the future can be implied by the spot interest rates for (1) the period starting today and ending at the same maturity of the forward and (2) the period starting today and ending at the start of the forward rate period (refer to Chapter 2, Figure 2.14). The second method is based on the corresponding Eurodollar futures contract, since the rate for the period starting today until the futures expire can be calculated as 100 minus the Eurodollar contract price. The reason this is a forward rate rather than a spot rate is that the expiration date of the futures contract is the date that the purchase of the security is initiated. Until the contract expiration date, only a right to the contract is owned, and income accrues. Since a three-month forward rate is the rate from some future date for the next 90 days, the contract for purchasing a three-month security on the contract expiration date replicates the same cash flows and the same forward rate. The forward rate is known as a rolling rate because the six-month forward quoted today is not the rate for the same period as the one quoted tomorrow. For example, suppose the three-month forward rate quoted today is the rate that starts June 1 to run until August 31. Tomorrow, the three-month forward will be for the period from June 2 to September 1, and so on.

Forward rates, then, are calculated according to the implications of today's yield curve and today's spot rates or are calculated on the basis on today's futures prices. Due to arbitrage possibilities, the forward rate will not vary far from either of these levels, all of which converge at the expiration date of the futures contract. However, there is a strong expectations factor that can be included in the rate. Both expectations of the shape of the yield curve in the future and expectations for the base level of interest rates will influence where you think rates will be. This can influence the price of the futures contract, which will influence both the corresponding forward and the forward rates near those dates. The theoretical value of forwards is always a bit approximate in any case, because the market price will vary according to the specific settlement dates ranging around a periodic settlement. For example, if we compare rates for a 1 x 4, the rates will vary according to whether the settlement date is before a major economic announcement or after. Since the differential between the contract rate and the reference rate can jump significantly on the day PPI or unemployment figures are announced, there will be an additional risk premium included. See Figure 6.2 for the calculation of estimated rates and how they are used over the course of a typical week.

Futures

While forward rates are tightly controlled by arbitrage possibilities and consensus risk premiums, there is more leeway in the futures markets. First, there is more than one method used to value futures contracts. Therefore, while these models may be close, their inputs might vary enough that one person's buy is another person's sell. There is also a

Figure 6.2.   Pricing an FRA

As an example, let's calculate an approximate rate for 9-month LIBOR. The equation is

$$9\text{-month LIBOR} =$$

$$\left(\left[(1+\tfrac{.0657}{4}) \times (1+ \tfrac{.0717}{4}) \times (1+ \tfrac{.0739}{4})\right] -1\right) \times \tfrac{4}{3}$$

$$=.0538 \times \tfrac{4}{3}$$

$$=.07167=7.167\%$$

The rates are given by the next three front month Eurodollar futures contracts. For this nine-month forward rate, the start date will be the date the front month Eurodollar contract expires, and the termination date will be an additional nine months in the future.

The theoretical rate is 7.167% for that period of time as calculated on a Monday. However, if there is an auction on Wednesday that increases the supply of low-risk 6-month paper in the market, the forward rate quoted may well increase to 7.20%. Then as the dollar rallies at the end of the week, which increases demand for dollar-denominated securities, the yield offered might fall to 7.15%.

more varied market of players, so the size of the risk premium will have a chance to move significantly as well.

The value of a futures contract is heavily dependent on the underlying security. Therefore, the factors to be compared and contrasted are the security itself (which can take several different forms), whether or not the security provides income and how much, the timing of any income payments, and the form of redemption for the contract at the expiration date. The cost-carry model of pricing is most accurate for financial futures securities that have a liquid underlying market and a relatively fixed supply. Treasury bill futures fit these criteria because the auction amounts are announced a week before the event and any last-minute changes are usually of a fairly small percentage. The model is fairly simplistic, as it merely adds a funding factor to the cash price. The implication is that cash must always be cheaper than the futures, as a cost-of-funds factor must be added to cash to derive the futures fair price. However, there are arbitrage opportunities implied if price moves away from this. For example, if there is an inequality, then you should be able to sell one side and buy the other simultaneously to lock in a profit.

Selling 3-month cash treasury bills at 94.00 and buying the near treasury futures contract at 94.19, when the funding rate is .6% monthly, generates this equation:

$$\text{Cash} + \text{Carrying Cost} \approx \text{Futures Price}$$
$$94.00 + (.6 \times 3) \approx 94.19$$
$$94.18 \approx 94.19$$

By using this formula and purchasing futures while simultaneously selling cash, we can make one basis point of riskless profit.

June 1—Sell 1 futures contract at a price of 94.19 with a face value of $1,000,000.

June 1—Borrow $940,000 for three months at .6% monthly.

June 1—Buy 100 3-month treasury bills (each bill has a face value of 10,000) at a price of .9400 to pay out $940,000.

September 1—Deliver the bills to the exchange to close out the futures contract sale. Receive $941,900.

September 1—Pay back the loan of $940,000 plus $1,692.00 in interest.

September 1—Riskless profit of $208.00.

Of course, one basis point profit does not pay for commissions, margin requirements, or the time spent doing the transaction. However, the example indicates how the cost-carry approach works. Thus, the cash/futures price relationship will tend to follow this arbitrage formula.

Valuing futures with income flows is more complex. We need to add a variable: the accrued interest earned on the security. In the case of note or bond futures, there will be interest accrued from the last coupon date that is paid at the futures settlement date. The relationship between this factor and the financing rate will influence the cash/futures price relationship. If we define the financing rate as r, and if c represents the current yield, that is, the coupon rate divided by the market price of the security, then we can note the following: (1) if c is greater than r, the futures price is less than the cash price, (2) if c is equal to r, the futures price will equal the cash price, and (3) if c is less than r, the futures price will be greater than the cash price.

This relationship between the financing rate and the coupon rate is known as the carry. There are two possibilities: either we borrow the funds to buy the cash bond and sell futures or we buy futures and sell the cash security, investing the funds received for the cash from the cash settlement date until the futures settlement date. When we add this accrued-interest factor to the Treasury bill arbitrage equation, we see that repaying the principal and interest on the borrowed funds must equal the flat price of the bond futures contract plus accrued interest on the cash bond at settlement. See Figure 6.3 for equations and an example.

Given a pricing equation, the futures price moves from this level for several reasons. The first reason has to do with the financing rate. There is a difference, or spread, between the cost of borrowing and the returns from lending. This accounts for a range of accurate futures/cash price levels where the returns from arbitrage are too small to be transacted. Second, the risk premium and expectations premium can move price. The arbitrage is based on the current cheapest-to-deliver security. If the market is anticipating that a sufficiently large move in price will cause another bond to become the cheapest-to-deliver, the market may not wish to undertake the arbitrage with the concurrent risk that it would need to sell the current cheapest-to-

Figure 6.3.   Valuing Futures on Income-Producing Securities

For income producing securities, the principal is the same, but the time value of the accrued income generated by the security must be factored in. This makes the equation appear:

$$\text{Futures Price} \approx CP + (CP \times r \times t) + \Sigma \frac{CF_t}{(1+r)^t} + \lambda$$

where CP = Cash Price
      r = Funding rate
      t = Time
      CF_t = Cash flow received at time t
      λ = Random factor

Lambda, the random factor, is to account for any difference between expectations and the actual amounts needs to do the trade. Usually it approximates zero.

For an example, let's look at the case where the long bond has a coupon of 8.125%, a price of 96.28125, the comparable futures contract has a price of 92.875, and the funding rate is .6% monthly. Suppose the time frame is one year.

$$92.875 \overset{?}{=}$$
$$96.28125 + (96.28125 \times .072) - \left[\frac{4.0625}{(1+.036)^{.5}} + \frac{4.0625}{(1+.036)^{1}} + \frac{4.0625}{(1+.036)^{1.5}} \right]$$
$$96.28125 + 6.93225 - [3.9913 + 3.9213 + 3.8525]$$
$$92.875 \approx 91.448 + \lambda$$
$$\lambda \approx 1.427$$

This example approximates a real-life example. The larger than expected difference comes from approximating dates and the amount of income received. Also, there may be a partial payment due when the futures contract expires. This part of a coupon payment has not been included. Still, the real-life case approximates the expected answer.

deliver and buy another if that move occurred. In that case, the market is refusing to participate in an arbitrage that has an accompanying large basis risk.

Swaps

The most common method used to price a swap is a cash-flow model called the Generic Equivalent Cash-Flow Approach (GECA). The GECA method is becoming more common because it can be adapted to more complicated swaps than the simple example that will be discussed here. This model is a variation of the cash flow model used to price fixed-income securities and equity securities.

To demonstrate the GECA method, consider a swap with the floating side at index level, which means that the swap pays a particular rate without any additional spread and that the payment dates correspond to the reset date. This manipulation of the swap permits us to look at it as a floating-rate annuity. With the addition of the notional principal to the cash flows, the floating-rate cash stream becomes a floating-rate note priced at par. For the purpose of valuation, we view the swap as the exchange of a floating-rate security for a fixed-rate security. From the perspective of the cash flows, the fixed-rate payer is selling a fixed-rate security and buying a floating-rate security. Since we have already arranged that the floating rate stream equates to a floating-rate note with a price at par, then the all-in cost of the swap is determined by the value of the fixed-rate cash flows. We look at the cash flows for the fixed side and calculate the internal rate of return. This measure is the all-in cost. By using this method, we can avoid a difficulty in pricing swaps: how to price-in the uncertainty attached to a floating rate stream of payments. This method includes that particular risk premium in the fixed-rate side. The desirability or undesirability of holding a floating-rate stream is determined by how the fixed-rate is bid to offset it. If holding fixed is more attractive, the floating receiver can pay a lower fixed-rate coupon. If receiving floating is more attractive, the floating receiver must pay higher coupon. Thus, the uncertainty of the floating-rate stream is transferred to the fixed side, which we price.

We also stipulate that the prices of the two contrived securities we are exchanging are equal, so that no cash changes hands on the settlement date. This allows us to pretend that the annuities are actually fixed-income instruments. We want to ensure that the net of the prices of the two securities at settlement is zero and that the net of the two principal repayments at maturity is zero. Determining the internal rate of return is not unlike calculating the yield to maturity for a bond. we discount the fixed-rate cash-flow stream according to the required rates of return associated with different time horizons. Then, the premium paid or discount received is the difference between the two prices. If fixed price minus floating price is negative, then the payment is made by the floating-rate receiver. See Figure 6.4 for a summary of the process.

However, most swaps are not the generic type. There are a number of slight modifications that can occur to make pricing more difficult. On the floating-rate side, most swaps today are quoted with spreads attached to the index, for example, LIBOR plus 30 basis points. We might also see lags or mismatches between reset dates and payment dates, which is called a payment-frequency mismatch. There also may be inconsistencies with calculation methods when one rate is based on actual/365 and the other rate is 30/360. This is known as a day-count mismatch. There also may be occasions where the index resets more frequently than the index maturity, such as when the 90-day LIBOR is reset monthly but is paid quarterly. This is a reset-frequency mismatch. Also, just as there are securities with odd-date coupons, some

Figure 6.4.   Summary of Swaps Pricing Using GECA

1. Calculate the cash flows on the floating-rate side and the fixed-rate side.

2. Add the required flows to make the swap a generic index flat.

3. Calculate the net analytic flows equaling the contractual and adjustments cash flows for when the swap matures.

4. Calculate the Present Value of the floating coupon due next, and add in the par amount appropriately discounted.

5. Find the amounts received by the fixed-rate payer that equals the value of the floating-rate note. Add in any discount and subtract any premium.

6. Find the internal rate of return. This is the all-in cost.

swaps may have situations entailing one odd-dated coupon. This might occur when the normal reset period is 92 days, but the first period is either 110 days or 85 days.

This usually happens in the first period. This is referred to as a long or short first floating-rate period. On the other hand, the fixed-rate side is less subject to unusual structures, but there can be variations in payment frequency, odd first periods, and day-count mismatches on the fixed side.

For the swap itself, there are only two fairly common differences from the generic swap described above. First, there may be modifications in settlement date. Five days after contract date is the usual date to settle swaps. However, it is not that rare to look for odd settlement dates around holidays or before key economic numbers are announced. Second, there may be variations in the payment amount. One of the pre-conditions to using the GECA method is that no payment is exchanged on settlement date, that is, that the two security equivalents are equal in price. This situation is a par swap. However, there are also nonpar swaps. In addition, if the two securities are equal in price but that price is not par—an even swap—there will be valuation implications because of amortization/accretion of the premium/discount. When the prices are both nonpar and not equivalent, we refer to the situation as being a differential swap. See Figure 6.5 for a way to classify swaps according to pricing difficulties.

Caps and Floors

Caps and floors are much more difficult to price than a swap because a major component of the price is the seller's perception of volatility and how likely it is that the instrument will be exercised. A cap or floor will decrease in price as they move out of the money until they reach a fixed rate. That rate will be the minimum price, because the cap or floor seller will not assume a contingent obligation for free, regardless of how slim the probability is that he will have to pay out.

One way to determine if a price is acceptable to you uses a modification of the GECA method used for swaps. You calculate the internal rate of return on the cash flows, which is the same as pricing an annuity. However, you are buying (or selling) a call option on this annuity, so you can then use the Black-Scholes option pricing model or the Cox-Rubenstein model using the current implied volatility to value

Figure 6.5.   Classes of Pricing Methodologies

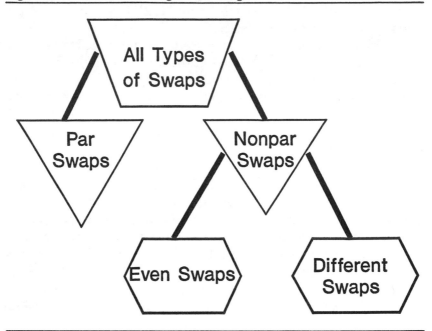

this present value. The details of this model are discussed in the next section. While this price may not compare with the market, it will give you an idea of a theoretical price.

Options

Three main methods are currently used to price options: the binomial, Black-Scholes, and Cox-Rubenstein options pricing models.

The binomial options pricing model is a single-case version of the Cox-Rubenstein model for options pricing both of which approximate the Black-Scholes options pricing model under most circumstances. These models evaluate the price of call options, then use the value of the calls to derive the value of the puts. There is also the Ho-Lee model for pricing options on securities, but this is less commonly used because of some practical difficulties. No model works perfectly, and we often see games-playing account for variations from the theoretical value as expectations and new information pass into the marketplace.

The games-playing will depend on the position of the market-markers' underlying book and whether they are trading the options or using them to hedge.

Binomial options pricing model. The binomial options pricing model (BOPM) is the basic model. This model contains key underlying assumptions of a random (efficient) market and of symmetrically probable price moves. In actuality, there are circumstances where volatility is non-symmetric due to expectational components, such as in an up market where the increase in volatility is less for price increases and more for price decreases. This model acts much like the future pricing model, in that there is an assumption that riskless profits will always be arbitraged away by the market.

One way of looking at this model is to construct a riskless hedge for when the option has one time period left before expiration. For example, if we purchase the security and sell calls against it, there are two possible outcomes. In the first, the security increases in value, so the calls increase in value, as well. In this case, the security purchase will make money and the short call position will lose money. However, since the calls are covered, the worst case loss on the calls is to see them expire worthless. Any additional loss is netted out by the cash security position. In the second outcome, the price of the cash security declines and so the value of the calls declines. The cash position loses money and the short call position earns money. However, the maximum profit to the short call position is the premium received when the position is initiated. See the Figure 6.6 for the various potential payoffs.

The covered call strategy achieves a maximum profit of the premium received for writing the call. Let the strike price of the call option equal K, the market price of the security equal S, and the premium received for writing the call equal P. Then when S is greater than K at expiration date, the investor delivers the stock to the owner of the call and receives K. His total earnings are (K + P). However if S is less than K at expiration, he sees a loss of (K − S) on the security, but the loss is offset by P. To avoid riskless arbitrage profits, the price of the calls must be such that the purchase price of the security minus the hedge is equal to the lower price of the security in one period when the calls would expire worthless. For this we need to calculate the hedge ratio to find out how many calls we will need to offset the security. The hedge ratio can be calculated by using the ratio of the differ-

Figure 6.6.   Probability Distribution of Covered Call Strategy

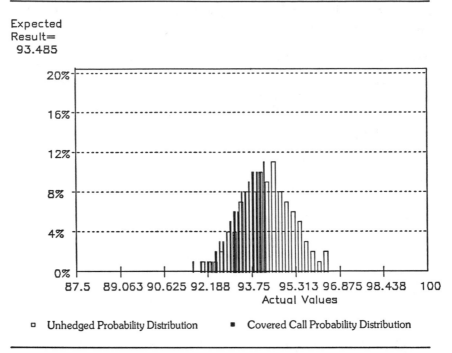

Expected
Result=
93.485

■ Unhedged Probability Distribution   ■ Covered Call Probability Distribution

ence between the two call values and the difference between the two security values. That is, if the security is priced at par when the position is originated and we sell call options with a par strike price, those par calls are the item we are trying to price. As a guide, they are at-the-money with one period left to expiration, so they will be priced at-the-money plus the time-value component to the price. If the security rallies to 103, then the call price will increase to around 3. Equally, if the security price falls to 97-00, then the call price will be zero. Therefore, the hedge ratio is calculated as:

$$HR = (3 - 0)/(103 - 97) = 3/6 = .50.$$

This means that each call will offset only 50% of the underlying cash security, so we need to sell two calls to offset the purchase of one bond. There is another constraint to pricing this position: the future value of the initial investment must be equal to the hedged payoff for the investment one period from now (97–00), when the calls are worthless, to prevent another type of riskless arbitrage. The initial cost of borrowing the bond is 100% of the face value (priced at par), which will be offset by the premium received from selling the call options. To calculate the future value of this cost, we need to multiply by $(1 + r)$ where r is the required rate of return for the investment. In this case, let's use 8.20% annually, or 2.05% for the quarter. For this calculation,

$$(100\text{–}00 - 2\,CV)(1 + r) = 97\text{–}00.$$

Thus, the call value at the time of purchase (CV) is equal to 2.47. This formula calculates the price as a percentage of the face value of the underlying security, so a call option price of 2.47 is $247 for each $10,000 bond. To show how different investors can calculate cost differently, let's look at including the cost of borrowing to buy the underlying cash security. Suppose the cost of borrowing is 9.50% annually. Borrowing $10,000 for a quarter will mean a future value of $237.50 to be returned to the lender at expiration. This adds 0.2375% to the cost of the investment. That is, the equation for calculating the call option value becomes:

$$[(100 + .02375) - 2CV](1.0205) = 97\text{–}00.$$

This gives us a call value equal to 2.49% of the face value. This variation of valuing call options shows why arbitrage is profitable to some people some of the time depending on their relative cost of borrowing.

This equation can be put into another form that makes it easier to use. It also introduces the notion of probability and how directional probability can affect the price of an option. This will be important when we look at the Black-Scholes and the Cox-Rubenstein models. The probability that the price of the underlying security will either move up or down is equal to one, since we have eliminated the case of the price being unchanged. This means that we can calculate the conditional or implied probability for the price movements. This uses Bayes' Rule and looks at how one event can affect the chance of another event occurring. This conditional probability is also affected by the required rate of return for investments. Note that some models use the risk-free rate instead. This rate is usually approximated by the rate for 90-day Treasury bills. In this case, we can use the above annualized required return, which is 2.05%, for the period, and the conditional probability p for price to move higher is:

$$p = (1+r) - \text{(lower price)}/\text{(higher price} - \text{lower price)}$$
$$\text{or } p = (1+.0205) - (.97)/(1.03 - .97) = .8417.$$

This is the likelihood that the price of the underlying will increase. The chance of price falling is $1-p$, or .1583.

We can use this conditional probability to calculate the price of the call option in the above example. The chance that price will increase multiplied by the increased price minus the chance of a price decrease multiplied by the lower price is present valued to calculate the price of the call. Thus, $[(.8417)(3) - (.1583)(0)]/(1.0205) = 2.47$. This is the same answer as calculated above, but it is in an easier form to use.

Now let's look at the case when there are two periods left before expiration. Using the same assumptions as in the one-period case, we can see that after two periods the underlying security can be priced at 106.09 (up in both periods), 99.91 (up in one period and down in the other), or finally 94.09 (down in both periods). Therefore, at expiration the call value will be either 6.09 or zero. The question then becomes what it is worth to us today if in two periods the underlying will be valued at either 6.09 or zero.

Basically, we work backwards. We use the model above to calculate the value of the call option one period before expiration, then use that answer and work the model again to calculate the price today, two periods before expiration. In one period, the value of the call option will be:

$$[(.8417)(6.09) - 0]/(1.0205) = 5.02.$$

If we put it into a simplified arbitrage form, the value is calculated as:

$$(103 - 2CV)(1.0205) = 94.09,$$
$$\text{or } CV = 5.40.$$

This simplification involves assuming only a worst case price, so the example may be somewhat overpriced.

The 5.02 outcome is the value of the call option one period from now, assuming that the underlying has not declined in price so that the value of the call is zero. To calculate the price we will pay for the call today, we use the model again for the case where the call value is 5.02 or 0 in one period:

$$CV = [(.8417) (5.02) - 0]/(1.0205) = 4.14.$$

If you wish to engage in some arithmetic, the binomial formula can be used to give us one equation for the two-period model. It looks like this:

$$CV = \frac{p^2 \, CV_{uu} + 2p \, (1 - p) \, CV_{du} + (1 - p)^2 \, CV_{dd}}{(1 + r)^2}$$

where p = Implied probability
CV_{uu} = Call price after two increases
CV_{du} = Call price after one increase, one decrease
CV_{dd} = Call price after two price declines

We can work this equation with the above example. Remember that $p = .8417$ and $(p - 1) = .1583$. Since the call will expire worthless in the case of the underlying price equaling 99.19 or 94.09, the last two terms or parts of the equation are equal to zero. This makes the equation much easier, and it becomes:

$$CV = [(.8417) (.8417) (6.09) + (0) + (0)]/[(1.0205) (1.0205)]$$
$$= 4.14.$$

We can use put-call parity to value the put option with a par strike price for this security. The value of the put is equal to the value of the call minus the price of the security plus the present value of the amount borrowed to purchase the security. Therefore, with a call valued at 4.14, and a price of the security at par or 100, the present value of the strike price is $100/(1 + .02050)$, or 97.99 and the price of the put is 2.13.

Black-Scholes options pricing model. The Black-Scholes options pricing model (BSOPM) approaches the valuation problem from another viewpoint.[1] When it is profitable to exercise a call, its value will be the difference between the underlying security's price and the present value of the exercise price. If the call is not profitable to exercise, the equation still holds true, but the value falls under the lower limit of zero. We can make the difference equation hold true for both extreme cases by multiplying each of the two items by a factor. This process is called weighting. In other words, when the exercise is unprofitable, the weights would be zero and the equation would come out to zero. When the exercise is clearly profitable, the weights would be one and the value formula would hold to its original shape. Thus, we might infer that the weights for the two variables would range from zero to one, depending on the likelihood of exercise being profitable. The Black-Scholes options pricing model clearly defines these weights, so it gives an exact value for the call option. This model is rather complicated and has a set of rigorous assumptions to go along with it. Some of the assumptions are intended to keep the model as simplistic as possible. For example, these assume that the model includes no taxes or other transaction costs and that there are no restrictions on short sales. While this is relatively the case in fixed-income markets, it is not true for equity markets. Another assumption is that "riskless borrowing and lending" is available at continuous rate r. For fixed-income markets, we note that the rates to borrow and the rates to lend are neither riskless nor equivalent. It always costs more to borrow than it pays to lend at the same risk level; banks make money by assuming a credit risk to gain the positive spread in rates between borrowing and lending. A less important assumption for the model is that the portfolio can be adjusted instantaneously. The assumptions that can cause the model to mis-value the option are two: (1) that the option can be exercised only at maturity and (2) that there are no cash flows paid on the security over the life of the option. The latter is seldom true for fixed-income securities unless, for example, the security pays in January and June and the option we are valuing has a life from February to May. But again, these models were developed for use in equity markets, which generally have a lower relative yield, even though they pay more frequently.

One last assumption, although not noticeably as important as the

---

[1] Fisher Black and Myron Scholes, "The Pricing of Options and Corporate Liabilities," *Journal of Political Economy*, May 1973.

Figure 6.7. Call Prices Over Two Periods

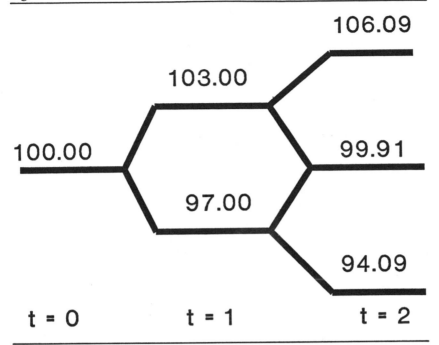

exercise date issue, is that the distribution of price over time is assumed to be log-normal. That is, there is an assumption that prices will form particular paths, so that the path will take on a particular shape when we look at price over time. Given that there is a strong expectational component to options trading, a single price-distribution curve may not be adequate. In addition, a log-normal distribution assumes that there is some probability, however low, that a security will reach any positive price. With fixed-income securities, there is a maximum price that can be achieved (the sum of the remaining cash flows) for all positive interest rates. In other words, the log-normal price-distribution path implies that sometimes interest rates will be negative, which is absurd. However, given the difficulty of finding another reasonable representative assumption for price distribution, this is adequate. This assumption is important because of what it says about how probable it is that certain prices will occur.

Using these various assumptions, the model incorporates the

weights for the two variables, the security price, and the present value of the exercise price. Its form is as follows:

$$\text{Call value} = [\,S \times N(D1)\,] - [\,(K \times e^{-rt}) \times N(D2)\,]$$

$$\text{where } D1 = \frac{\text{natural log } \dfrac{S}{K} + \left[\left(\dfrac{r+V}{2}\right) \times T\right]}{(V \times T)^{.5}}$$

$$D2 = D1 - (V \times T)^{.5}$$

$S = $ Current Security Price

$K = $ Strike Price of call option

$T = $ Time until option expiration

$N(.) = $ Normal Distribution Function

$V = $ Variance of security returns

$e = $ Natural logarithm 2.718281828

This looks quite complicated, but if we simply weight the original formula of the difference between the security price and the present value of the strike price, then we can look at the two weights and define them. The weight factor attached to the security price is the regular normal distribution function, and the weight factor attached to the present value of the strike price is the normal distribution function multiplied by a natural log constant in order to make the distribution log-normal. For the log-normal function, we use an inner variable upon which to base the distribution. This inner variable is the difference between the security price and the variance of the log-normal distribution, Variance multiplied by Time. For the first weight, the normal distribution function is performed on a more complex inner variable. This inner variable contains the ratio between the security price and the exercise price, which is a measure for how in- or out-of the money the option is. It also includes the extreme levels for the risk-free rate under the volatility and time constraints we assume. These two items are summed and then discounted by the variance of the distribution.

See Figure 6.8 for an example of the calculation. As you can see, there is a small difference because of specific supply/demand inequities for that particular security or because of expectational factors or both.

There is a concern with the assumption that the option can be exercised only at the expiration date. An option with this type of exercise

Figure 6.8.   An Example of the Black-Scholes Pricing Model

Use the following values:

S = 96.09375
K = 96.00000
T = .25 (3 months)
V = 14.4% = .144
r = .065

D1 is calculated as:

$$= \frac{\ln\left(\frac{96.09375}{96.00000}\right) + \left[.065 + \left(\frac{.144}{2}\right) \times .25\right]}{(.144 \times .25)^{.5}}$$

$$= \frac{(.000976) + (.137 \times .25)}{(.036)^{.5}}$$

$$= \frac{.035226}{.189737}$$

$$= .1856$$

Then D2 =

$$= .1856 - (.144 \times .25)^{.5}$$
$$= .1856 - .189737$$
$$= -.004137$$

Then N(D1) = .8750 and N (D2) = .90
The last step is:

$$CV = (96.09375 \times .900) - [(96 \times e^{-.065 \times .25}) \times .875]$$
$$= 86.484375 - [(96 \times .98388) \times .875]$$
$$= 86.484375 - 82.64592$$
$$= 3.83845$$

So the price of the 96–00 call option when the security price is 96.09375 (at-the-money) is approximately $3.84. The exchange-traded price is 26 ticks, or .40625% of par. This translates to a price of $4.0635. So there is a small difference between the calculated value and the market price.

is known as an European option. However, the type of exchange-traded issue we deal with can be exercised on or before the exercise date and is called an American option. This is particularly significant when we consider that fixed-income securities have a cash-flow component affecting their value. When we look at equities, there are structural differences that make adjusting the BSOPM easier. For example, when you purchase a bond, you are entitled to the interest payments from the time you purchase it. For an equity, the payment goes in full to the owner on the ex-dividend date. As a result, there are specific price movements on stock that occur post-ex-dividend date. Since bonds start accruing on purchase date, there is no easily made adjustment to the received cash flows. Such adjustments also tend to undervalue the option.

Another problem is that this model assumes a constant volatility for the security. However, with fixed-income securities the price volatility decreases as the maturity date approaches. This, then, is not a constant number. However, since the life of exchange-traded options is three months or less, the variation in term-to-maturity should not differ significantly over the life of the option. This will not be true when you price longer life OTC options, however.

Cox-Rubenstein options pricing model. The Cox-Rubenstein options pricing model (CROPM) is a limiting version of the BSOPM.[2] Its added usefulness lies in recognizing that exercise before expiration can and will occur, and it values this early exercise more accurately. The CROPM is a binomial model, much like the expanded equation for the riskless arbitrage example of the BOPM. The CROPM is the model standardly used for the exchange traded fixed-income product, which has various futures contracts as the underlying, as opposed to the OTC versions that have cash securities as the underlying. Its major drawback is that the short-term rate is assumed to be fixed when evaluating the call option. In addition, the CROPM approaches the same answer as the BSOPM for a large number of time periods. The binomial lattice of probable options prices approaches a log-normal distribution as the number of time periods increases, so it has the same drawbacks as the BSOPM in many cases. However, because the bi-

[2] John Cox and Mark Rubenstein, *Options Markets* (Englewood Cliffs, NJ: Prentice-Hall, 1985).

nomial model is a numerical method, it can be used for American-exercise options.

Another advantage to using the CROPM is also related to the numerical methodology used. Because the option price is determined period-by-period with conditional probabilities, securities with cash flows can be evaluated. The BSOPM, on the other hand, does not include the effect of cash flows.

Other models formulated by R.P. Clancy[3] and by Lawrence Dyer and David Jacobs[4] used a binomial model, but they were based on log-normal distributions of yield rather than a log-normal distribution of price. This has the advantage of translating into a symmetric price distribution curve, rather than a positively skewed curve. It also sets maximum price at somewhat less than the sum of its remaining cash flows (discounting). In addition, the translated symmetric price distribution allows for a negatively skewed curve for securities with short maturities and low convexity and a positively skewed curve for longer term bonds with higher convexity, of which both assumptions are intuitive and logical.

Pricing considerations. With all the advantages to the other models, why does anyone use the BSOPM? The reason relates to three primary advantages. First the BSOPM is the most familiar. As you grow to learn the model and its advantages and shortfalls, you learn to use it as a tool rather than as an absolute answer or a mysterious "black box." Second, the BSOPM has the advantage of continuous pricing. The lattice approach from the binomial methodology treats price change in rather sudden intervals, as discontinuities rather than gradual change. As a result, when you try to measure the risk exposure of a portfolio including options, a binomial model will also cause the risk posture of the portfolio to change abruptly. Finally, the log-normal distribution approach of the binomial model implies a flat yield curve and parallel moves in the yield curve. This does not accurately describe the real world and also leaves the model open to riskless arbitrage opportuni-

---

[3] R.P. Clancy, "Options on Bonds and Applications to Product Pricing," *Transactions*, vol xxxvii, 1985.

[4] Lawrence J. Dyer and David P. Jacobs, "Guide to Fixed-Income Option Pricing Models," *Handbook of Fixed-Income Options*, ed. Frank Fabozzi (Chicago: Probus, 1989).

ties. The BSOPM does not imply a flat yield curve, although it too, assumes parallel yield curve moves.

The arbitrage-free binomial model has a "no riskless arbitrage" constraint included.[5] This is more a complicated version of our first example done with conditional probabilities but is based on yield rather than price. It is difficult to use and is heavily dependent on the length of the period used to evaluate the price. The shorter the term, the fewer discontinuities there are and the more refined it is. Using it is not significantly different from our first example.

Options pricing theory has come a long way since 1973, when the BSOPM was first published upon the opening of the CBOE. We can expect it to continue to develop. Most of this development currently is focused on the role of expectations. Also more work needs to be done to make the models easier to use and cheaper to run.

[5] Lawrence J. Dyer and David P. Jacobs, "An Overview of Fixed-Income Options Models," *Handbook of Fixed-Income Securities*, ed. Frank Fabozzi (Richard D. Irwin, 1991), 761–765.

CHAPTER 7

Conclusion

The underlying focus of this text is the entire process of making a hedging decision. Do you want to hedge? Are you instead being paid for the risk you have assumed? At what stage do you want to re-evaluate your risk? If you hedge, how much risk do you want to transfer to another party? How much do you want to pay to reduce your risk? If you hire consultants or experts, how should you evaluate their decisions?

An entire field of study is devoted to decision-making under uncertain circumstances. There are two divisions in the field: normative decision-making, which examines how people should make decisions and descriptive decision-making, which examines how people actually make decisions. The descriptive study tries to identify the things that are the base for a decision; while the normative study tries to teach how to form a "better" decision. However, it is usually difficult to determine what makes one decision better than another. That is why I have been emphasizing the concept that a better decision is one that is either less expensive or more convenient. When ambiguous terms as "better" are used for goals, then gradations of choice become equally ambiguous.

However, there are certain practices in decision-making that lessen the time spent "second-guessing" a decision once it is made. For example, listing all the choices and then ordering them according to some pre-specified priorities can quickly narrow the field of acceptable choices. Quite often, this first priority list will provide three or four choices that have different advantages and disadvantages. You can then quickly choose one and not worry that a "better" choice was missed. This is referred to in the literature as "complete ordering." A second practice is to treat all choices that result in the same reduction of risk as being equal. That is, the decision to use futures or forwards is "equally good" if the reduction in risk exposure is the same. Thus, this risk strategy requires a second prioritizing to decide whether to emphasize cost reduction or convenience, but it is irrelevant to the primary decision—risk modification—which product is used. This is known as the irrelevance of identical outcomes.

There are also the concepts of admissibility and independence. Admissibility is where one decision or class of decisions is strongly better than another. This is why the ordering of choices is a key process. Due to admissibility, one choice will generally be judged the "best." However, due to independence of tastes, this best decision will not be the same for all parties. In a way, that is why trades can be completed: there are as many "best" decisions as there are market participants. In some cases, risk reduction is expensive primarily because so many participants view the same strategy as "best." This is another example of admissibility, as well.

Another difficulty in decision-making is to accurately measure the perception of risk. I have concentrated on separating this into two parts: (1) viewing risk as uncertainty and (2) measuring uncertainty as a probability distribution of returns. But to some, this has acted instead to measure uncertainty, while the true "risk" lies in whether the returns truly are random or not. While I have looked at the behavior of a range of prices, there is a sector of the market that sees risk differently. Their risk is whether or not one can assign probabilities to outcomes. Since this sector perceives risk as a different issue, then their decision-making will differ, as well.

There are several ways to examine how people perceive risk, and both are tied to different views of the marginal utility of wealth, that is, how much utility each additional increment of wealth gives. If each additional dollar is viewed as being worth less than the previous one, then we speak of declining marginal value. In 1948, Friedman and Savage hypothesized that the marginal utility increased for a specific range of wealth before declining at a later time. If each additional dollar is worth more than the previous one, then it implies that, although you are unwilling to share a lottery ticket for a million dollars, you might be willing to share a ticket worth $100,000. Von Neumann and Morgenstern, on the other hand, suggest that wealth utility is maximized at some point. After you reach a maximum utility, then no additional risk is worth accepting, regardless of the potential reward.

These different ways of valuing each additional dollar might explain some behavior that otherwise looks irrational. For example, in the transferal of risk from one party to another, Investor Bigbucks may not want any additional risk, no matter what the potential reward, and will be willing to sacrifice all of the upside return to eliminate that risk. He is an example of the maximized utility of wealth. Investor Millionaire wishes to transfer most of his risk, but he wants to keep some of the upward potential. He exhibits the declining marginal utility of wealth, but it is not yet at the maximum. Investor Middlebucks has a large appetite for risk and assumes much of the excess of Millionaire and Bigbucks. He is in the part of the curve where the marginal utility is increasing. However, he will not accept the small pieces of the risk package. These small pieces are taken by Investor Littlebucks, who is more concerned with the amount of the investment and the reward potential for a limited investment. This is because he also has an increasing marginal utility of wealth, but starts from a different initial position. Figure 7.1 shows a theoretical path for current wealth versus the risk appetite for additional wealth. I've indicated where all of our investors are along the curve.

The idea of utility is intuitive and so is helpful in general analysis. However, it is difficult to measure the relative "usefulness" of something for different people. The way that a measure will change for each investor introduces subjective probability. In this idea, the probability that an event will occur is based on perceptions of the event rather than on the independent behavior of the event itself. This means that different investors will have different opinions of the probability that an event will occur, even if they use the same methodology.

All of these elements taken together mean that, if there are spots of increasing marginal utility of wealth, then a person can be subjected to accept unfair gambles. This fills in the last portion of the market.

Figure 7.1.   Appetite for Risk at Different Levels of Wealth

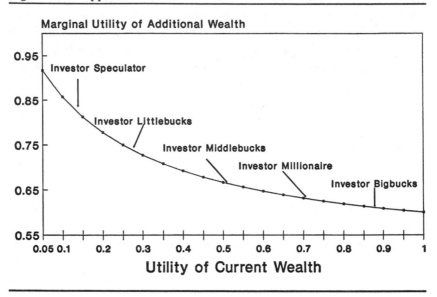

There is a theoretical base for the investor in the market that accepts "unfair" gambles. An unfair gamble is one where the investor accepts a gamble in his favor but at odds where he has a greater than 50% chance of losing. It is considered more important to add the next dollar to wealth than to lose the last dollar he added to wealth. We can call him Investor Speculator.

Another important issue has less to do with appetite for risk, but deals with the overall view of price action. If your time frame is intermediate to longer, and if you believe that long-term perceptions of the value of an asset change only gradually, then you look to place concave payoff schedules. That is, a buy-and-hold portfolio is your preference. As a corollary, hedging is less important, because your perception is that price deviates around the mean. This is called regression to the mean. For this viewpoint, event risk is the thing to be hedged.

However, if your viewpoint is for a shorter term, or if volatility is troublesome, or if you believe that price trends can be sustained, then hedging is more worthwhile. If price action can be directionally sustained, then hedging becomes worthwhile. This view looks for convex payoff schedules. This is a situation where buying and selling on price break-outs will pay off.

Quite often, though, a hedging decision will be put off because the decision-makers feel uncomfortable with the issues. They excuse the lack of a decision by pointing out that profit margins are designed to pad against volatility or they comfort themselves with the notion that it all evens out in the end. Perhaps it does. However, if your time frame for a profit does not allow for too many consecutive quarters with poor profits, then you really can't afford to wait for the "end" and hedging might reduce volatility. Moreover, while profit margins do allow for some minor price moves, you should know at what point those profit margins are being squeezed. Even if the hedge program is not implemented, it may behoove you to have a plan in reserve. When prices realign themselves, opportunities can be lost if you do not have at least a bare-bones plan available.

In general, no one objects to reducing risks, as long as the protection is sufficiently inexpensive. But how do we judge whether the hedge has done its job? And while we can distinguish which hedging alternative is least expensive, how do we know if they are all too expensive for the protection offered? The answers are all somewhat ambiguous and, of

Figure 7.2.   Risk Equilibrium Line: Risk-Free Rate Plus Risk Premium

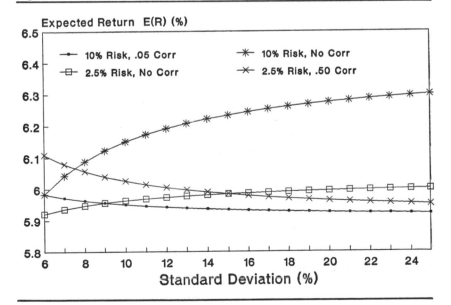

course, open to interpretation. However, there are a few ways to measure the effectiveness of a strategy. If we look at the overall performance of a security or asset as a combination of conservative intrinsic value (where below market rates are assumed to be the long-term average) and a risk premium, then an equilibrium line can be designed for the instrument. This equilibrium line will designate a frontier between expected return and excess risk for the item. It looks like the curve designating an optimal portfolio. The line can be used for ballpark estimates of how much upside return can be sacrificed to limit downside moves. If the market price for the strategy costs more, then the risk should be tolerated since the protection is overpriced. The equilibrium is a line drawn by the sum of a base "risk-free" rate and a risk premium multiplied by the risk of the asset. This gives us an assured rate of return—normally the 90-day T-bill by proxy—and a risk-adjusted premium. The risk of the asset is the covariance of the asset and the total

Figure 7.3.   The Sharpe Measure of Risk

This is a measure of excess return divided by the standard deviation of the portfolio. The equation is as follows:

$$S = \frac{(R_p - RFR)}{\sigma_p}$$

where R_p = Portfolio Return
RFR = Risk Free Rate
σ_p = Standard Deviation of Returns for the Portfolio

As an example, suppose you earned 15% on your portfolio, and your competitor earned 22% for the same period. The proxy for the risk-fee rate is at 5.90%. The standard deviation of return for your portfolio was 18%, and that of your competitor 25%. The Sharpe Measure is calculated as:

$$S_A = \frac{(15.00 - 5.90)}{18} = .5055$$

$$S_B = \frac{(22.00 - 5.90)}{25} = .644$$

In this example, your competitor took greater risk, but was compensated for doing so.

market divided by the standard deviation of the total market. The total market for this measure will depend on the portfolio. It might be equities only, fixed-income only, or an attempt to build a balanced index just for measurement purposes. The risk premium is the market price per unit of risk assumed. The multiplication of these two pieces results in a total market price for the risk assumed. The risk premium is measured by the excess returns over the base rate divided by the standard deviation of the total market. When we take this risk amount and add in the expected return for the total market, the result is the equilibrium line. When the market offers returns above the line, that much return can be sacrificed without a penalty. See Figure 7.2.

Another way to judge effectiveness is by using William Sharpe's risk-penalty measure. This will vary from investor to investor, as it is defined as the square of risk divided by the risk tolerance of the investor. Sharpe uses the standard deviation of returns as the measure of risk, and the risk tolerance is on a scale from 0 to 100. By taking the expected return and subtracting the risk penalty, we can derive a measure of the portfolio's utility. See Figure 7.3. By plotting the risk equilibrium line and the portfolio utility for various hedged portfolios, we can find a cross-section to indicate the most attractive portfolio.

There is a difficulty attached to hedging, as the proof is in the pud-

Figure 7.4.   Risk Management Decision Tree

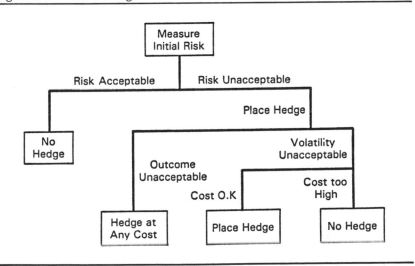

ding, and sometimes the various risk premiums can change both in magnitude and in direction. For example, a long corporate bond position can be hedged by holding a short bond futures position. However, suppose that fears of a recession cause yields to fall and credit spreads to widen. In that case, the hedged position would generate a loss as prices increased. However, the underlying cash position could also lose money, as the widening credit spread would see corporate bond prices fall. This is hardly less risky than holding just the corporate bonds. Another example is when cash, FRAs, and Eurodollar futures are used in combination. A customer of a money center bank purchases an FRA from the bank, then the bank hedges the FRA with Eurodollar futures. The futures are a mark-to-market item generating gains and losses today, while the underlying FRA is not payable or receivable for another three to six months. The future value of any

Figure 7.5.   Transferring Risk

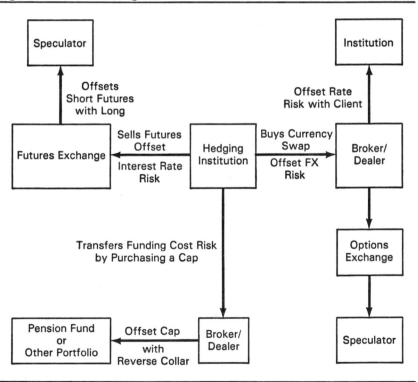

losses on the futures should be incorporated into the costs of the FRA. Since the future value of the gains or losses on the futures portion can swing so widely, and since there is the compounding effect, it is very difficult to measure its effectiveness exactly. This variability of future value is why the stacking process is so popular. By altering the size of the hedge—in effect managing the hedge ratio—this sort of basis risk can be minimized.

Admitting that the hedging process is imperfect, why should you bother? Partly due to competition, since everyone else is hedging, and partly to change floating costs to fixed costs. A general rule of thumb, which has many exceptions, is that most costs are better fixed and most revenues are better floating as long as the average revenue is at or below the fixed rate. Therefore, using derivitives to transform costs is good for the overall health of your company.

I hope that this text has clarified some of the decision-making for derivatives or at least examined the variables. See Figures 7.4 and 7.5 an overview for the entire process. Risk management is still at the stage of being as much art as science. Remember that you are trying to solve problems. The solution that is most convenient in terms of manpower, that has fewer commission costs, and that does not require a new computer will probably fit the bill.

REFERENCES

Brown, Stephen J. and Mark P. Kritzman *Quantitative Methods for Financial Analysis* 2nd ed. (Dow Jones-Irwin, Homewood, Ill.) 1990.

Clancy, R. P. "Options on Bonds and Applications to Product Pricing" *Transaction*, volume xxxvii, 1985.

Diamond, Peter and Michael Rothschild eds. *Uncertainty in Economics* (Academic Press, New York) 1978.

Fabozzi, Frank J. ed. *Handbook of Fixed-Income Options* (Probus Publishing, Chicago) 1989.

Fabozzi, Frank J. ed. *Handbook of Fixed-Income Securities* 3rd Ed. (Business One Irwin, Homewood, Ill.) 1991.

Gibson, Rajna *Option Valuation* (McGraw-Hill, New York) 1991.

Ho, Thomas S. Y. *Strategic Fixed-Income Investments* (Dow Jones-Irwin, Homewood, Ill.) 1990.

Kapner, Kenneth R. and John F. Marshall *The Swaps Handbook* (New York Institute of Finance) 1990.

Kreps, David M. *Notes on the Theory of Choice* (Westview Press, Boulder, Co.) 1988.

Maginn, John L. and Donald L. Tuttle *Managing Investment Portfolios—A Dynamic Process* 2nd ed. (Warren, Gorham & Lamont, New York) 1990.

Natenberg, Sheldon *Option Volatility and Pricing Strategies* (Probus Publishing, Chicago) 1988.

Platt, Robert B. *Controlling Interest Rate Risk* (John Wiley & Sons, New York) 1986.

Reilly, Frank K. *Investment Analysis and Portfolio Management* 2nd ed. (Dryden Press, New York) 1985.

Schwager, Jack D. *A Complete Guide to the Futures Markets* (John Wiley & Sons, New York) 1984.

Schwartz, Robert J. and Clifford W. Smith Jr. ed, *The Handbook of*

Currency and Interest Rate Risk Management (New York Institute of Finance) 1990.

Schwartz, Edward W., Joanne M. Hill, and Thomas Schneeweis, *Financial Futures* (Irwin, Homewood, Ill.) 1986.

Smith Jr., Clifford W., Charles W. Smithson, and D. Sykes Wilberforce *Managing Financial Risk* (Harper & Row, New York) 1990.

von Neumann, John and Oskar Morganstern *Theory of Games and Economic Behavior* (Princeton University Press, Princeton, N.J.) 1947.

GLOSSARY

Adjusted Internal Rate of Return. the rate of return on a project that results when the cash flows are reinvested at a rate of return not equal to the project's internal rate of return. Large variances between Internal Rate of Return and adjusted ROR are caused by exposure to reinvestment risk.

American Option. the right to buy or sell an asset at a prespecified price for a period of time. The American option can be exercised at any time up to expiration date.

American Window. an exercise alternative for captions and floortions that allows exercise at any time until expiration while the maturity of the underlying cap or floor remained fixed.

Arbitrage. the act of locking in profits by exchanging assets without incurring risk. Opportunities usually arise through pricing errors.

Arithmetic Mean. a calculation of the mean or average that assumes all values to have equal weight.

Asked. also known as the offer, this is the seller's quotation of the price of a financial instrument. It is the price that must be paid by a possible purchaser of the instrument.

Asset. a class of positions on the balance sheet that indicate obligations due you by others.

Asset Swaps. a term used when a swap is applied to an asset to change the rate of return from a fixed level to a floating rate. It is also used when a currency swap is used as a method of changing the return from one currency to another.

At-the-money. when the strike price of an option is near the current market price.

Average. also known as the mean or expected price.

Balloon Payment. typically, a payment on a fixed-income security that is larger than the usual coupon payment. It is often used to refer to the lump-sum principal repayment at maturity.

Basis. the difference in price between a futures contract and its underlying cash security.

Basis Point. one one-hundredth of a percent, a measurement used frequently in yield calculations and interest-rate sensitivity analysis.

Basis Risk. the risk assumed when assets are based on one floating rate index and liabilities on another; also the risk assumed when hedging a cash instrument with futures contracts.

Basle Agreement. an agreement reached in 1989 between the central banks of 12 countries to standardize reserve requirement rules on a risk-adjusted basis by 1992. At that time regulated banks will need to have an 8% ratio for capital reserves to total assets and a 4% ratio of tier-one capital to total assets.

Bear Spread. an options strategy using combined calls and puts that experiences the greatest return when the price of the underlying instrument declines. This strategy also experiences the greatest risk when the price of the underlying instrument increases.

Bid. the other side of the asked price; the price that those interested in purchasing the instrument are willing to pay.

Binomial Options Pricing Model. a valuation model for options that assumes that changes in prices follow a binomial distribution with random direction to the moves. The value of the option is computed by working along a path tree. Prices are assumed to move either up or down each period, and periods are treated as being discrete rather than continuous.

Black-Scholes Option Pricing Model. a valuation model for options that assumes that asset prices change continuously and that arbitrage opportunities cannot exist. The value depends on the price of the underlying asset, the exercise price, the risk-free rate of return, the time to expiration, and the standard deviation of the underlying asset.

BP. an abbreviation for basis point.

Bull Spread. an options strategy combining puts and calls that offers the greatest risk when the price of the underlying instrument declines and that experiences the greatest return as the price of the underlying instrument increases.

Bullet. a lump-sum repayment of a loan or fixed-income security that occurs at maturity.

Butterfly. a class of options strategies consisting of two calls and two puts with different strike prices and/or maturity dates. It can be structured in either a bullish or bearish fashion.

Call Option. a contract that gives the owner the right, but not the obligation, to purchase an asset for a pre-specified period of time.

Cap. an option that provides a maximum upside risk for funding purposes, but allows the holder of the cap to join in the benefits of a downward move in rates.

Capital Adequacy. the notion that all on-balance-sheet and off-balance-sheet items exert a certain credit risk so that a certain amount of capital, known as a loan loss reserve, must be held to offset potential losses.

Caption. a contract providing the right, but not the obligation, to buy or sell a cap. The term, exercise price, and strike price are all pre-determined. Exercise alternatives include European, American, and American window.

Causal. a statistical relationship that implies that the occurrence of one event leads to or causes another event.

CBOE. Chicago Board Options Exchange, a part of the CBT regulated to trade standardized options contracts through the Option Clearing Corporation, or OCC.

CBT. Chicago Board of Trade; a futures exchange that deals in financial and agricultural commodities. Best known for their bond contract.

CFTC. Commodity Futures Trading Commission; an independent government agency with the regulatory power over the U.S. futures exchanges.

CME. Chicago Mercantile Exchange; a futures exchange that deals in domestic and international financial contracts. Best known for their Eurodollar contract.

Collar. a financial instrument combining a cap and a floor. The purchaser of the collar buys the cap and sells the floor. Owning a collar locks the investor into receiving a floating interest-rate limited on the top by the strike price of the cap and banded on the bottom by the strike price of the floor.

Compounding Periods. the number of periods in a year in which a financial instrument pays interest.

Compound Options.   options that have other options as their underlying security. Examples are captions, floortions, and swaptions.

Concave Payoff Strategies.   asset allocation strategies that work best when the asset returns converge in value. This results in rebalancing by selling the higher priced asset and using the funds to invest in the cheaper one. These are a class of range-trade strategies.

Contract Month.   the month specified in a futures contract in which receipt or delivery of the underlying instrument takes place.

Conversion Factor.   a factor applied to cash bonds with coupons other than 8.00% so that they can be used in delivery for the CBT bond futures contract.

Conversion Factor Model.   a method of calculating the hedge ration where the hedge ration is set equal to the conversion factor.

Convexity.   a measure of a financial instrument's price sensitivity to changes in yield.

Convex Payoff Strategies.   a class of asset-allocation strategies that work best when the returns on the asset classes diverge. It uses techniques such that the lower priced asset is sold and the funds are used to buy more of the higher priced asset. This is an example of portfolio insurance and is used in trending markets.

Correlation Analysis.   a statistical process that measures the direction and strength of the relationship between two things, usually events or financial instruments.

Cost of Carry.   the average interest rate paid to borrow money or funds for investment purposes.

Counterparty.   one of the two firms participating in a swap.

Coupon Security.   a security that pays interest between the issue date and the date of maturity based on a pre-determined interest rate. Most bonds are coupon securities.

Covered.   when an options or futures position is offset by the cash underlying instrument; e.g., owning cash government bonds when short bond futures contracts is a covered position.

Credit Risk.   the repayment risk assumed that a borrower will repay his loan as specified.

Currency Swap.   an agreement between two parties that details the exchange of a flow of payments in one currency for a flow of payments in another currency. Typically, this includes the interest payments and principal amount for a fixed-income security.

Dedication. a portfolio-management strategy used in asset/liability management that involves matching or "dedicating" certain incoming cash flows with certain outgoing cash flows. This offers protection from interest rate chances.

Defeasance. in finance, a strategy to end one liability by replacing it with another. The term is used when pension plans lock in a better reinvestment rate than the actuarial assumption by purchasing a floor.

Delta. the change in the price of an option for a given change in the price of the underlying security. The measure is used to indicate sensitivity of the derivative to changes in the underlying and is known as the neutral hedge ratio.

Dependent Variable. the y in the regression equation; the variable that is affected by changes in the other variable(s). It is also the variable we are trying to forecast.

Derivative Security. a security that acts as a substitute for another security, known as the underlying. The derivative instrument substitutes by providing rights and occasionally obligations to the purchase and sale of the underlying instrument.

Deviation. the difference between a particular occurrence and the average value of that occurrence. This measure changes for each observation.

Diffs. futures contracts used to hedge the differential between the short-term rates in two countries; there are Eurodollar/Euromark, Eurodollar/Euroyen and Eurodollar/short sterling varieties.

Discount Formula. the equation used to calculate the present value of a future cash flow.

Discount Rate. the assumed reinvestment rate used to calculate present value.

Dispersion. the variation of payments around a portfolio's duration.

Dispersion Measures. statistical measures to indicate how different observations of a sample differ from the underlying universe's central tendency. They include variance and standard deviation.

Dual-Currency Options. one of a class of options of which an option-linked loan is an example. Which currency will be ultimately received is uncertain. This type of option makes sense for multinationals that are indifferent to the currency received and that like the flexibility.

Dual-Index Floater.   a security that pays interest at a rate determined by which of two pre-specified indexes is higher. For example, there are short-term commitments that pay the higher of 3-month LIBOR or 3-month Treasury bills plus a certain number of basis points.

Duration.   the weighted average of the cash flows for a security, measured in years. The duration of a zero-coupon security is equal to the maturity. Duration decreases as the coupon increases and increases as maturity increases.

Estimation Risk.   the risk that the parameters to determine price are in error and that the price estimate deviates significantly from the actual price.

Eurodollar.   a dollar issued overseas, generally in London. It is a common denomination for securities and time deposits.

European Option.   the right, but not the obligation, to buy or sell as asset at a pre-specified price on the expiration date of the contract.

Event.   a particular occurrence; the outcome of a forecast or change in interest rates.

Exercise Price.   a pre-specified price at which an asset can be bought or sold by the owner or an option. It is also known as the strike price.

Expected Price.   the mean of a range of possible prices for an asset.

Expiration Date.   the date on which an option contract or swap expires or matures.

Face Value.   the principal value of a financial instrument. In a bond, it is the amount the holder will receive at maturity.

Fair Option Value.   the theoretical price of an option determined by using a probability-driven options model, such as Black-Scholes.

Federal Reserve Bank.   the central bank for the United States, which has the responsibility of managing money supply and regulating national banks.

FHLBB.   Federal Home Loan Bank Board; previously the regulator for the thrift industry, it has been replaced by the Office of Thrift Supervision.

Floor. an option that provides a minimum lower rate for funding beyond which the seller of a floor cannot benefit from decreased rates. However, a pension fund may choose to own a floor to lock in a minimum re-investment rate.

Floortion. the option to buy or sell a floor at some time in the future. They come with expiration choices of European, American, or American window.

Forward Exchange Agreement. a contract to buy or sell currency at an agreed-upon exchange rate at a specific date in the future.

Forward Yield Curve. a term structure of interest rates calculated using the forward interest rates for different maturities. It gives an expectational component to the usual yield curve.

Forward Rate. the future interest rate implied by the current yield curve. For example, if a one-year instrument has a rate of 6% and a two-year instrument has a rate of 8%, an investor will expect to be able to purchase a one-year security today and a one-year security one year from today so that the compound return over the two-year period would equal the current rate on the two-year instrument. The one-year forward would be 10.04% based on the equation $[(1.08) \times (1.08)]/(1.06) - 1.0 = 10.04\%$.

Forward Rate Agreement. a contract to purchase or sell securities as a pre-arranged rate at a specific date in the future.

Funding. the act of borrowing funds for investment purposes; it is related to the cost of carry.

Fungible. exactly interchangeable. For example, a buy of Eurodollar contracts on the IMM can be offset with a sell of Eurodollar contracts on SIMEX. The two contracts are *fungible*.

Futures Contract. a contract that provides the holder an obligation to buy or sell a financial instrument at a specific date in the future. Futures are exchange-traded instruments and are required to meet certain pre-specified standards.

Future Value. the dollar amount of an investment at a specific time in the future. The growth rate of the investment will depend on the reinvestment rate of the investment.

Gamma.   the measure of the rate of change of delta, defined as the change in delta for a one-unit change in the price of the underlying. It is also known as the curvature of the option.

Hedge Ratio.   a measure of how many of a specific derivative security are required to provide one underlying security with risk protection. There are a number of models available to gauge this measure.

Immunization.   a fixed-income investment strategy designed to insulate a portfolio from changes in interest rates by controlling the portfolio's duration and/or cash flows. A portfolio has approximate immunization for a term if its duration is set equal to the length of the term. It protects by matching capital gains/losses to increases/decreases in reinvestment income.

Implied Volatility.   the future volatility of prices of an asset derived from the forward yield curve and the price at which the options for the asset are trading.

Independent Variable.   the x in the regression analysis; the variable which, when it changes, produces accompanying changes in the dependent variable.

Interest.   dollar earnings of an investment for a specific period. It is paid by the borrower as a cost of funds and received by the lender as compensation for assuming credit risk.

Interest Rate Swap.   An agreement between two parties to exchange the interest payments of two different fixed-income securities. They can be fixed-to-floating or floating-to-floating. No principal is exchanged.

Internal Rate of Return.   the discount rate that makes the present value of an investment's net cash flows equal to the present cost.

In-the-Money.   a reference to an option with the difference between current market price and strike price giving an intrinsic profit. For example, a call with a strike price of 94–00 and a current market value for the underlying of 94–24 has an intrinsic value of 24/32. As this is profit and greater than zero, the option is in–the–money.

Intrinsic Option Value.   the market value of an option minus the strike price, or the difference between the strike price and the current market value of the underlying. The intrinsic value cannot fall below zero.

Inverted Yield Curve. a term that applies when short-term rates are higher than long-term rates.

Kappa. a gauge of volatility of an option. It is measured as the change in the price of the option for a given change in volatility. It is also known as vega, zeta, or sigma prime.

Liability. a section on a company's balance sheet indicating future cash outflows that the company is obligated to meet.

LIBOR. the London InterBank Offer Rate; a series of interest rates offered from overnight to about five years out in which major banks are willing to make Eurodollar-denominated deposits to other major banks.

Linear Regression. a method of analysis that tries to find a straight-line relationship between one event and another.

Liquidity. a measure of how quickly an asset or liability can be converted into cash without significantly moving price from its bid/asked level.

Long. a strategy in which a position or the right to own a security is entered because you think the price will increase.

Look-Back Option. a type of call or put that provides the right to buy or sell the lowest or highest price for the underlying instrument during the time period that the option contract runs.

Margin. the equity required to collateralize an investment; it is more typically used today to define the cash payment needed to maintain an open futures or options position at one of the exchanges.

Marked-to-Market. an accounting method that treats all price variations in a security from the last period to the current period as realized income. It works as though each position were closed out and reopened at the market levels current at the accounting period. It tends to subject the income accounts to additional volatility.

Mean. see Average.

Median. the middle value of a set of data, such that half the members of the set are above the median and half the members are below.

Mode. the most common value in a set.

Modified American Option. an option contract that is available for exercise only on specific dates during its life. An example is the put option attached to some bonds in which the bond may be sold back to the issuer on certain prespecified dates at a pre-specified strike price.

Naive Hedge Ratio Model.   a model of evaluating the hedge ratio in which the ratio is set equal to one.

Naked Option Strategies.   a strategy in which the underlying security is not owned by the holder of the option. A naked put exposes the holder to limited rewards and unlimited risk.

Net Present Value.   the difference between the principal and income cash flows for a financial instrument after the original investment is subtracted when the cash flows are discounted at a specified interest rate.

Normal Curve.   a probability distribution curve in which the mean is zero and the standard deviation is one. It is a standardized version of a probability curve and can be used in statistics to estimate the likelihood of seeing prices above or below an estimate.

Notional Principal.   the amount of money on which interest payments are based in an interest-rate or currency swap. The notional principal is not exchanged between counterparties.

Novation.   a term used in the Basle Agreement that permits the netting of two currency payments only when both the currencies are the same and the date of exchange is the same.

Off-Balance-Sheet Financing.   a method of financing, such as a swap, that is not treated conventionally on the balance sheet. There are advantages to this, as key financial ratios are not affected by financing decisions.

Offset.   the right to net assets versus liabilities of the same counterparty.

Options.   the right, but not the obligation, to purchase or sell an asset. Options come in two forms, European and American, which have different exercise alternatives.

Out-of-the-Money.   an option in which the intrinsic value is less than zero; i.e., where the strike price is above the current market price of the underlying instrument for a call and the strike price is below for a put.

Path-Dependent Options.   options based on an average rate at expiration rather than the prevailing spot rate.

Plain Vanilla. a term used when the structure of a derivative instrument or a financing deal is the simplest or most standard of its type.

Portfolio Insurance. a convex portfolio strategy for asset-allocation that involves selling the cheaper asset and using the funds to buy the richer asset. It works best in a trending market.

Premium. the upfront price of an option.

Present Value. the amount of money needed today for an investment to reach a specific level at some time in the future. It can also be viewed as the value as measured today of a cash flow to be received in the future.

Principal. the face value of a financial instrument or its initial value.

Probability Distribution Curve. a curve that describes the relationship between a particular price for an asset and the probability of that price occurring.

Process Risk. the risk entailed by the change of input prices during the process of producing a good. This risk is the same whether the good is a manufactured item, a service, or financial product.

Protective Put. a strategy that involves buying a put for which the underlying asset is already owned. The strike price is slightly below the expected price and limits the possible loss at a cost of a portion of the upside potential.

Put Option. a contract giving the holder the right, but not the obligation, to sell a security or asset.

Put/Call Parity. a relationship between prices of puts and calls so that riskless arbitrage is not possible. It is the basis for synthetic securities. The premium for the put of an asset will equal the premium for the call minus the investment in the underlying plus the present value of the strike price.

Range Forward. a contract used in foreign-exchange agreements that pre-specifies a maximum and minimum exchange rate for a future transaction. If the spot rate on two days before the termination date falls within that range, then it becomes the transaction rate. Otherwise, the rate becomes the maximum or minimum specified, whichever is closest to the market value.

Rebalancing. the act of buying and selling assets to bring the ratio of assets to total portfolio position back into the desired range.

Reinvestment Rate.   the rate of interest at which the cash flows of an investment are invested when received.

Reinvestment Risk.   the risk that future cash flows will be reinvested at a lower interest rate than currently anticipated.

Rho.   the expected change in the value of an option when applicable market interest rates change a small amount.

Risk Premium.   the additional monies required to make assuming a risk attractive.

Safe Harbor.   transactions that have no legal or tax consequences or penalties; this term is also used when assets are moved from a more volatile to a less volatile sector of the market.

Scenario Analysis.   the analysis of "what if" conditions and the probability associated with conditions to arrive at an expected price for an asset.

Short Position.   a transaction in which the investor sells an instrument he does not own in expectation that the market price will fall.

Skewed Probability Distributions.   distributions of data that are non-normal, usually with the differences from normal concentrated in one area of the probability distribution curve. Variances above the expected price are positively skewed; variances below the expected price are negatively skewed.

Spreadlock.   a commitment for a period in the future to enter into a swap at a particular pre-specified spread to an index. The index itself is pre-determined, although the rate is not. However, the spread above or below the index is determined. For example, a spreadlock might be to enter a swap in 30 days based on paying fixed and receiving prime minus 100 bps.

Spreads.   the price differential between two similar securities. For example, March and June Eurodollar contracts or Eurodollars versus T-Bills.

Spreading Strategies.   trading call or put options with different exercise prices but with the same expiration date; any strategy involving an expectation of pricing changes between similar instruments. This is a class of lower risk strategies.

Stack.   adding to a futures or forward position as time moves on in order to match more exactly the derivatives position to the underlying. For example, an amortizing mortgage will see a hedge that gradually decreases in size as the principal is paid down (reverse stack); a pension fund may add contracts to a hedge as futures liabilities to workers increases (stack).

Standard Deviation. a measure of variability or volatility of price given as the square root of the variance. It is measured in the same units as the interest rate variable.

Straddle. an options strategy consisting of owning both a put and a call on the same underlying and usually at the same strike price. It can be structured to be either mildly bullish, mildly bearish, or neutral.

Strike Price. also known as the exercise price.

Strip. (1) a series of forwards or futures spread over a number of different maturities; (2) an options position consisting of two puts and one call.

Swap. a contract for the exchange of cash flows between two counterparties. Standard versions are fixed-rate-to-fixed-rate, fixed-rate-to-floating-rate, and floating-rate-to-floating-rate. There are both interest rate swaps and currency swaps.

Swaption. the right, but not the obligation, to purchase or sell a swap at a pre-determined date.

Synthetic Securities. a position in cash, options, and the underlying security that replicates the cash flows of a particular single-option position.

T-bill. see Treasury Bill.

Term Structure of Rates. also known as the yield curve; a method of graphing interest rates versus maturity.

Treasury Bill. fixed income obligations of the U.S. government issued at a discount for a maturity of not more than one year. These are coupon securities.

Treasury Bond. fixed income obligations of the U. S. government issued at par for a maturity between 7 and 30 years. These are coupon securities.

Truncated Distribution. a probability distribution curve for a position or portfolio in which the tails are cut off, or truncated, because of the addition of options into the position or due to the presence of arbitrage opportunities.

Underlying.   the security acting as the base for a derivative instrument.

Value.   the theoretical worth of a position, which can vary significantly from the market price.

Vega.   see Kappa.

Volatility.   the variability of the price of an asset over time; often measured in terms of standard deviation.

Yield.   the return on an investment; yield can be measured a number of different ways.

Yield Curve.   also known as the term structure of interest rates; a plot of yield to maturity as a function of time to maturity. There are versions of yield curves calculated on the basis of zero-coupon securities, coupon securities, and forward rate agreements.

Yield to Maturity.   the internal rate of return for the cash flows of a fixed-income security. It is also the discount rate where the net present value of the cash flows is equal to zero.

Zero-Coupon Bond.   a debt instrument issued at a discount and consisting of a bullet payment at maturity.

Zero-Coupon curve.   often the zero-coupon curve reflects a lack of liquidity in this market. It is used primarily for pricing swap hedging programs.

Zero Curve.   a type of term structure of interest rates; it uses zero-coupon securities rather than government coupon bonds to eliminate any yield differences due to reinvestment risk premium.

Index